The Offshore Racer

Ted Jones   **The Offshore Racer**

Quadrangle/
The New York Times
Book Company

Copyright © 1973 by Theodore A. Jones
All rights reserved, including the right to reproduce this book or portions thereof in any form. For information, address: Quadrangle/The New York Times Book Co., 10 East 53rd Street, New York, New York 10022. Manufactured in the United States of America. Published simultaneously in Canada by Fitzhenry & Whiteside, Ltd., Toronto.

Library of Congress Catalog Card Number: 73-79916

International Standard Book Number: 0-8129-0385-4

Design by Paddy Bareham, Planned Production

To BJ, Doug, and Bill

Contents

	Introduction	ix
1	The Great Ocean Race	1
2	Getting a Berth	9
3	Personal Equipment	15
4	Organization of the Crew	23
5	The Skipper and the Watch Captains	35
6	The Cook	41
7	The Navigator	49
8	Racing Strategy	65
9	Helmsmanship Upwind	89
10	Helmsmanship Downwind	109
11	Sail Handling	125
12	Spinnaker Handling	145
13	Heavy Weather Racing	169
14	Survival Storms	175
15	Safety	183
16	Health	199
17	What It's Like	205
18	A Philosophical View	251
	Appendixes	
I	Bill of Fare, Yacht *Astral*	263
II	Marine Weather Information (U.S.)	267
III	Navigator's Checklist	271
IV	Navigator's Equipment Checklist	273
V	Sources of Supply	275
	Bibliography	277
	Index	279

"Tomorrow or the next day the sun will shine and dry your itchy, salty clothing."

Introduction

This is a book about offshore racing. It concentrates on the people who sail offshore—who they are, how they got interested, how they got started, what they need to know, and where and with whom they sail. It is designed to have something for each specialist, be he skipper, watch captain, navigator, foredeck hand, or cook. This is *not* a book about equipment, design, rigging, sails, or rating rules. These subjects are planned for a subsequent companion volume on the offshore racing yacht. This is the "how to do it." The next book will cover the "what to do it with."

The overriding theme is seamanship, which to me also includes the ability of the seaman to do all the things, direct and indirect, that will make a boat sail her fastest. Most expert seamen I know sail fast. They don't know any other way. To sail slowly or inefficiently is to be unseamanlike. The sea demands this kind of efficiency, and to be timid or indecisive is to invite disaster.

The racing sailor will go to great lengths to get the maximum speed from his yacht. He will take risks that the cruising sailor or passagemaker—even the commercial seaman—will not take. But the racing sailor must know the limits of his yacht and crew, and these limits must *never* be exceeded. No prize is worth risking the yacht or her crew through imprudent seamanship, but the line that divides viable risks from foolhardiness is a fine one. The purpose of this book is to help the reader improve his seamanship, so that he may extend his limits and sail faster—safely.

It is assumed that the reader already has a fair amount of sailing experience, either sailing cruising boats in sheltered waters or racing in a one-design class. For this is not a how-to-sail primer. The raw beginner would do better to start with a more basic text, get his feet wet in a small boat, and learn to handle it with confidence. Such preliminary training, which can take anywhere from one or two months to a year or more, depending upon the amount of dedicated effort, will prepare him for offshore sailing. He will also learn lessons that might escape him if he attempts to sail a large boat at the beginning.

One of the great fascinations of offshore sailing is the wide diversity of knowledge that it requires. Except for the fact that he usually pays the bills, the owner is no more important—nor does he need to know much more—than the newest crew member. When offshore, everyone must know as much as possible about helmsmanship, sail handling, navigation, weather, strategy, and safety. Ideally, everyone aboard should be able to do everything, and while there will be specialists in charge of different departments—the foredeck boss knows the most about spinnakers and headsail trim, the navigator knows the most about position finding and strategy, the cook knows the most about the galley and feeding hungry sailors—everyone should be able to pitch in anywhere when needed. It is a small team that sails offshore, and there is no room for rigid specialists or prima donnas.

I have attempted to set down all I have learned about sailing and seamanship offshore in twenty years of "big boat" racing. Of course, I do not presume to know it all, and like most authors I have sometimes awakened abruptly at night realizing that I have forgotten some detail. Surely, I have been telling myself, I will blunder and leave out something important, showing my ignorance or, worse, lack of attention. I am now committed, but enough eyes have seen the manuscript to make me reasonably certain that nothing vital is missing.

Most of us do not sail by ourselves, and few could singlehandedly write a book on as complicated a subject as offshore racing. One does not learn about sailing through mystical experience. One learns the hard way through countless experiences, and these experiences are shared with others. Everything I have written about I have learned either directly from others or through sharing their experiences. So it is my many shipmates over the years who have contributed most of what is written here.

At the risk of slighting some past shipmates, I will mention those who have helped me the most. There are five skippers—Dick Sheehan, Dick Nye, Fred Lorenzen, George Moffett, and Humphrey Simson—who provided the yachts and the racing opportunities and with whom I have sailed many thousands of miles. Without them there would be no book. There are eight shipmates—Walter Fink, Bill Gray, Barney Compton, Alan Gurney, Seth Hiller, Bruce Kirby, Joe Mac Brien and Tom Norton who have shared their

INTRODUCTION

expertise on many races. Knowingly and unknowingly they have contributed immeasurably.

Alan Gurney, Joe Mac Brien and Seth Hiller were of specific help. Alan, who designed *Windward Passage* and many other famous yachts, was the first to see the completed manuscript. He was extremely helpful with technical advice and suggestions for corrections and improvements. Joe, who is probably the most thorough navigator I have sailed with, provided many ideas and procedures for the chapters on navigation and strategy. Seth is, likewise, a man of many talents. A professional architect, a gifted artist, and an accomplished offshore sailor, Seth drew the excellent illustrations used throughout the book.

My good friend, word wizard, and sometime shipmate, Jack Wisner, provided early encouragement and advice on organizing the material.

Finally, and most important, is Dorcas Jones who has shared— and sometimes endured—twenty years of sailing with me. Not only has she been invaluable as a critic, making suggestions to improve meanings or to make them more clear, but she performed the time-consuming, thankless, but very necessary task of transcribing the original manuscript from xxxxx's, scratches, and strikeovers into a legible document. Without her help, encouragement, and particularly her considerable knowledge of the subject, there would be no book.

So, there are many people—some famous, some unknown, some well remembered and some all but forgotten—who should be credited as co-authors of *The Offshore Racer*.

Ted Jones
Rowayton, Connecticut
4/22/73

The Offshore Racer

Ticonderoga. (George Smith)

Chapter 1 The Great Ocean Race

Honolulu
July 16, 1965

Mr. L. Francis Herreshoff
The Castle
Marblehead, Massachusetts

Dear Mr. Herreshoff:

John Barkhorn of Honolulu greeted us upon our arrival today and told me that he had sent you the newspaper clippings of what I now call the "Great Ocean Race." I am not alone in this because when and where else have two ships sailed over 2,400 miles of ocean, never more than a few miles apart, and finished within five minutes and both in record-breaking time?

As you know, this race has been going on for fifty years. There have been large ships in it. The 161' schooner *Goodwill* has run it several times; the two 350' square-rigged Japanese training ships ran it in 1959. Many big schooners of more than 100' have now run the course. None had ever equaled the time of the ketch *Morning Star*, a 98' ship with a crack crew that set the record in 1955, beating all previous records by nearly a whole day!

This year two ships, your *Ticonderoga* and *Stormvogel*, broke the all-time records and finished within five minutes of each other. After more than 2,400 miles, *Stormvogel* came out of a rainsquall about 75 miles from Honolulu and downwind from us. When she saw us, she reached up and crossed our stern within about 100 yards. From this point, we started a whole new race, boat for boat in the middle of the Pacific Ocean.

As you well know, a great many people believe that *Stormvogel* is capable of higher speeds, under certain conditions, than any sailing vessel ever built. She is a foot longer than *Ticonderoga*, her aluminum masts are as tall or taller, and she has a fin keel like a Star boat. She is the product of several designers and was built by the owner, Cornelius Bruynzeel, in South Africa. I became acquainted with Mr. Bruynzeel after we got here. Oddly enough, he is in the timber business in South Africa, which also happens to have been my business. He is indeed a very fine gentleman and sportsman. He tells me *Stormvogel* has attained speeds of 22 knots, momentarily, under wind and sea conditions that permit her to surf. I believe him.

Few will believe it I'm sure, but *Ticonderoga* will surf, too. In this race we far exceeded our previous top speed, which was 17 knots. We hit 18½ and then twice exceeded the limits of our electronic speed indicator, which goes to only 20 knots.

When we first saw *Stormvogel* 75 miles out, we had just been able to get sights and determine that we were on our course within a degree or two of Koko Head. It was late afternoon, and although we didn't know it then, *Stormvogel* was uncertain of her proper course to the finish and therefore elected to come up to us, feeling that they could beat us in a boat-for-boat race to the finish and be safer than pursuing her own course to the finish. Actually, they were right. Our course was correct and proved so hours later when we picked up Makapuu Light just off our starboard bow, bearing 227° magnetic and right where we figured it would be.

Since they were downwind from us, their course, had they maintained it, would have been low of the mark. When we saw them, they were close with a spinnaker and gaining ground rapidly. We knew we had to do something, so we dropped our spinnaker and put on a reacher, headed up to windward about 15°. Soon they followed suit, changing course about 20°, and reached up to us at tremendous speed, passing our stern within 100 yards. Then they changed to our course, but lost ground.

Next they altered course again and went further up to windward. We guessed correctly that they wanted to change their angle to be in a running position with the wave direction directly down to the mark—Diamond Head. The wind by this time was at least 30 knots, and as we approached the Molokai Channel, it increased to 40 knots (about standard for this stretch of water where the wind funnels between the great mountains of the Hawaiian archipelago).

From this position *Stormvogel* came back down, and in all my sailing I have never seen anything like her performance. We started to surf. The seas were mountainous. We never went under

11 knots and on the waves were getting 14–16, even at times 18 knots! Yet *Stormvogel* was closing rapidly. She must have been getting her 20-knot spurts.

We simply kept ahead by staying with our shorter course. She sailed *miles* further in these last few hours to the finish line. But when she came back down from way up to windward, we still had our 100-yard lead. At Koko Head, six miles from the finish, we jibed from port to starboard tack.

I have great admiration for the aptitude and precision of the America's Cup sailors. They are artists. But we are in a different business. Accomplishing a dip-pole jibe at night in 30-foot seas, 40 knots of wind, with a 3,800-square-foot, 2.2-ounce Dacron spinnaker is not exactly child's play. Add to this a thirty-year-old ketch with a bowsprit that takes the man on it under water, a rainsquall, jury-rigged spinnaker hardware to replace the regular spinnaker pole gear that ripped right off the mast three days before, and the sum total is a situation that comes under the heading of "amateur sport" and offers security somewhat less than a foxhole in South Vietnam. A professional seaman wouldn't attempt it. Good sense and the union rules wouldn't permit it.

The *Ti* rolled her windward rail under a couple of times, the spinnaker pole came out of the jury rig on the mast, and went *overboard*, but they got it back. The helmsman, Bob Dickson, was able to steer a course to follow the spinnaker. It never collapsed, and these boys got the pole back and connected it to the mast and the spinnaker clew again. We changed course 25° and pulled away from *Stormvogel*, passing the Diamond Head buoy by a few feet.

It couldn't have been more exciting if we'd staged it from a prepared script. Even from a script, no one would have believed it anyway.

This was the greatest crew I have ever sailed with. Being the oldest man aboard, I managed gracefully to avoid engaging directly in the foredeck exercises. The boys let me off, thank the Lord, and I was perfectly content with this arrangement. I just tended to my navigating and tailed the occasional line. These boys were magnificent, and I can't say enough about them. In Bob Dickson and Chip Cleary, we had a couple of old hands who were wonderful watch captains and the quarterbacks for every maneuver we made.

During the race, we knew from available weather information that there was a tropical disturbance off the coast of Mexico. Usually these recurve from a starting point off Nicaragua and hit the mainland of northern Mexico. Not much is said about these storms since the population and traffic along the coast of Mexico is insignificant compared to that of the Gulf and the Caribbean. So no one much cares. But in Mexico these are well known, and there is no West Indies' hurricane any more fearful or awesome than a Mexican "chubasco," as they are called there. Twice in the last century one of these things has not recurved, but has made its way across the Pacific and hit Honolulu. No one liked to acknowledge this, and to think that it might happen during a race was out of the question.

But we watched it on the weather map, and it happened! The Weather Bureau finally admitted that "Beatrice" had been born. Her existence was made public when her center was at lat. 21° N long. 137° W, heading for just north of Honolulu at a speed of 12 knots.

We knew it was there. Any sailor knows that when you see huge cross-swells from a quarter different from either the present or prevailing wind, things are just not right.

We turned down 1,000 miles from Honolulu, hoping to sail the "edge" of the hurricane. We figured we were in the northwest to westerly quarters of it. We also figured that its counterclockwise winds should supplement the normal 12- to 15-knot Trades.

We were right. The wind built up to 50 knots dead aft. That's when we hit our 20 knots plus. The surfboarders say that they get "locked in" on a wave. That's what we did. We flew a 4-ounce Dacron storm spinnaker of about 60 percent area and *full* main, no reefs, mizzen sails furled. We "locked in" twice on two giant waves, and the speed indicator banged right up against the pin—20 knots *plus* we don't know how much, and the old *Ticonderoga* stayed with the wave.

Wave speed—what's that? The crew were like maniacs, like dope addicts. I don't know whether this was surfing or what it was! The water flew off the bow like it would off a PT boat. Finally she'd break in a smother of foam. At least once, the spinnaker, instead of pulling, was plastered against the mast. I've heard about the old ships "sailing under." Is this the way you do it? If it is, we just about made it. Finally, the 4-ounce spinnaker exploded into confetti, the main ripped from leach to luff halfway up, and the madness was over.

The gooseneck was ripped loose from the mast; the poles, spinnaker bells, and the cars went into orbit and overboard. We put on a staysail and jib and, meanwhile, Signode strapped the boom hardware back on and made up a sort of charm bracelet out of

Bob Johnson.

cable clamps and jib track cars to hold the spinnaker pole. We sailed more than 250 miles during this twenty-four-hour period, half of it with no main. We really didn't hurt anything. The helmsmen were so good that they kept her on the track; no broaches, no knockdowns. We were in the water and had gone over her—she didn't leak, and nothing pulled loose. Nothing was hurt but some hardware.

Mr. Herreshoff, this is one great ship. What other ship of *any* length has averaged *over* 10 knots for 2,400 miles under sail? Bear in mind that we had some six and seven knots in our sailing. At the start of the race, we fell into a hole and were dead in the water for over an hour, during which even the small boats all passed us.

With this crew and the shape we have her in, we're ready to race anything, as far as they want, in the tradewinds, reach and run. Pass the *Cutty Sark*. Where is she?

The master and crew of the *Ticonderoga* salute you, and henceforth the name Herreshoff shall be spoken aboard with the accord due the immortals of the sea: Herreshoff, Columbus, Henry the Navigator, Magellan (and in that order!).

> Sincerely,
> Robert Johnson
> Portland, Oregon

Who wouldn't have liked to have been aboard "Big *Ti*" and to have lived the "Great Ocean Race"? Yet how would you have gotten aboard? What would you have had to know? What would you have had to do?

It should be quite obvious that you simply don't go to a "yacht store," buy a *Ticonderoga,* and take off for Honolulu. A few people have tried it that way, but they have not won a Transpac Race and some have even perished along the way. The fact is, there is a considerable amount of experience and knowledge, not to mention money, that must be acquired before you can attempt to duplicate the feat of Bob Johnson and his boys.

It would seem a great deal simpler if you could be content with being among the crew. Great, but do you walk up to a Bob Johnson and ask to be invited aboard? You could, but he would want to know what you could do for him. How good a shipmate are you? With whom have you sailed? Are you a good helmsman, foredeck expert, navigator, cook?

The knowledge and abilities expected of an offshore racing crew are vast. Not only do shipmates demand competence from those with whom they sail, but the sea itself is a demanding master—and it is the master, not the servant, of all who venture forth upon it. The sea will snap at the first missed step and may turn even a small error into a major catastrophe.

The neophyte racing car driver does not start by driving at Indianapolis; the would-be mountain climber does not start by climbing Mt. Everest; the beginning skier does not start by skiing The National; the potential offshore racer does not start by commanding *Ticonderoga*. There is much to be learned; there is much experience to be gained. Like the racing car driver, mountain climber, and skier, the offshore racer starts at the bottom and works up. If you really want to race offshore, there is no other way to begin.

Somewhere in the maze of yachts, spars, and rigging someone needs you. (Chris Caswell)

Chapter 2 **Getting a Berth**

If you owned an airline, Peter Bowker is just the sort of fellow you'd want selling tickets, which is what he once did. He is congenial, witty, affable, intelligent, and relaxed. He is just the sort to do his job well and create a good impression for his company. He must have been a valuable asset to his employer, but he doesn't have an employer anymore.

Peter Bowker was in his early thirties when he took advantage of airline employees' liberal travel benefits to take his "holiday" from England to sunny Miami. While wandering around the docks one day admiring the graceful sailing yachts, Peter got to talking with one of the owners—something very easy for someone who is congenial, witty, affable, intelligent, and relaxed—and soon he was sailing aboard his newfound friend's offshore racer.

That did it. Peter was hooked. To hell with selling airline tickets and being nice to dull, complaining people, thought Peter, and he's been on "holiday" ever since.

Today, Peter Bowker is one of the most sought after crew members in the offshore racing circuit. He has raced in just about every offshore race one could name, from Sydney to Hobart, from Bermuda to Copenhagen, from Los Angeles to Hawaii, and from Buenos Aires to Rio de Janeiro—to name only the big ones. Name any big, well-known offshore racing boat and chances are that Peter has raced on her. He has been aboard the record-setting yacht each time the previous record has been broken in the Miami to Montego Bay, Jamaica Race. He has shipped aboard as bilge boy, watch captain, cook, navigator, and skipper, and his vast experience has led him to the prestigious position of navigator/tactician aboard an America's Cup contender. Wherever there is something important going on in offshore racing, you will find Peter Bowker among those participating.

John Bolton, an Australian, is a junior Peter Bowker. John was chatting with an acquaintance in a London pub when the acquaintance asked him if he'd like to go for a sail. "I don't know anything about it," John replied, "but what the hell...."

John's first sail was a transatlantic passage aboard the famous 73' *Ondine*, which was on her way to Florida for the Southern Ocean Racing Conference after a summer of campaigning in Europe. John's been sailing ever since.

Hugh Calder, an engineer from New Zealand, had an agent who used to find him jobs at the end of offshore races. Hugh's reputation as being a top-notch offshore hand, and available, spread worldwide. Someone would always know where to find him, whether it was London, Montreal, or Copenhagen, and Hugh would have a good berth.

Hugh would sign on to sail in a race such as a Transatlantic, quit his job, and have his agent look for employment while he was racing on the ocean. Hugh got married in England after the 1966 Transatlantic Race. He bought a boat and sailed it home to New Zealand.

You don't have to be a Limey, an Aussie, or a Kiwi to go offshore racing. Nor do you have to change your life as these three men did, but you do have to make at least a short-term commitment. How one gets started—makes the necessary contacts—is, however, largely a matter of luck.

Many people get started just as Peter Bowker did, by hanging around where one is likely to meet the right people and by making friends with them. Sooner or later—often much sooner than one might expect—someone will need a crew member at the last minute. You must be ready to make a pier-head jump, and if you are enthusiastic, willing to learn, and easy to get along with, you very likely will be asked again.

The John Bolton method of picking up a berth at a pub is not recommended. True, it worked out fine for John, but for many, the associations made under such circumstances may not be the most reliable.

One would-be seafarer met a fellow at a bar on Lexington Avenue in New York. "I'm the captain of the *Cotton Blossom*," the fellow declared. After getting further acquainted, he said they were leaving from Stamford, Connecticut and sailing to Florida the following day and would the would-be seafarer like to join them. "Sure," said the w-b s. The next morning he took a train to Stamford and showed up with his duffel aboard the *Cotton*

GETTING A BERTH

Blossom. The "captain" he'd met at the bar was nowhere around; no one had ever heard of him. *Cotton Blossom* was there all right, but she was securely battened down under winter cover and frame, certainly not fit for a sea voyage that day.

There is another good reason to avoid frequenting the bar on shore. Offshore sailing puts a great strain on even the best of relationships. Living in close quarters, often under conditions of strain and fatigue, can quickly make enemies out of the best of friends. Each crew member must be aware of this. He must keep his temper and his emotions in check and make allowances for the foibles of his shipmates. He also must make every effort to keep his own peculiarities from irritating others. Then, too, it's good practice to be wary of going offshore with someone you don't know well enough to know if they are reliable and congenial.

Most people who want to go offshore racing get started by racing inshore on day or short overnight races. Those who have had small-boat racing experience will find it invaluable when they are learning to handle the lines and gear of a larger boat.

I got my start this way and was very lucky to start at the top. I had told a friend of mine who was sailing on the New York Yacht Club Cruise that my summer job had suddenly terminated and that I was available. There was no room on his boat, but luckily he found someone looking for a crew the night before the first run and suggested to the skipper that he call me.

I was at dinner, getting lectured by my family, who wanted to know what I was going to do with myself for the rest of the summer, when the phone rang.

"This is Dick Nye," the voice said. "I own a boat named *Carina*, and I understand you might be available to sail with us." Would I! *Carina* had won the Bermuda Race a month earlier, and I knew very well who Dick Nye and *Carina* were. I was packed and on my way in minutes. I raced with *Carina* the balance of the summer, and have raced with the Nyes in other *Carinas* and in other seasons since.

All the incidents recounted so far would make you think that one can get started racing offshore only by accident. This is largely true. One needs to know someone who knows someone else, or one needs to be at the right place at the right time, and have a knack for making friends quickly and for making a good first impression.

There are organizations, yacht clubs, and associations one can join that often will lead to introductions to the owners of offshore racing boats. One such organization is The Corinthians with headquarters in New York City and members spread throughout the northeastern United States. The Corinthians' *Yearbook* states:

> The Corinthians is a noncommercial membership association of amateur yachtsmen. Its primary objectives are to promote sailing, to encourage good fellowship among yachtsmen afloat and ashore, and to serve as a "clearing house" between non-boat-owning amateur sailors and boat owners needing occasional amateur hands for cruising and racing. The organization is equally concerned with both the beginner and the trained sailor.[1]

The story of The Corinthians is interesting, particularly for the would-be crew member seeking a berth on an offshore racer. The association is unique as far as I know, but its organizational format could easily be followed in other areas. While membership is restricted and potential new members must be recommended, screened, and voted upon as in most clubs, the restrictions are neither social nor ethnic (women, however, are not eligible). According to their by-laws, "Any gentleman of acceptable character and personality, experienced or interested in yachting, is eligible for membership." All they ask, in effect, is that a member be a "good shipmate," which is the least anyone ought to expect of a crew member for an offshore passage.

> The Corinthians was organized in February 1934. The Association is founded upon the theory that there are many boat owners desirous of finding congenial and capable shipmates and the companion theory that there are many men who do not own boats, some of them experienced seamen who welcome an opportunity to get afloat. The soundness of the idea is proven by the steady growth of the Association; this year, our thirty-sixth, there are almost 700 members.
> The establishment of two branches has been the only major change in the Association since its founding. In 1957, the membership voted to change the By-Laws and add Article XIV, to authorize having "Fleets" at the discretion of the Afterguard (governors). Two Fleets were immediately authorized and established in Boston and Philadelphia; they are known, respectively, as the New England Fleet and the Phila-

---

[1] The Corinthians' *Yearbook* (New York, 1971).

GETTING A BERTH 13

delphia Fleet. In this, the fourteenth year of their existence, both Fleets are active and flourishing.

The Corinthians Activities

Crewing.—Crewing is still the major activity of The Corinthians. While the Crewing Committee is frequently the marriage bureau that brings crews and owners together, many crewing arrangements are made directly between members. Each spring, the committee sends crewing questionnaires to all members to determine their qualifications and availability of berths or desires to crew, and the committee uses these to mate available hands with open berths. The Fleets have their own Crewing Committees and may handle local calls within their own membership or circulate a call to the entire roster of the Association. Crew calls, which are sometimes accepted from boat owners who are not members, have ranged from a Saturday afternoon race to a voyage across the Atlantic or South Pacific. They offer nonowner members an opportunity for a summer or winter vacation cruise, and enable owners to crew their boats with congenial cruising companions.

Shore Activities.—The Shore Activities program is another major function of The Corinthians. From October through May, a series of "Gams" is held; a Gam is a dinner meeting followed by a talk, generally by a member, or a movie, on a subject of interest to sailors. The New York Gams are held monthly from October through May. There is a "Ladies Night" in February. The two Fleets schedule their Gams, in Boston and Philadelphia, from late fall to early spring. In addition, various Rendezvous are scheduled each year, both afloat and ashore. The Philadelphia Fleet's annual Rendezvous is held on a raft of sailboats in a harbor in Chesapeake Bay and the New England's annual get-together is the same, in the Cape Cod area. The New York group stages two Rendezvous each year; the spring Rendezvous is a floating raft, while the fall party goes ashore for a dinner at a yacht club, both in western Long Island Sound.[2]

The Corinthians' shore activities program serves the very important function of providing a way for prospective crew mem-

[2]*Ibid.*

bers and owners to get acquainted. In actual practice this serves as the primary source of berths, with owners and crew members arranging their own schedules. The Crewing Committee more often takes care of last-minute calls.

The Corinthians also sponsors local races and has developed programs to interest juniors and college students in offshore racing boats and cruising auxiliaries.

There are other organizations, of course, which can provide the non-boat-owning sailor a chance to get afloat. The Little Ship Club, in England, is similar in some respects to The Corinthians. Some clubs, like England's Royal Ocean Racing Club, own offshore racing yachts that they charter to members at reasonable rates.

As many ways as there are to get started in offshore racing, there are still no guaranteed methods. Each of those described above has its drawbacks: namely, the necessity of relying on chance and the necessity of knowing someone in order to get into a club.

It is particularly hard for women to get offshore berths since they are excluded from many clubs and are discriminated against by many offshore sailing people. Women tend to be thought of as ship's cooks, and when they are included in crews, that is almost invariably their berth. Yet some of the best, most knowledgeable, most aggressive crew members I have sailed with have been women. Some of the best helms*men* are, in fact, helms*women*. Owners, skippers, and male crew members of offshore racers who shun having women in their crews are depriving themselves of some very good shipmates.

Many men, however, feel that they are or would be inhibited by the presence of women aboard—that they would have to watch their language or that they would be offensive in some other way to a woman. Yet surely any woman who agrees to sail offshore with a boat full of men realizes that she is going to hear language that she wouldn't hear at a debutante ball. She also realizes that she can't be offended by such incidents as members of the crew relieving themselves over the rail or appearing on deck half-naked. These are unavoidable necessities of the sport, and the good female crew member learns to adjust. Women enjoy the same excitement, exhilaration, beauty, and challenge of sailing offshore as do men. There is no valid reason why they should be excluded.

So, male or female, if you have a hankering to go offshore but find it difficult to get a berth, by all means persevere. It can be difficult, admittedly, but once you make it, you'll be very glad you kept trying!

Chapter 3 **Personal Equipment**

The would-be crew member who wants to go offshore racing must have certain personal equipment and special clothing. The owner of the boat normally does not supply these essentials.

The beginning offshore sailor needs to buy the kind of clothes that will keep him dry. Purchase of the proper clothing will constitute a sailor's greatest expense. For example, if you haven't spent between $60 and $80 on a jacket, pants, and boots, you can count on getting wet offshore. Don't waste your money on something that will do only half the job. You'll be glad you bought the best when the weather turns cold and nasty.

There are many different types of foul-weather gear, but I prefer a heavy-duty separate jacket and pants set. I once wore a pullover-type jacket, believing that it would keep me drier than a fly-front jacket. More recently I have used a fly-front jacket, which closes with snaps and has a large, overlapping flap inside. This jacket is much easier to get on and off than my old pullover, and for that reason alone, I wouldn't go back to wearing a pullover even if it is drier. I can't say from experience that it is, although in theory it must be.

One thing I don't like about wearing some jackets is that there is no way to close the sleeves so that water can't run down your arms when you raise them. Jackets with sewn-in elastic wristbands can help prevent this annoying problem.

Most jackets have hoods, although some people prefer the fisherman's "sou'wester" hat. Hoods tend to restrict vision to the side and up.

For trousers, I use high, bib-front, heavy-duty suspender pants of the same material and make as my jacket. Your pants should be high enough front and back to keep water from seeping through the fly-front jacket or from getting under the back of the jacket when you bend over.

Boots, foul weather gear (inside boots), floater jacket, personal rescue light, rigging knife, and duffel bag on the dock waiting to be taken aboard. (Ted Jones)

PERSONAL EQUIPMENT

Fly-front foul-weather jacket with hood. Safety harness pulls from high on chest to avoid pulling wearer "stern first" as some waist level belts might. (Ted Jones)

There are several one-piece suits available which in theory, at least, will keep you drier than a two-piece suit. However, I find them cumbersome to climb into and out of, and most I have seen are of the lightweight variety, which usually don't do the job. When shopping for foul-weather gear, you should check to see that the garment is waterproof. Some impregnated fabrics *look* waterproof but leak in heavy or continous rain and spray. Needless to say, leaky foul-weather gear is worthless.

Some people believe that heavy-duty foul-weather gear will be excessively hot in summer weather, but I have rarely been too warm when I found it necessary to don the "oilies." If it is raining, it is usually cool enough so that you are happy to have on the extra layers of clothing. Remember that you're likely to work up a sweat in the lightweight suit as well, and a lightweight suit probably won't keep you dry. Another solution is to wear a bathing suit or shorts that you don't mind getting wet, and then drying yourself off later.

You also will need a pair of sturdy boots to keep your feet dry. There are low boots that fit over the shoes, low boots that are worn over the socks, and high boots that are worn over shoes or socks. I prefer high boots worn over socks. Then if I fill my boots with seawater, I don't also soak my shoes. The high, stiff boots are warmer and do a better job of keeping the feet dry. It's good practice to wear foul-weather pants *over* your boots to keep the water out; an elastic band will help to hold the pants tightly over the boots. Boots that get soaked with salt water probably won't dry out for the rest of the passage.

Most sailors already have a pair of good deck shoes, but a second pair (in addition to the boots) ought to be available. Wear your deck shoes at all times! When I took mine off one hot day, I broke my toe doing nothing more strenuous than going down the companionway. If I had worn my deck shoes, this accident would not have happened. I normally wear a pair of sneakers and keep a pair of oxfords with deck soles in reserve. I wear the oxfords when traveling to and from a race and use them as shore shoes, thereby eliminating the need for a *third* pair of shoes.

What one packs in his duffel depends largely on the kind of weather expected and the length of the passage. In the tropics one can, obviously, get along with fewer heavy clothes, but don't be lulled into leaving all your wool clothes at home. At least one pair of wool socks, a wool sweater, and warm wool pants should be packed as a hedge against those not-so-rare cold nights.

It may be helpful to work up a packing list of specific clothing and equipment before each trip. This will help you avoid the frustrating problem of discovering, when you're miles at sea, that you've left something you need ashore.

As a general rule, I try to pack two of everything I think I need, in case I get completely soaked while fully clothed. Sometimes this rule has to be tempered by the lack of stowage space, so maybe you'll have to take one sweater instead of two. Extra clothes can be left in your duffel and be stowed somewhere out of the way if they won't fit into your locker.

Don't take a lot of gear you don't need. Have pity on your skipper and your shipmates who have to cope with your mountains of gear. Extra clothing not only gets in the way, but adds

PERSONAL EQUIPMENT 19

extra weight that the boat need not carry. Remember, too, *you* have to carry your duffel to and from the boat!

Other items of clothing I prefer, in addition to normal socks and underwear, are turtlenecks (at least one), which will keep cold winds and water trickles from shivering your neck; wool socks, which will keep your feet warm even when they get soaked; thermal underwear, which is light but warm; a wool watch cap, which will keep your head and ears warm at night; and a wool sweater. Don't forget gloves; you'll feel miserable if your hands are constantly wet and freezing. Fisherman's rubber gloves with wool inserts do a great job, but they are stiff and may make it difficult to handle the lines. Then, too, loosely fitting, soft material can get caught on the lines so that you might suddenly find your hand starting to go through a turning block or around a winch. Perhaps the best kind of gloves for the job are a pair of lined leather ones that you can take off when you are handling lines and put back on when you are steering or aren't busy.

You will not be expected to provide your own life jacket or safety harness. However, some crew members who prefer a particular style or brand often bring their own. Most life jackets that are provided are the cumbersome Coast Guard-approved types. So if you like the security of wearing a flotation jacket routinely while on watch, you should bring your own.

There are a number of jackets available that double as a warm garment and a flotation coat, due to the particular unicellular foam sewn inside. Several of these double-duty jackets are Coast Guard approved. There are also jackets designed for small sailboats which provide an adequate amount of buoyancy and yet do not restrict movement as most of the "approved" jackets do. Most of these life jackets may be worn over or under foul-weather jackets. New U.S. Coast Guard regulations recognize a few jackets developed by the North American Yacht Racing Union (NAYRU) that are comfortable to wear while working on deck.

If the race is to be an especially long one—such as a Transatlantic Race, which may take several weeks—your skipper may recommend that each crew member buy inexpensive underwear which can be thrown overboard when soiled. The objective is to dispose of dirty clothes which could cause clutter in duffels or in lockers below.

You will, of course, need certain personal care items. Be sure you have a compact toilet kit for toothbrush, toothpaste (the skipper may object to your using his, and besides, you might not

A typical "floater" jacket with unicellar foam sewn inside to provide flotation as well as warmth. Some of the latest types (like this one) are U.S. Coast Guard–approved "personal flotation devices." (Ted Jones)

like the taste), shaving gear, etc. I like to be clean shaven and have found a battery-driven electric razor convenient. It has shaved me every other day for three weeks on one set of four penlight batteries.

One necessary item that I often forget to pack is a towel. Don't rely on your skipper to provide one—although there are usually extras aboard well-found yachts. When I remember, I take a fairly large one for toilet use and a smaller one to wrap around my neck under my foul-weather jacket to keep the drips out in really hard weather.

Don't forget about sun protection! A sun hat with a brim all around protects not only your eyes and nose, but also the tops of your ears and the back of your neck. Long hair also will protect your neck, but it won't do much for your eyes and nose. Bring your own preferred type of sunburn lotion. Even though you may not be bothered by the sun normally, exposure to tropical sunshine for many hours (under some watch systems you may be exposed

PERSONAL EQUIPMENT

for as long as ten hours in one day) can cause serious burns. You should use a protective lotion that totally blocks ultraviolet radiation and not a *tanning* lotion, which may not afford enough protection under intense sun conditions.

If you require any special medications, you must provide them. In addition, notify your skipper or the crew's medical officer (see Chapter 16) regarding the type of medicine you have and why you need it. This applies to anything stronger than aspirin, including seasickness remedies. If you become incapacitated, someone should know what you need and where it can be located.

Packing a lot of gear can be difficult, especially when boots, foul-weather gear, flotation jacket, and deck shoes will almost fill a large duffel. I find it helpful to roll my clothing in tight wads and to stuff the duffel bag while it stands vertically, closing the zipper gradually until the duffel is filled up. By filling all the cracks and crevices in this way, you can get a surprising amount of gear in a normal-size duffel bag. If your boots won't fit, stuff your foul-weather jacket in one boot, your pants in the other, tie the boots together with a string (some have grommets on top for this purpose), and carry them over your shoulder. When flying

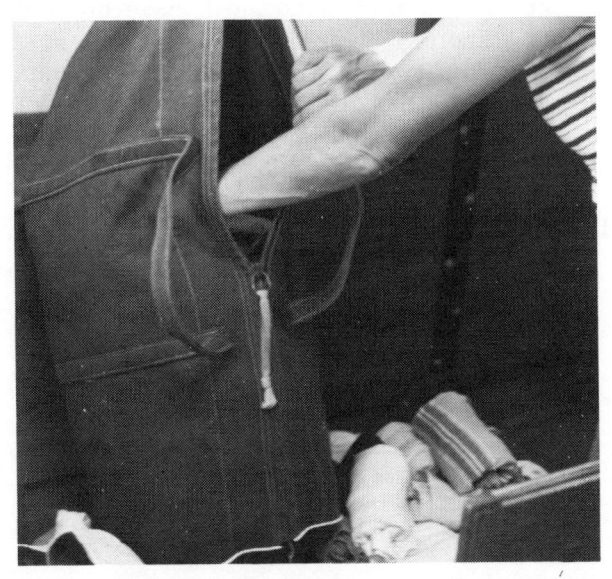

The recommended way to pack a duffel. (Ted Jones)

to a race, don't check your boots as baggage or you may arrive minus part of your foul-weather gear.

A good-quality rigging knife should be carried at all times—either a folding one in a pocket (with a lanyard) or a sheath knife in a belt—worn outside foul-weather gear. A three-inch blade should be the minimum size, and a proper sheath knife is better than a pocketknife. Good sheath knives are available with marlin spikes and with pliers as well. The trouble with some is that they stick up over the belt and dig into your ribs. Try them all for comfort as well as quality before you buy.

I have trouble keeping stainless steel blades sharp. However, I have found that a slightly rough edge—as it comes from a grinding wheel rather than a stone—cuts lines more effectively than a fine edge.

I always carry sunglasses, but I try not to use them unless it's absolutely necessary. If I wear sunglasses as a matter of course, my eyes become accustomed to them, and I find I need them all the time on sunny days. Rather, I keep the sunglasses in reserve for those occasions when I have to squint into the sun while watching the luff of the spinnaker—or when the glare is such that I cannot see without them. A brimmed hat will often cut the glare enough so that sunglasses are unnecessary.

If you smoke cigarettes, by all means bring your own. There are no sundries stores at sea. Your shipmates will have brought their own and, no doubt, carefully figured out just how many packs they need to complete the voyage. If you bum from them, they won't make it. I would hate to be the cause of a shipmate's nicotine fit. Better you should have your own nicotine fit or use the opportunity to quit smoking. Cigarette ash makes a mess both on deck and below, so any ship will be cleaner if there are no smokers aboard. However, good crew members being hard to find...

Chapter 4 **Organization of the Crew**

Windward Passage and her 20-man crew. (Chris Caswell)

Unlike the two- or three-man one-design racing crew, each of whom often has a set of specific duties, the offshore racing crew members must be more diversified. Each member of the crew will be expected to perform a variety of duties while on watch and in case of an "all hands" call-up. Remember that in a long race the boat must be sailed continuously for days at a time. It is not possible, therefore, for the skipper or owner to be the only helmsman or for there to be only one foredeck man or one winch grinder. There must be several good helmsmen, several good foredeck men, several good winch grinders. Ideally, every member of the crew will be able to do an excellent job at any task that may be required of him during a race.

Offshore crews are usually divided into watches. Half the crew will be working the boat while the other half sleeps, relaxes, or eats. Each watch has a "watch captain," who is in command of the yacht while his watch is on duty. If there is an even number of crew members, the owner or skipper will usually take one watch, acting as its watch captain, and assign his second in command as watch captain of the other watch. Conventionally, watches are referred to as the "starboard watch," captained by the skipper or senior watch officer, and the "port watch," captained by the second in command or junior watch officer. In practice, these are formal distinctions only, but they serve to identify the chain of command if some emergency or dispute should require a clear statement of who is in charge. Hopefully, there won't be any outright disagreements, but one must be realistic and acknowledge the possibility.

If there are eight men as the total crew for an offshore race, four will be assigned to each watch. These four men together must be able to perform any normal function that will be required during their watch. They must be able to make rapid headsail changes, reef and shake out, set and take in the spinnaker and staysails, and, of course, steer. However, there will be times when they can't perform some of these tasks without help—a squall comes up and sails must be gotten in quickly, a gear failure requires immediate attention—the possibilities are almost endless. Bear in mind that a boat with a crew capacity of eight might require six crew members for a short, around-the-buoys race, and that four crew members will be hard pressed at times to get everything done. This is racing, after all, and not only must sails be set and doused, but these tasks must be done as quickly as possible to minimize the time lost. When a particular task cannot be done quickly enough by the watch, one or two crew members from the other watch can be called to help. Otherwise, it is an all-hands call and everyone must turn to.

Large yachts will have more all-hands calls than small yachts. Some of the over-60-footers I have sailed on require all hands for such routine tasks as headsail changes and spinnaker sets, takedowns, and jibes. Yet a rough race can be a grueling experience if one is constantly called out of his bunk to give a hand to the watch on deck. Watch captains should be thoughtful of their fellows below and make sure a call-up is absolutely necessary before calling all hands. Two or more interrupted off-watches in a row can exhaust the crew. If it happens to both watches, the racing will surely suffer, and the safety of the yacht may be jeopardized. Proper rest is absolutely necessary, as fatigue is perhaps the greatest cause of lost races, broken gear, and injured crew members.

Nevertheless, one must realize that such call-ups are necessary, and one must try to take them in stride. I recall a race many years ago aboard Dick Nye's second *Carina*. It was a short overnight race of sixty miles on Long Island Sound, and since *Carina* had several Transatlantic, Fastnet, and other important trophies to her credit, we didn't exactly stand in awe of our anticipated sixty-miler.

Shortly after supper when everything was squared away and *Carina* was sailing nicely under spinnaker, our watch turned in, supposedly until midnight. I had just gotten to sleep when I was awakened by sensations of violent rolling and shouts on deck. A cold front had come through, and the wind had shifted instantly from 15 knots from the southwest to over 35 knots from the northwest. We scampered on deck just in time to see the spinnaker disappear from its tapes, and we all turned to to get the boat jibed, cleaned up, and new sails set. The job done, we returned below to go back to sleep.

Crash!

Seemingly minutes later we shot out of our bunks again. *Carina* was screaming along before the wind, and her mizzenmast was lying in pieces amid a tangle of sails and rigging around the helmsman's ears. So we turned to once again—to clean up the new mess.

By the time we had retrieved the sails, cut away the rigging and stowed the pieces, and were ready to go back to the sack, Dick announced, "Well boys, it's midnight, time for your watch."

It just didn't seem fair. We had gotten no rest at all when we were supposed to be off watch, and here we were rounding the mark and facing four hours of cold, tough thrashing to windward. Of course, the other watch was just as tired as we were, and it *was* their turn to rest, so we took over without complaint.

In the end, it was worth every minute of being tired and cold. In spite of our difficulties, we finished first and won our class. Incidentally, this particular race gave the annual Indian Harbor Yacht Club's Fall Stratford Shoal Race the nickname "Gearbuster," which has stuck over the years.

Sometimes crews are organized so that one or more members stand out of regular watches. The skipper may use this arrangement in order to be "on top" of any critical decision that might arise in either watch. Obviously, the skipper can't remain on duty all the time, but he usually can rest during periods where nothing much is likely to happen. In this way the skipper makes himself available when he is needed most.

It is often a good practice for the navigator to stand out of the watch system. When celestial observations are made, the navigator must be up at specific peroids during the day and night to take his sights. He also needs time to work out his calculations. It is much easier on the navigator if he can be free from other duties to work on his primary task. As will be brought out in a later chapter on navigation, a good racing navigator will be at his job continually; he will get little enough rest doing the navigating without having to stand a watch, too.

The other person who legitimately may stand out of watch keeping is the cook. Long races, particularly long races on large yachts, put a special burden on the logistics of feeding the crew. Cooking and cleaning up the galley can be a demanding and nearly full-time job. Like the navigator, the cook must carry out his duties at specific times so that it often works out best if he does only his job and does not have to stand a watch. Chapter 6 will discuss the duties of the cook.

Whenever one or more people are left out of the regular watch system, they can be used to supplement the watch on deck when additional manpower is needed. If one additional hand is needed, call the cook; if two hands are needed, call the cook and the skipper or the navigator. This eases the burden on the other watch and allows them to get the full benefit of their rest period. The skipper, navigator, and cook can make it up later if they need more rest.

Watch Systems

The normal two-watch system calls for "four on and four off," with each alternating every four hours. This system of watch "tricks" is probably as old as sailing itself and is the basis of the "ship's bells" that strike every half-hour from one to eight and thoroughly confuse the landlubber. In early seafaring days the bells were used to count the watches—one bell was sounded after the first half-hour had passed, two after the second half-hour, etc.—until eight bells (four hours) sounded the change of the watch. The watches changed at midnight, 0400, 0800, noon, 1600, and 2000 each day.

Most offshore racers use some modification of the two-watch system, since four on/four off watch tricks mean that each watch has the same time periods each day. So that one watch doesn't get stuck with the dreary watch between midnight and 0400, a system of rotating, or "dogging," the watches is often used. The simplest dogging device is to split the 1600 to 2000 watch into two watches of two hours each. However, even this has its disadvantages in that during this period neither watch has an opportunity to get any meaningful rest. It does help overcome a second problem—feeding the watch at normal eating hours—because the crew can be fed at 1800 instead of either 1600 or 2000.

Variations of the so-called Scandinavian watch system take advantage of the normal alertness that most people have during daylight hours by lengthening the daylight watch and shortening the night watch. The most common of these systems has two six-hour watches during the day and three four-hour watches at night. These watches may begin any time, of course, but most crews prefer to have the six-hour watches from 0700 to 1300 and 1300 to 1900, with four-hour tricks from 1900 to 2300, 2300 to 0300, and 0300 to 0700. This allows mealtime to fall at convenient

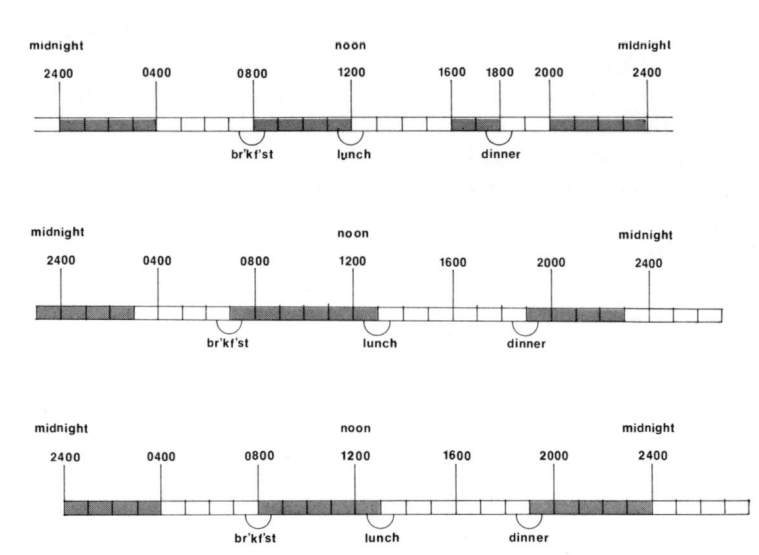

The basic four-on/four-off watch system (top) with the 1600–2000 watch split or "dogged" so that the watch periods rotate each day. An improvement on the basic watch system (middle) is the 4-4-6-6-4 routine with the first watch beginning at 2300. Mealtimes come at six-hour intervals. The 4-4-5-6-5 watch system (bottom) allows a long rest period between the five-hour watches or two long rest periods either side of the six-hour watch.

hours and automatically dogs the watches so that neither watch gets stuck with more night watches than the other.

An additional advantage of the modified Scandinavian watch system is that it provides a longer rest period during the day. Conversely, the system has the disadvantage that if there should be a long call-up during either six-hour watch, the called watch will have missed its best opportunity for rest before the long afternoon trick (if called up during the morning) or the two night watches (if called up during the afternoon).

Another modification of the Scandinavian watch system is the 4-4-5-6-5 arrangement. The daylight hours are split into five- and six-hour watches. Starting at midnight they progress as follows: 0000 to 0400, 0400 to 0800, 0800 to 1300, 1300 to 1900, and 1900 to midnight. This system dogs automatically and accommodates the normal meal hours. It also provides a long six-hour rest period between the five-hour watches or two five-hour rest periods either side of the long six-hour watch. Thus, if call-ups are necessary, there is an early opportunity to catch up on missed rest.

Some crews find this system complicated at first, but once it is

ORGANIZATION OF THE CREW   29

in full swing it works very well. I prefer this system to others I have been shipmates with. Its only disadvantage seems to be that the hours on duty during the normal twenty-four-hour day are not the same. The first watch is on for fourteen hours and off for only ten hours from midnight to midnight the first day, although the time off gets made up the second day. In actual practice, this doesn't seem to matter. It does mean, however, that this watch system is not practical for races of much less than three days' duration.

A watch system using an uneven number of crew members, which gives four hours on and six hours off with two crew on

CREW	MARK	TED	JANET	KAREN	JOHN	GENE	CHUCK	PK
BERTH	Q.B.	Upper	Stbd.	Port	Q.B.	Upper	Stbd.	Port
MIDNIGHT	●	●					●	●
1	●	●	●					●
2	●	●	●	●				
3		●	●	●	●			
4			●	●	●	●		
5				●	●	●	●	
6					●	●	●	●
7	●					●	●	●
8	●	●					●	●
9	●	●	●					●
10	●	●	●	●				
11		●	●	●	●			
NOON			●	●	●	●		
13				●	●	●	●	
14					●	●	●	●
15	●					●	●	●
16	●	●					●	●
17	●	●	●					●
18	●	●	●	●				
19		●	●	●	●			
20			●	●	●	●		
21				●	●	●	●	
22					●	●	●	●
23	●					●	●	●
MIDNIGHT								

Mark Baxter, owner of *Chimera,* uses a variation of the four-on/four-off watch system in which a fresh crew member comes on deck each hour. This system does not dog, and mealtimes fall at inconvenient hours for some crew members. This system is only suitable for races of two days duration or less.

watch (with a total crew of five), also has been used. Using the conventional four on/four off system, Crew A takes the midnight to 0400 watch starting out with Crew E, who is relieved by Crew B at 0200. A is relieved by C at 0400, while B is relieved by D at 0600. E relieves C and A relieves D to complete the sequence. This system also dogs itself.

Still another watch system, used by former CCA Commodore Fred Adams' *Katama* in the 1963 and 1966 Transatlantic Races,

	MARK	TED	JANET	KAREN	JOHN
MIDNIGHT	●	●			
1	●	●			
2		●	●		
3		●	●		
4			●	●	
5			●	●	
6				●	●
7				●	●
8	●				●
9	●				●
10	●	●			
11	●	●			
NOON		●	●		
13		●	●		
14			●	●	
15			●	●	
16				●	●
17				●	●
18	●				●
19	●				●
20	●	●			
21	●	●			
22		●	●		
23		●	●		
MIDNIGHT					

The four-on/six-off watch system is possible with an uneven number of crew members. Fresh crew members come on deck every two hours. As in *Chimera*'s routine, mealtimes are inconvenient for some crew members, and there can be no particular watch captains. This system is good for long offshore passages.

ORGANIZATION OF THE CREW 31

	MARK	TED	JANET	KAREN	JOHN	GENE	CHUCK
MIDNIGHT	•	•	•				
1	•	•	•				
2	•	•	•				
3	•	•	•				
4					•	•	•
5					•	•	•
6					•	•	•
7					•	•	•
8	•	•					•
9	•	•					•
10	•	•					•
11	•	•					•
NOON			•	•	•		
13			•	•	•		
14			•	•	•		
15			•	•	•		
16	•					•	•
17	•					•	•
18	•					•	•
19	•					•	•
20		•	•	•			
21		•	•	•			
22		•	•	•			
23		•	•	•			
MIDNIGHT					•	•	•
1					•	•	•
2					•	•	•
3					•	•	•
4	•	•	•				
5	•	•	•				
6	•	•	•				
7	•	•	•				
8				•	•	•	
9				•	•	•	
10				•	•	•	
11				•	•	•	
NOON							

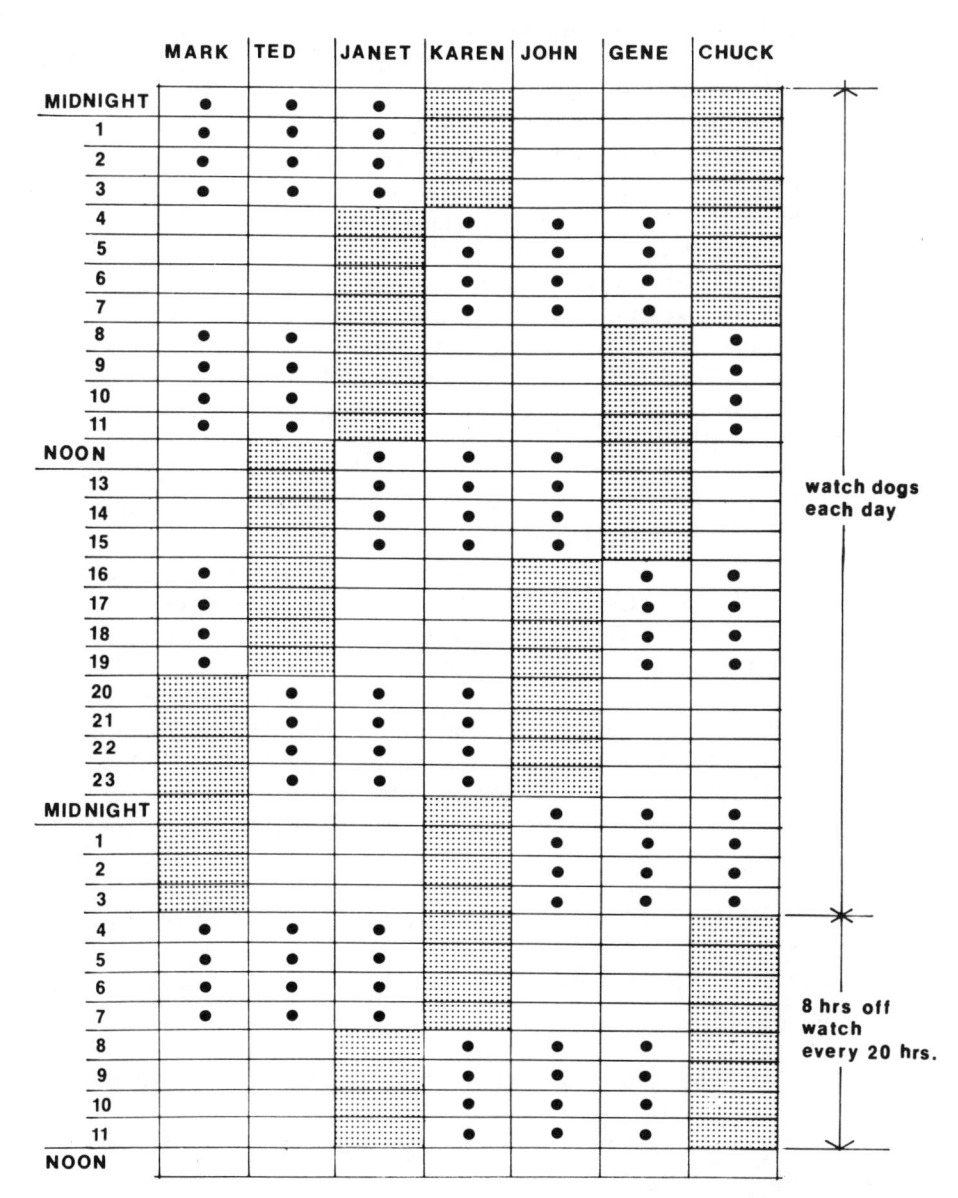

watch dogs each day

8 hrs off watch every 20 hrs.

Katama's watch system appears to be extremely complicated because it performs several important functions. Each crew member has eight hours off every 20 hours. Mealtimes are at eight-hour intervals dividing the day equally. The system dogs automatically. Three crew members are on deck at all times while four are off. In case of a call up, the crew member with the eight hours off is called first. This system is suitable only for races longer than three days duration.

involves an uneven number of crew members and provides each man with an uninterrupted eight hours of rest every twenty-two hours. It is based on the four on/four off system, with three crew members on watch at all times and four off at all times. For example, on watch from midnight to 0400 will be A, B, and C, while D, E, F, and G are off; from 0400 to 0800 D, E, and F are on, while G, A, B, and C are off (G having had eight hours of rest). From 0800 to 1200 G, A, and B are on, while C, D, E, and F are off (C having had eight hours of rest), and so forth.

This watch system is self-dogging, and the eight-hour rest period also rotates as the days progress. Mealtimes on *Katama* were at 0400, noon, and 2000, providing even eight-hour periods between meals. Like the 4-4-5-6-5, Adams' system is suitable only for races of long duration.

With a full eight hours uninterrupted rest each day, there is less likelihood that crew members will need sleep at other off periods. Hence, they have a chance to help with minor ship's husbandry chores, or they can read, listen to the radio (with earphones, please), carve scrimshaw, or whatever else they like, if it does not disturb either the watch on deck or those sleeping below.

A great deal has been written about watch systems that the uninitiated might think is superfluous. In my opinion, not enough thought is given to watch systems and the benefits they can deliver in helping to keep the crew rested and happy. In the long run, an alert, spirited, and well-fed crew is the crew that will be in the best position to take advantage of their breaks and thereby win offshore races.

One of the nice touches aboard *Carina* was the relaxed informality in the watch system. Shortly before the start of a race, or sometimes even just after the start, Dick Nye and his son Richard would have a public conference in the cockpit that would go something like this:

Dick: "Why don't we start watches at 1500? I'll take the first one until 1900."

Richard: "Okay, then why don't you take Bill, Ted, and Al with you, and I'll have George, Fred, and Frank on my watch."

Dick: "Fine with me. That okay with you fellas?"

Thus, watches and watchmates were established in a way that made it seem that it didn't really matter who was on what watch. It ought not to matter, but often it does. The watch detail *was* thought out in advance—if only roughly—when crew members

ORGANIZATION OF THE CREW

were invited for the race. It must be if one is to have a balanced and efficient winning crew, but the effect of this conversation on new crew members not only established an informal atmosphere aboard, but also instilled the confidence in the crew members that each was being relied upon as much as the other.

I have sailed aboard boats which were run in a very formal way. When you came aboard, you were shown to your assigned locker; the watch billet was posted above the navigator's desk along with a bunk assignment. Even your towel and its rack were labeled in the head. This may be necessary in a large boat with fourteen in the crew, but in a smaller boat this kind of regimentation can cause the crew members to develop animosity toward the afterguard and apathy toward the race:

"I'm just here to pull the strings. I'm not a part of the team. I'm just another body. I won't be consulted at decision time. My experience as a helmsman (foredeck man, tactician, etc.) is not appreciated. I'll just do what is expected of me and try to enjoy the ride."

If these feelings are allowed to develop, the reaction of the crew, when the chips are down and extra effort is needed, is likely to be: "Go to hell!"

This rarely happens aboard boats run like *Carina* because everyone feels important and a part of the team. When extraordinary effort is called for, it is given without a second thought. Everybody pitches in, and gladly. When the job is done and the crew members collapse, wet and tired, to recoup their strength, it is with feelings of deep satisfaction of having worked together and overcome a difficult situation.

I don't mean to knock organization. It is necessary to have a permanent locker, bunk, and towel, but the crew members should pick them out themselves on a first-aboard, first-choice basis. The skipper, watch captains, and navigator are "first aboard"—having organized the prerace planning—so they probably have already staked out their claims to special lockers and bunk requirements suited to their duties and equipment.

Even the best-run boats will have their problems—I don't think the Nyes would mind my saying that I've participated in a couple of panic parties on *Carina*. There have also been disagreements, but the well-run boat will rarely receive less than 100 percent effort from its crew. Let one or two crew members feel that they are in some way "lower-class citizens," though, and you will destroy morale and decrease your chances for top racing efficiency.

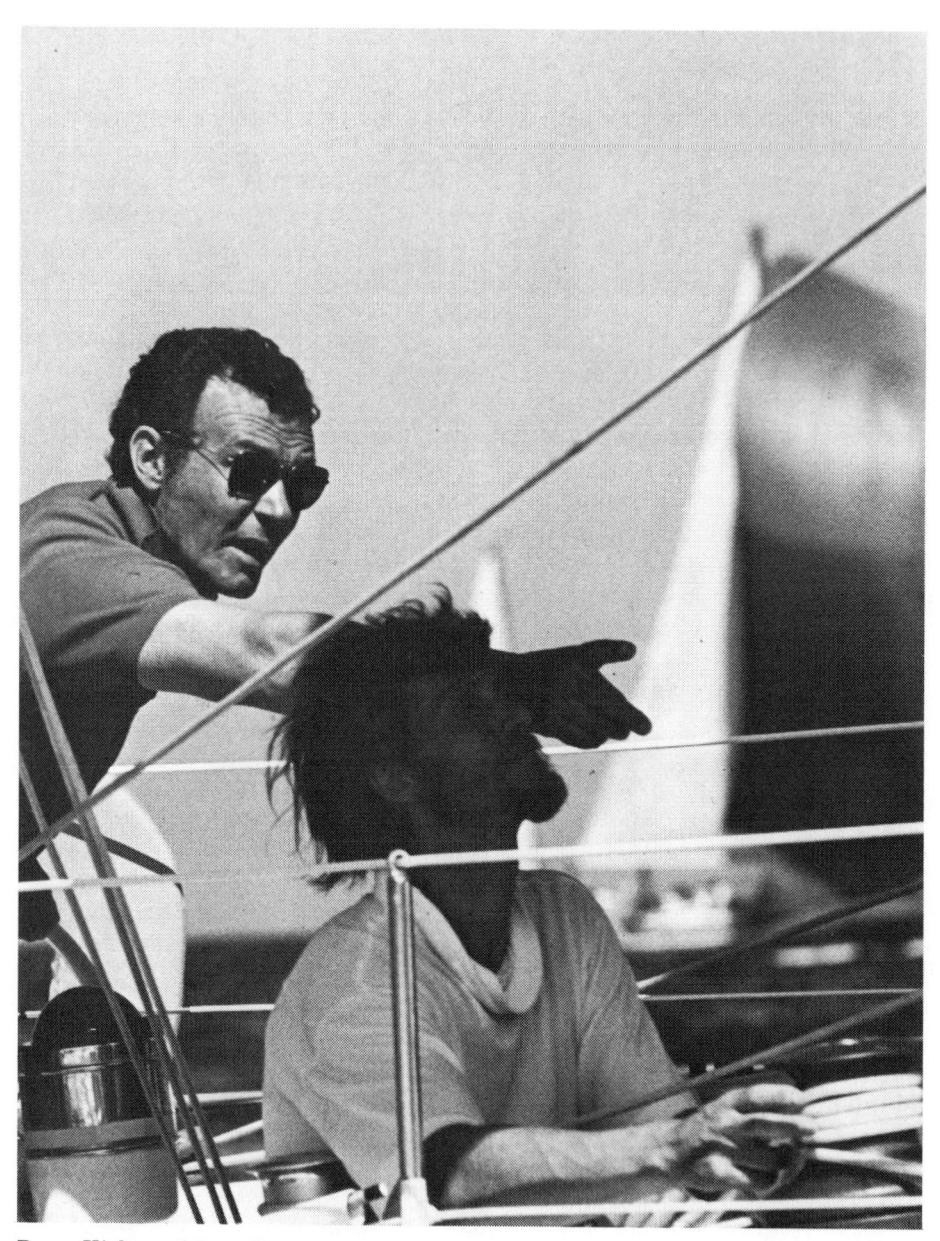

Bruce Kirby and Lars Bergstrom.

Chapter 5 The Skipper and the Watch Captains

In most cases the primary requirement for becoming a captain is ownership of the boat. This is only fair because, after all, there must be some rewards for the fellow who pays all the bills. Ideally, the person in command should know more about the yacht and about racing the yacht than anyone else aboard. He cannot be *only* a superior helmsman, navigator, or strategist. He cannot be expected to be a superior everything, of course, but he must, ideally, have considerable working knowledge of everything that goes on aboard his yacht. In this way, the captain will quickly earn the right to command and the respect of his crew. The bill-paying captain, a captain by proclamation only, invariably will be held in contempt by his crew.

Unfortunately, many captains are captains by proclamation. The simple fact is that often the person who pays the bill has been so busy earning money that he hasn't had much time to become an expert seaman. Of course, this is not always the case; there are many wealthy people who *are* expert seamen. But even a captain who is not knowledgeable can be a good one. The good captain knows his limitations and gathers around him people who have the type of knowledge he lacks.

The absolutely essential quality that any captain must possess is good judgment. I know of several very successful offshore racers whose captains know very little about the sport except that they enjoy it and learn more every time they race. Yet by knowing how to rely on skilled crew members for specific information, these captains are able to arrive at a decision tempered by their own good judgment. In many cases, a crew may feel slightly contemptuous of the captain's lack of knowledge. However, if his judgment is above reproach, he soon will have earned his right to command. Good judgment is the most important attribute of a good captain because the ultimate decisions that determine race strategy, navigation, crew morale, the settlement of disputes, and ultimately, the safety of yacht and crew can be made only by the *one* person in command. This requires the ability to sift through all the alternatives that a given situation presents and to pick the best one.

Note that the title of this chapter refers to the "skipper" and not the "captain." I prefer the title "skipper" because it has a gentler connotation than "captain." We all sail for fun, and the more relaxed we can be, the more fun we will have. Therefore, if we can ease any feelings of oppression that the word "captain" might arouse, that is all to the goood. I am not suggesting that the responsibilities of command be undermined in any way, for whether he is called "Captain," "Skipper," or "Shit Head," *The Man* is still in command. He is an autocrat—an absolute dictator. When he says, "Do it," it must be done. There can be no argument with his authority.

The best skipper, however, will be the one who doesn't have to say, "Do it." He should have those delightful qualities of leadership that allow him to be relaxed and "one of the boys," yet at the same time be able to retain the authority of the commander. His crew will quickly learn the difference between, "Sam, do you think we ought to take the spinnaker down?" and "Hey, guys, I think we ought to take the spinnaker down." Both are casual statements, but the latter is a command, while the former is a reminder, a suggestion, or a question.

Part of the skipper's responsibilities is to be certain that each crew member knows what is expected of him and his shipmates, too. For example, the skipper should make it clear that Sam is in charge of the foredeck, Mike is the navigator, and Sandy is the cook—and for heaven's sake stay out of his galley!

The skipper's job is really very simple. If he stays out of the way, and nobody notices him until he steps up to accept first prize, he has done his job to perfection. That is an oversimplification, of course, because no one *wants* a skipper who is a nobody. However, if he is not obvious about being in command, yet is, in fact, commanding, everyone will have a good time, the skipper included.

There is no way to play down the responsibility that the skipper must bear alone. He is responsible for the safety of the yacht and her crew, and this responsibility cannot be delegated to any other person.

Yet the skipper cannot be on deck every minute of the day and night, so someone must be able to act—routinely—in his place.

That person is the watch captain. When his watch is on duty, the captain of the watch assumes the authority of the skipper. Note well the difference between "authority" and "responsibility." The authority granted the watch captain allows him to act in the skipper's place, to make decisions which he feels confident to make, decisions which he is sure will be the same decisions the skipper would make. He is responsible to the skipper for those decisions, but the skipper's ultimate responsibility cannot be delegated. If the watch captain makes the wrong decision, the skipper is still responsible for the *consequences* of the decision. If the watch captain feels that he is not capable of making a decision, or if he wants to consult the skipper to be sure he is in agreement, then the skipper should be awakened and apprised of the situation. It is perfectly normal and acceptable for the watch captain to make a decision and to conduct his watch however he sees fit, even if the skipper is on deck. The watch captain may assume that he is in command unless or until the skipper tells him otherwise. If there is any disagreement with the action the watch captain takes while the skipper is on deck, the skipper will normally exercise his authority as commander.

The watch captain may consult with the navigator while the skipper is asleep. The navigator is on a more or less equal level with the watch captains in the chain of command, though he is responsible to the skipper. However, any decisions are made by the watch captain, not the navigator. The navigator's position is an advisory one unless the skipper designates him as his second in command.

This arrangement may appear much too formal and military to the crew whose primary objective is to have a good time, but the transfer of authority from skipper to watch captain to crew is one that must be understood by all hands. This does not mean, however, that all must be "aye, aye, sirs," complete with snaps to attention and clicking of heels. The carrying out of orders by the chain of command may and should be as informal as possible without sacrificing the primary goal of maintaining discipline.

On a well-run yacht, the chain of command may work this way:

Watch captain to navigator: "Hey Charlie, we just got headed five degrees, and the blue sloop that was behind us and to windward tacked. Waddya think, should we tack and cover him?"

Navigator to watch captain: "Well, we are very nearly on the rhumb line on this tack although there are some indications that we might get a favorable current if we went over to the south a few miles. You could give it a try if you want and keep lookout for a header on the other tack. I can keep working with the Loran to see what current there is, if any."

Watch captain to navigator: "Okay, I think we'll tack and cover this guy and see what happens."

Skipper (getting out of his bunk) to watch captain: "Hey Sam, we tried that two years ago, and the damn current never materialized. Let's stay on this tack. Let the blue boat go. If you get headed some more, then you might consider tacking. *(Climbing back into his bunk)* Give me a call in a couple of hours if something doesn't come up before that."

This dialog represents the chain of command in action. It was informal, but not without attention to authority. The watch captain asked the navigator for advice, received it, and made a decision. The skipper, having overheard the conversation, assumed command momentarily and overrode the watch captain's decision before returning command to him. Everything was done on a friendly basis. The ultimate decision was based, rightly or wrongly, on a combination of the information at hand and previous experience. Nobody got uptight or argued; nobody's feelings were hurt.

This sort of command system can work only where there is some requisite experience in each position and where each person recognizes and respects the other's experience. It is absolutely essential that each person deal with the other fairly and that there be no attempts to undermine the authority of another crew member.

The skipper has the final duty as chief morale officer. He must not undermine the authority of his watch captains by consulting with one of his watchmates. If the skipper wants the opinion of another crew member, he should ask the watch captain, "What does Fred think?," rather than ask Fred directly. The watch captain can then say, "Hey, Fred . . ." and thus get Fred's expertise into the system. This may appear very stilted and formal, but when practiced by the experienced, tactful skipper, such formalities pass unnoticed. It is only when protocol is ignored that it becomes noticeable.

The watch captains must be careful in their dealings with the navigator and the other crew members to make certain that they do not undermine the authority of the skipper. A statement like: "Waddya say we crack off ten degrees and set the chute while old 'Blue Balls' is down there asleep?" will do nothing to inspire the watch with confidence in their skipper. If the watch captain thinks cracking off and setting the chute is a good idea, he simply should go ahead and do it. If he thinks the skipper would disagree, he either should not do it or wake up the skipper and ask him. Any attempt to improve his own image at the expense of the skipper's is a ground for demoting the watch captain to "bilge boy" or recommending him to duty aboard a rival yacht.

Kittiwake's crew examines pile of food that must go aboard prior to the Transatlantic Race. (Ted Jones)

Chapter 6 **The Cook**

Eating well is absolutely essential for a healthy, strong, and happy offshore racing crew. Poor or insufficient food can cause sickness or the old sailing ships' malady, scurvy (vitamin C deficiency), to develop. Poor or insufficient food also can contribute to seasickness and fatigue and affect crew morale, especially when the food is badly prepared.

To get good food into the crew, someone must cook it. This is an obvious statement, but all too often the preparation of food on an offshore race is left to chance. The best solution to the problem of who shall cook is to find an experienced offshore racer who is also an experienced chef, who has cooked before offshore, and who doesn't mind doing it and nothing else. This solution also presupposes that your boat is large enough to carry a crew member who does not regularly participate in sail drill—hence does not stand a watch. I strongly recommend a full-time cook if there is room aboard the yacht.

The person who signs on as cook must have an absolutely iron stomach and be impervious to violent motion, lack of air, foul odors, and disgusting sights. An example of the latter is the first mate as he crawls out of his bunk, wipes the drool from his scruffy beard, scratches his crotch, stares at the cook with bleary, red eyes, and says, "Good morning, Sweety, what the fuck's for breakfast?" If the cook can take this with a smile and remain standing in a galley tilted at a 45° angle while peering into a frying pan in which slosh two slimy eggs, and still manage to retort with a "Go back to bed, you ugly son-of-a-bitch," then he or she is a first-class sea cook. Of course, the eggs are cooked to order and done to perfection. If you can find someone like this, whether male or female, single or married, young or old, beautiful or ugly, sign him or her on for life!

There really are people like this. Such a person is Joan McKee, an English girl who has sailed Bermuda, Transatlantic, Fastnet, and innumerable RORC Races. Joan has sailed with the prime minister of England, and I'm sure that if it were within their power, the crews she has cooked for would have proclaimed her Queen. While I have had the pleasure of meeting Joan several times, I have, unfortunately, never had the pleasure of being shipmates with her. Those who have sailed with her report delicacies that would do justice to a fine French restaurant, yet Joan has the sensitivity to know when to serve a fancy meal and when to serve a plain, rib-sticking bowl full of stew that the crew can down in a hurry so as to get on with the race. And either meal may be prepared while thrashing to windward in a whole gale. Nothing can have a more salutary effect on a tired, wet, hungry crew than a chance to sit down below in a warm, dry cabin to a delicious feast carefully prepared and served by an attractive cook. Suddenly, the storm raging on deck is miles away.

Not all cooks start out as cooks. Sandy MacKenzie, who cooks for eighteen or twenty men aboard *Windward Passage,* once was a regular crew member, sailing frequently with Bob Johnson on *Zia* and *Ticonderoga.* In one race there was no one to cook, so Bob asked Sandy if he would like to do it. Sandy's been cooking exclusively, first for Bob Johnson and (subsequent to his death) for Bob's son Mark and the *Windward Passage* crew, ever since.

I have sailed with Sandy. While his meals may not be as sensational as those served up by Joan McKee, they are superb—particularly when one considers the size and number of *Passage's* crew, and the fact that Sandy does all his cooking on a standard three-burner stove with a small oven.

Not all experiences with full-time cooks turn out as well, and I know of two that were disasters because the cooks were unknown to the rest of the crew prior to the race. I will not identify the individuals or the races, except to say that both races were extremely long ones, which compounded the problems.

I was a party to urging the signing on of a cook whom none of us had ever met. This person came highly recommended, and we had visions of a second Joan McKee sailing with us. Our cook was supposed to be a reasonably good seaman, but, we soon discovered, could neither steer nor handle lines. We were not used to the type of food prepared, and when, after long suffering, we suggested with our greatest tact that a slight change be made (onions only once a day instead of at all three meals) the cook became incensed. "You don't like my cooking!" was the stormy retort.

THE COOK

In addition, the galley was constantly a mess, matches were struck on the plexiglass window—leaving great scratches—and one by one the cook found reasons to fault each member of the crew. The crowning blow came two-thirds of the way through the race when the cooking gas ran out because the cook had not followed instructions for shutting off the stove. We were fortunate that we didn't blow a great hole in the ocean and disappear, as we must have had gas escaping into the bilge. As it turned out, we did have an explosion, but not from gas.

When the gas finally ran out, we were forced to attempt cooking, quite awkwardly, inside the charcoal cabin heater. We suggested to the cook that a can of spaghetti be heated inside.

"Be sure you put a hole in it first!" we warned.

"Yes, of course, do you think I'm stupid?," was the reply.

Boom! The stove exploded in a cloud of ashes, hot coals, and spaghetti. The stove door hit one of my watchmates on the back as he was crawling out of his bunk and it landed in my lap. Fortunately, no one was hurt and there was no damage, but what a mess! You guessed it—the cook had forgotten to put a hole in the spaghetti can.

The only thing this cook was good for was to act as a focus for our animosity. None of the sailing crew had a harsh word for one another the whole voyage, although we all had harsh thoughts and even a few choice words for the cook.

The following horror story comes to me secondhand. The crew had been sworn to secrecy, but several of us got one of them drunk in Bermuda and were alternately entertained and sickened for several hours while he spilled the whole sorry tale.

It seems the original cook had to back out at the last minute, and in something of a panic the skipper signed on a likely-looking prospect a few hours before departure who claimed to be an excellent cook with experience at sea. There was no time to check references, and the story was accepted at face value since no one had any reason to doubt it. After all, why would someone lie if he were to be found out in a matter of hours and have to live with the consequences perhaps for weeks?

When it came time to cook the first meal, the skipper asked, "Okay, Cookie, what's for dinner?"

"I can't cook," was the reply.

"Waddya mean, 'can't cook'!" said the skipper. "Didn't you tell us you were an experienced sea cook, and didn't we sign you on to do just that?"

"Well, it's too rough [they were still in relatively calm water, close to shore]. You don't expect me to cook when it's rough, do you?"

"Get your ass down there and *cook!*"

"No, I can't."

It was not a very pleasant beginning for a long voyage, but worse was yet to come.

Alternate arrangements were made for cooking with some of the other crew members taking turns. The erstwhile cook was assigned to a watch, and all went relatively well—although relations were decidedly strained—until the first call-up. While the watch turned out in their skivvies to reef, ex-cook took the time to don boots and foul-weather gear and was about ready when his watchmates, cold and wet, reappeared below, the job completed.

Later, when sent forward to help change a headsail, ex-cook clutched the mast trembling with fear. Ex-cook, it seemed, was absolutely terrified of the ocean and refused ever to go forward of the mast again. Yet this person had represented himself not only as an experienced cook but as an experienced seaman—a former boat owner with a new ocean racer on order.

It would be hard to imagine a more worthless individual aboard an offshore racer, particularly on a long race. The effect of this experience on the rest of the crew was frightening and was epitomized by the statement of a normally nonviolent crew member who at one point said to ex-cook, "Don't you ever get between me and the rail."

The implication was clear enough, and the ex-cook (by this time terrified and intimidated by the crew as well as the sea) was truly lucky to survive the voyage. When they reached their destination, he was summarily ordered off the boat, and as he passed through the cabin with his duffel, he was swung at by each of the other crew members—none of whom, probably, had ever hit another person in anger before.

If it is not possible to find a good cook or if the yacht is too small to carry someone to do only that job, it doesn't mean that the crew must dine on second-rate rations. While not everyone can cook well and some people cannot work in the galley without being seasick, there are usually one or more members of the crew who do enjoy cooking, are good at it, and don't get sick. If there are several talented "cooks" aboard, it is best that they be on different watches so that the cooking chores don't always fall to the same watch.

Normally, the watch off duty before the meal will prepare it, and the watch coming off will clean up. If there are those who can't cook but can work in the galley without becoming seasick, they can share in the cleanup detail when it's their watch's turn, thereby further spreading the workload. When several cooks are aboard, they tend to compete so that each succeeding meal becomes better and more elaborate—a good rallying point for the crew.

Occasionally the skipper will stand out of watches and double as the cook. Some skippers prefer it this way simply because they enjoy cooking. The skipper normally is in on the planning of meals, the purchase of stores, and stowage, so it is logical that he probably knows more about the cooking operation than anyone else aboard.

If there is no regularly assigned cook, but the job is allowed to rotate among different crew members, it is most important that detailed menus be prepared, outlining not only what to cook but how to cook it and where the supplies are stowed.

What to Cook

Once the cooking duties have been assigned, there still remain many important questions about the types of meals to serve under particular conditions, the kinds of foods that can be carried, and the places where food can be stowed.

The cook should not be overly concerned with turning out gourmet delights. Good, simple, wholesome food and plenty of it should be the rule. It doesn't hurt to use imagination to add interest to an otherwise dull succession of meals—mandarin oranges in a salad was one nice touch on *Astral*'s menu (see Appendix) for a Bermuda Race. Exotic foods and excessively spicy foods should be avoided. Whereas plain food often can settle a potentially seasick stomach, fancy, spicy food can upset it.

If the galley is small and the stove minimal, interesting and varied meals can be made available by precooking them ashore and reheating them at mealtime. Prebaked casseroles—prepared under the supervision of a capable shoreside chef—can make "Cookie" into "Pierre of the Ritz" in the eyes of his shipmates; all he has to do is reheat and serve. *Voilà, c'est magnifique!* Similarly, precooked roasts and canned hams can last for many meals and may be served hot, reheated in a pan with gravy (something out of a can, not Grandma's secret and fussy recipe), or cold (good for rough weather when it would be difficult to use the stove). Meats that are easy to prepare in a frying pan, such as steak, hamburger, and pork chops, can round out the menu, and many crews dine the first night on "take-out" fried chicken that has been bought just before leaving the dock (although some object to the grease it is fried in).

I once dined on guinea hen, shot by our skipper and cooked at home by his wife. It was a little fussy eating, especially when we bit into the bird shot, but otherwise a delicious meal. Good for morale, too; what other yacht in the race was dining as well?

Canned vegetables are the most convenient. They are easy to stow, easy to prepare, and keep indefinitely. Frozen vegetables are okay, but they don't last as long and clutter up the icebox.

Potatoes keep well, can be served in a variety of ways, and are easy to stow. Canned potatoes are even easier.

Radishes, carrots, and onions keep well and can be served raw in salads or (carrots and onions) cooked. Lettuce is great in salads and sandwiches, but cabbage keeps longer and can be served raw or cooked. Eat the lettuce first on a long race and save the cabbage for later on.

For desserts, canned fruits, cakes, and cookies are simple and easy to store.

Sandwiches are a staple lunch item, but unfortunately keeping the bread fresh is not always so simple. On the Transatlantic Race in 1966, however, we used canned bread, which lasted well for several weeks. The "good" breads—those made with natural foods and few preservatives—don't last as long as the soft, economy-size sandwich loaves.

Luncheon meats—bologna, smoked ham, chicken, salami, and liverwurst (if the crew likes the stronger meats)—that come presliced and packaged are an obvious choice for sandwich meats. Also consider canned Spam, deviled ham, and chicken spreads. Mayonnaise makes a good spread, but it must be kept cold once it is opened. Oleomargarine keeps better than butter and is neater.

Lots of peanut butter and jelly should be available for between-meal snacks and standby meals. One shipmate literally lived on peanut butter for the entire transatlantic passage. He didn't like many of the meals that were served, being an admittedly fussy eater. He was a good shipmate, however, and when we were down to our last jar of peanut butter, we hid it from the other watch so he wouldn't starve.

Breakfasts should consist of eggs, cooked as many different ways as the cook can dream up. One good wrinkle is to fry an egg in the center of a piece of bread which has had its middle removed. Bacon will last quite a while if it is kept cold. Canned bacon will keep indefinitely. Cereals, either hot or cold, are okay, but they

THE COOK

require milk, which is bulky and doesn't last long. Powdered milk is a good substitute, but it requires fresh water—an item usually in short supply—to mix it.

Frozen or concentrated juices should be avoided for the same reason: they use up the precious water supply. Canned juices are a better choice since they supplement the water requirements of the crew rather than making demands upon it.

Water must be carried to last throughout the entire voyage, plus a comfortable reserve (30 percent extra is not excessive). There should be enough aboard for one quart per man per day, and it should be stored in separate tanks or other containers—not all in one tank—in case the tank is holed or becomes contaminated. Beer and soda are convenient to carry and stow and make excellent supplements to the water supply. Vegetables may be cooked in seawater, and dishes can be washed in seawater to conserve the fresh water supply.

Between-meal snacks are very important. The night watch will particularly appreciate it if the cook has left some packages of dried raisins ("power pellets") or candy bars in the galley. They are excellent sources of instant energy, and raisins (as well as dried prunes) act as laxatives. Coffee, tea, and broth with crackers, pilot biscuits, and cookies can help turn a miserable night watch into a bearable four hours.

Before the cook decides on what foods to serve, he should check with the entire crew to see if anyone has any particular dislikes or aversions to specific foods. One shipmate couldn't eat peanut butter. It made him instantly and violently ill. We found out that he wasn't kidding one day when we buttered his jelly sandwich with the same knife that had been used for peanut butter. He couldn't taste it, but he became ill almost before he had swallowed the first bite.

It is always helpful (and essential for long races) to write out a detailed menu for each meal to be served during the passage. (*Astral*'s menu is reproduced in the Appendix.) This should be done well in advance so that special foods, like canned butter, bacon, and bread, can be ordered. If many crew members will be sharing the cooking chores, the menu should include brief instructions on preparing the meal and list each item and where it is stored. Some owners have special bins available into which complete meals can be packed. All the cook need do is open the appropriate bin to find all the ingredients for Thursday's dinner.

Cans stowed in bilges should have their labels removed and their contents marked with indelible magic marker. Otherwise, the labels will soak off in bilge water and the crew will spend the rest of the voyage eating "canned surprises."

If it is necessary to wrap food in plastic bags, remember that they should not be thrown overboard. The sea is the world's garbage pail; it can recycle almost anything we throw into it from a yacht, but it can't recycle plastics.

Long races, such as a two-week Transpac or three-week Tahiti or Transatlantic Race, present two particular problems: how to keep perishables and how to get enough food stowed aboard to last for the duration of the voyage—plus a comfortable reserve. Mechanical refrigeration and freezers are one solution to the food storage problems posed by long voyages, but I know of several crews that had to eat steak three meals a day when the freezer broke down, and they still had to throw away a considerable amount of spoiled food. Relying on mechanical devices can be dangerous. Keep a reserve of canned food just in case.

If mechanical refrigeration is not available, dry ice may be used. It should be stowed in the bottom of the icebox and thoroughly wrapped in heavy, waterproof paper and/or plastic to help preserve it. Dry ice will last for five or six days, sometimes more. Keep fresh vegetables away from the dry ice so they don't freeze or become contaminated, and be cautioned that it may cause milk to become carbonated. The milk isn't harmed, but it will taste funny.

Eggs will keep for weeks if they have never been refrigerated, and months if dipped in paraffin. (See Chapter 17 to find out what happened to *Kittiwake*'s eggs in 1966.) Canned butter will last indefinitely.

For Transatlantic Races, *Carina* had coal for the cabin stove stowed in her icebox. The reasoning was that the ice wouldn't last long anyway, so why start out with any? The newest *Carina* has mechanical refrigeration.

To be happy, a sailor needs a full belly. The cook's job is, therefore, extremely important to the overall morale of the yacht. Most crews cope with most problems, but a crew that is fed lackluster meals by a cook who is uninterested in his job *will* become discouraged, disheartened, and antagonistic. Crews in bad humor do not win races. Good, plentiful meals, served by a congenial cook who puts imagination into them and keeps a neat galley will do wonders for morale.

A good cook can't win a race by himself, but he certainly can help. A bad cook can earn dead last all by himself.

Chapter 7 **The Navigator**

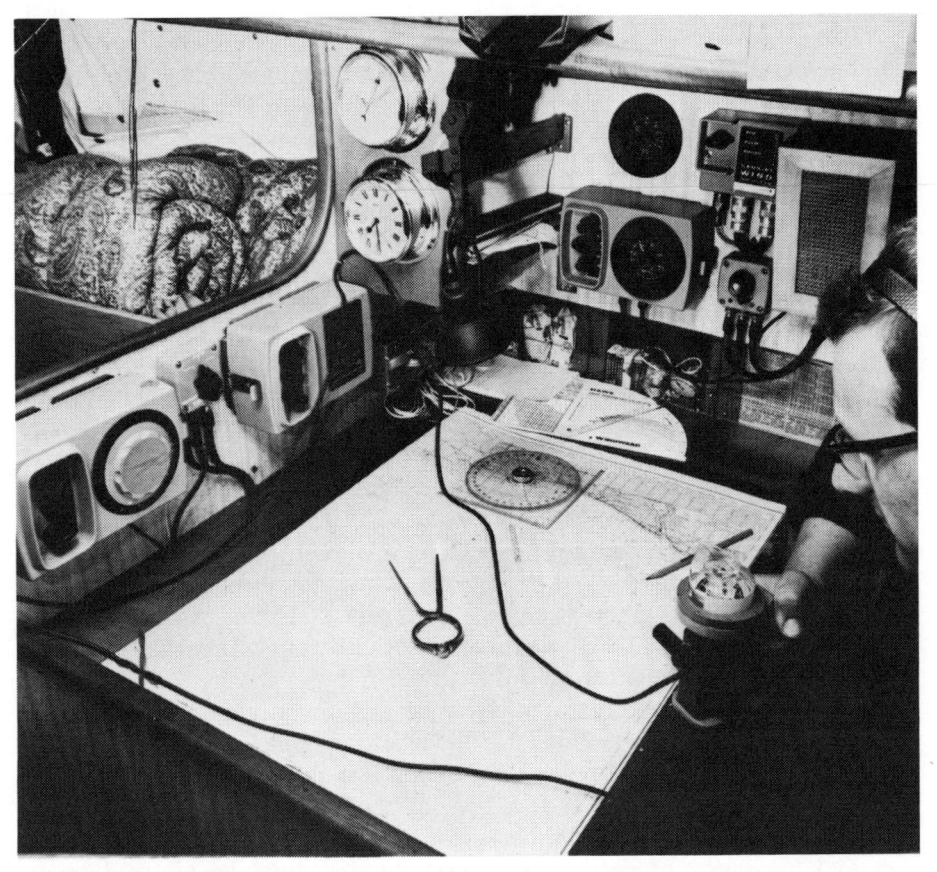

The navigator surrounded by the tools of his trade.

The traditional role of the navigator aboard an offshore racer is to keep track of the yacht's position. The modern navigator, however, if the yacht is to be among the winners, must go beyond his traditional role. He must figure out how to get from wherever he is at the moment to the finish line, in the shortest possible time.

"The principle of marine navigation," according to J. J. Mac Brien who navigates Ted Hood's famous *Robins*,"is always to have plenty of safety margin, whereas the *racing* navigator is zipping along past rocks half a boat length away." Therefore, the racing navigator has to work to much tighter tolerances. There is (or should be) less margin for error, hence a small safety margin, otherwise the yacht is not racing to her maximum potential. Racing navigators must be bold. They must take risks as a matter of course that would not be taken in normal cruising or passage making.

Mac Brien believes that good "racing" navigation is often bad navigation. As an example, he cites the 1972 Bermuda Race which finished in a gale at night with many yachts beating into a lee shore toward unmarked reefs. "If a merchant marine navigator ordered such a course," says Mac Brien, "he'd be relieved of his job, and rightly so." The prudent seaman would heave to and wait for daylight and better visibility *at least*.

It will be correctly surmised that the offshore racing navigator must have a combination of both skill and guts in large measure. In addition, of all the jobs aboard, the navigator's is the most specialized. He has his own special tools, a seemingly prodigious number of books and tables (see Appendix), his own work area, and a variety of delicate instruments. He must be allowed to do his work undisturbed, should have no other duties, and, if possible, should not be assigned to a watch.

Before adding to the mystique that has developed around navigation, let me point out that it is not the mysterious black art that some navigators would have their skippers and fellow crew members believe. This idea is a smoke screen put out by marginally competent people who don't want the crew to know that they don't know precisely where they are. Navigation is basically a simple, logical process. True, there is sometimes a bit of guesswork and intuition (intuition is based upon experience) involved, which makes it not an exact science but partly an art. But the knowledgeable, secure navigator will have the stability of character to admit, on those occasions when he isn't positive, that there is a small doubt as to the yacht's *exact* position. More likely, he will point to a spot on the chart and say, "We're here." How are you going to know if you aren't exactly "here"?

The navigator must use every bit of information he can obtain. Navigation is a twenty-four-hour-a-day job, which means the navigator should never stop working. So if he occasionally appears irritable and impatient with inane questions from the other crew members, he should be forgiven. Even better, the inane questions should not be asked. Navigation, done properly, is extremely demanding, but few navigators are as thorough as they ought to be.

To me, navigation is at the heart of offshore racing. It is the fascinating plotting board where, with all its ramifications, the battle unfolds. Flying a spinnaker when nobody else can keep theirs full, getting the most out of the boat when you're steering her to windward are exhilarating, necessary features of winning a race, but if the navigator doesn't put you in the right place, you're nowhere.

If you do not already possess the technical knowledge to become a navigator, this chapter will not make you into one. If, on the other hand, you have a working knowledge of the basics, I hope that reading this chapter and the following one can make the difference between getting there and getting there first. We'll begin by reviewing the basics, and then go on from there.

For the beginning navigator, whose needs are well beyond the scope of this chapter, there are many books devoted exclusively to navigation. The most prestigious, both in terms of size (1,524 pages) and content, is Nathaniel Bowditch's *American Practical Navigator* (U.S. Navy Hydrographic Office) which, although it was first published in 1802, continues to be the basic reference of navigation.

Several organizations offer courses in navigation. The most well known and most comprehensive of these is offered by the U.S. Power Squadrons (USPS) throughout the United States. The course is a four-year program consisting of courses in elementary piloting and basic seamanship, advanced piloting, practical celestial navigation, and celestial navigation theory and practices. USPS members with an "N" certificate (signifying completion of the four-year course) are among the most sought-after yacht navigators. A person who has gone through the entire four-year USPS course has been exposed to virtually everything he will need to know to navigate a yacht offshore (except the experience). Other courses, such as one offered by New York's Hayden Planetarium, are geared to practical celestial navigation and may be completed in a relatively short time.

There may be books and courses to teach the techniques and principles of navigation, but there is no text to teach *offshore racing* navigation. Speaking of the 1972 Bermuda Race, mentioned at the beginning of this chapter, Joe Mac Brien said, "You won't find a book which teaches you to make approaches like that!" There can be no substitute for experience and the good judgment and confidence that only experience can provide.

For the moment, let's put aside the second job of the navigator, getting from "here" to "there" in the shortest time, and concentrate on how he determines where "here" is. The navigator must know where he is or precisely where he was at a given time, in order to know how to get someplace else.

Two separate activities are often lumped together under the term "navigation." The first is "piloting," a term used for position-finding where reference to land and other objects of known position can be made. The second is "navigation," which includes position-finding by observing the position of celestial bodies, taking various kinds of radio bearings from transmitters whose locations are known precisely, taking soundings where depths are available on charts, and, of course, piloting.

The basic tool of the navigator is "dead reckoning" (DR). He may be far from the sight of land, or visual reference may be obscured by fog or darkness; clouds may prevent the taking of sights; he may be out of range of radio stations or the bearings may be distorted by outside influences; and he may be far offshore "off soundings," or have no means for measuring the water's depth. Still, the navigator has the basic means of calculating by dead reckoning—the time, speed, and direction run from his last known position—where he is.

THE NAVIGATOR

Dead reckoning is often not the most accurate means of position-finding, but it is always available. DR is used as the basis for more precise means of position-finding. It tells you where and in what direction to start looking for visual bearings. It is used in celestial calculations and in checking the accuracy of radio bearings (the least accurate and reliable of the navigator's tools). Using it as a starting point for the location of soundings, a navigator often can pinpoint a boat's position on a chart with no information available other than the DR position and the depth of water.

A line of position (LOP) results when a bearing is taken on an object whose position is charted or when a bearing is taken on a radio transmitter whose location is known. The bearing from the object or transmitter, taken by sighting across a compass rose, is a line, which should be drawn on the chart, from that object on that magnetic bearing. It is actually not a line but a cone (whose width in degrees depends on the accuracy of the bearing). Your position is somewhere within that cone. The angle of a celestial body, whose precise angle above the horizon at a given time on a given day is known (taken with a sextant), will also provide a line of position.

A fix is a point where two or more lines of position cross or where a depth measurement coincides with soundings along the line of position. Lines of position from any combination of observations may be used to determine a fix. The accuracy of the fix is dependent upon the accuracy of the individual lines of position. The more lines of position available, the more accurate will be the fix.

For example, if you cross a visual line of position, which may be accurate within a couple of degrees, and a radio direction-finder bearing, which may not be more accurate than plus or minus 5 degrees, your fix will be less accurate than if you crossed two good visual bearings. The navigator must have a feeling for the relative accuracy of his bearings (the width of the cone) so that he can evaluate the accuracy of his fix.

A check of the DR position can also be obtained by plotting a DR against a line of position. You know that your position is somewhere within the cone of the LOP, and you also know that you have traveled a certain distance along a certain course. If both are accurate, the DR position will fall on the LOP, and you will have reasonable certainty of your position—although, technically, not a fix. If the DR and the LOP are miles apart, something is wrong.

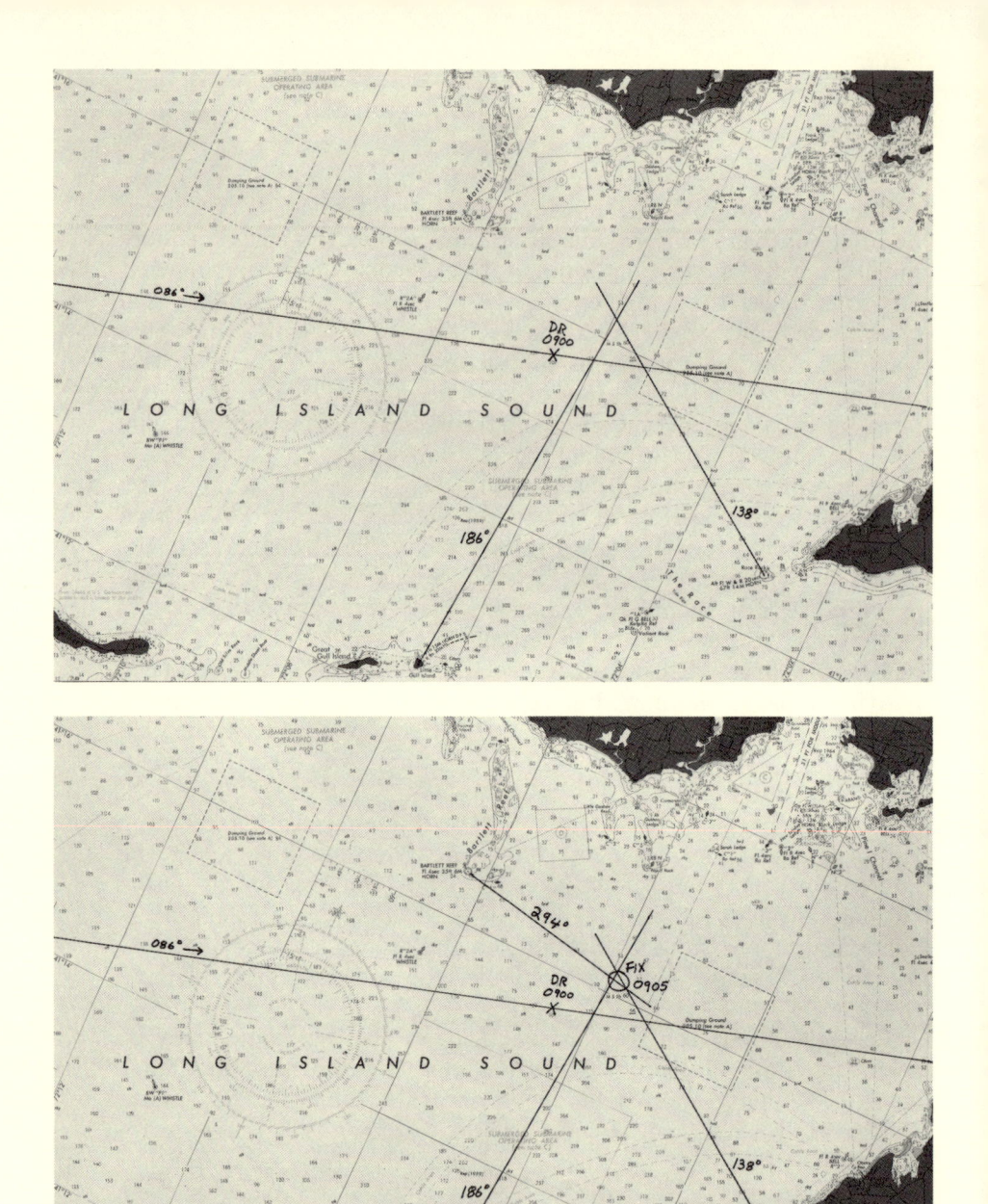

In a race down Long Island Sound through Fisher's Island Sound on a heading of 083 degrees, bearings could possibly be taken on Race Rock (138 degrees magnetic) and Little Gull Island (186 degrees magnetic), both with distinctive lighthouses. In the example shown, these bearings do not coincide with the 0900 DR position. A third bearing at 0905 from Bartlett's Reef (a small tower which might or might not be visible) would verify or deny the accuracy of the two previous bearings. If a bearing of 294 degrees was obtained from Bartlett's (as shown in the second drawing) the fix would be confirmed—the difference probably accounted for by a current set which can be considerable in this particular area.

Shallow angles between LOPs will magnify the error in the fix. Ideally, two lines of position should cross each other at a 90-degree angle and three should cross each other at 60-degree angles. Three LOPs will usually cross at different points, providing a triangle on the chart. Your position is most likely somewhere within that triangle, and the size of the triangle gives you an idea of the accuracy of your bearings. A small triangle means accurate bearings; a large triangle, inaccurate bearings.

Visual bearings are best taken with a hand-bearing compass. Remember that this compass is not compensated. There may be some deviation due to large metal objects nearby.

One day, when I was trying out a new, pocket-size, hand-bearing compass, I was mystified because my bearings were 20 to 25 degrees different from the simultaneous bearings the navigator was taking with the ship's regular hand-bearing compass. I was sitting in a very logical place from which to take a bearing; it was steady, I had something to rest my back against, and there was nothing in my line of sight. The only trouble was that I was leaning against the steel hydraulic backstay adjuster, which was throwing off my compass. Always double-check!

It is possible, of course, and often more convenient, to take bearings across the binnacle. These will not be as accurate as bearings taken with a hand-bearing compass, although deviation errors will have been eliminated.

Be sure you know the *exact* position of the object from which you take a bearing. Buoys and other floating marks can shift their position, but if all you have is a floating mark, by all means use it. A later bearing, even on another buoy, can be used with your DR plot to double-check the first buoy's position. The chances are small that both floating marks drifted out of position the same amount. If there is a discrepancy, you must then ask yourself which mark was out of position. You will be almost as badly off as if you had not taken the bearings in the first place. At least you *know* that you are in trouble, and you will look extra hard to find yet another object from which to take a bearing. If at all possible, however, don't settle for only two bearings!

Suppose you had a fix based upon a bearing on a lighthouse and a bearing on a buoy which had floated out of position. Obviously you would not be where you thought you were, but you wouldn't know it! If you can obtain a third bearing, it will tell you that something is wrong; that is, the three lines of position will cross at widely different points forming a large triangle. Still, you will not know, if two of your bearings were from questionable sources, which of the two is in error. If a fourth bearing can be obtained, and if it crosses two of the other three at nearly the same point, then you will be able to identify the spurious bearing and obtain a precise fix.

You should also use anything and everything that is available. In a race on Long Island Sound in our 26-footer *Trilogy*, we were suddenly enveloped in fog just before dawn. We had a fairly good idea of where we were, but we had no warning of the fog, and we did not have a precise fix. To make matters worse, our speedometer was inoperative! We had been sailing on course to the finish line, so all we could do was maintain this course and hope we could get a fix later.

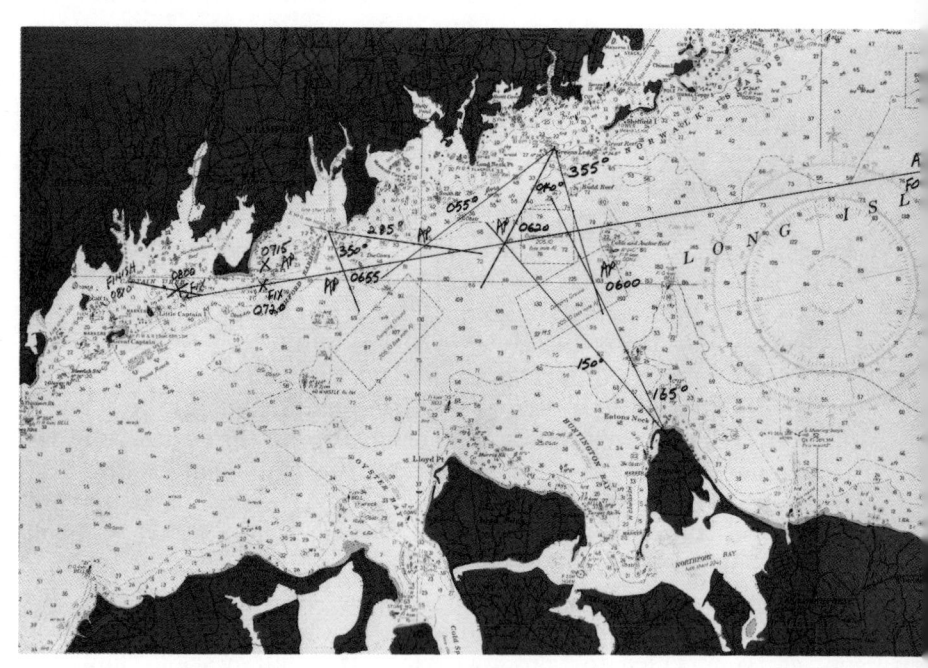

Trilogy's chart of the Long Island Sound race in which fog signals were used to confir approximate positions (AP). Fog set in without warning at 0435 about four mil southeast of the Norwalk Islands. Cable and Anchor Reef buoy was not seen, but f signals gave us an approximate position just past it at 0600. Subsequent audib bearings tended to confirm our estimated speed, and we were looking for either "C1" "N34" when we nearly sailed into grass off Greenwich Point at 0715. We obtained fix on "C1" at 0720 and continued to the finish line to cross at 0810. The saluti cannon for morning colors from Greenwich Harbor at 0800 caused momentary conf sion as we briefly thought that it could have come from the committee boat, signali a finisher. (From C. & G. S. Chart 1213)

Fortunately, the wind was light, and I could hear and positively identify the fog signals from Green's Ledge and Eaton's Neck. I took rough bearings *by ear*—turning my head until the sound was equal in both ears—as we passed, and later did the same thing with the Stamford Breakwater horn. These audible bearings were very imprecise, but they were all we had and certainly better than nothing. We were able to double-check our DR, although we could not get a bearing that would tell us if we were on track for the finish line. This was less critical.

We finally reached a point where, according to our *very rough* calculations, we should see either a buoy or shore. Sure enough, eel grass appeared out of the fog a few boat lengths ahead. We did a quick evasive maneuver, located the buoys, and went on in to the finish line, picking it up without further difficulty. We were the first boat to finish, and the sound of the gun pinpointed the finish line position for those around us who had been milling around helplessly in the fog.

We had a moment's confusion when we heard a gun well off to starboard.

"Could that have been the first finisher?" was our logical question. It didn't make sense, though, since we were now certain of our position and certain that the committee boat marking the finish line lay ahead.

After a few moments' thought and discussion among the crew, I happened to glance at my watch, which read 0800. Of course! The gun we heard was the salute for morning colors ashore at the yacht club. We were right on course, and in a few moments we heard the gratifying sound of a gun to salute *Trilogy* as she crossed the line first.

The lesson for me from all this was that you *can* use questionable information to advantage if it's the only information available. You must know the limitation of such information, however, and not expect too much.

Radio direction-finder (RDF) bearings are subject to so many errors that they are often of questionable value. The radiated signals get bent where they pass shorelines, and they also get twisted by the rigging. Radio direction finders should always be used in the same position aboard the boat and should be swung, like a compass, in good weather with visual reference to the transmitting antenna, on various headings. Still, be very suspicious of RDF bearings unless you get three or more to cross. Even then be suspicious! Use RDF bearings for verification and don't depend upon them for basic data unless you have positive experience with the particular RDF in its defined location on *that* radio station and *that* bearing. If you can satisfy all those requirements, okay—maybe.

Automatic Direction Finding (ADF) is nothing more than an expensive RDF. It is easier to use because it takes the bearing automatically. However, it is subject to the same externally influenced errors of RDF and is of questionable value, considering its relatively high cost.

OMNI is a variation of the RDF using the principle of an infinite number of radial bearings from the station. It is very accurate and easy to use. OMNI will give you a magnetic bearing to or from the station and tell you which it is, thereby solving the 180-degree ambiguity error of conventional RDFs. It will even indicate (roughly) how accurate the bearing is. The only troubles with OMNI are its very short range (line of sight) and, since it is intended for aircraft, the fact that the transmitter locations must be transferred from aircraft charts to nautical charts.

Loran is another electronic device that can be extremely accurate. Two transmitters are involved. To interpret the signals, the navigator aligns the waves from the two stations on an oscilloscope. Numbers are connected to knobs on the set, and when the waves are aligned, the navigator reads the numbers, which then identify a colored line on his chart. This line, although it does not appear straight, is an LOP. A skillful operator can obtain numbers from two sets of Loran stations to provide a very accurate fix at long range (the word "loran" is a contraction of "*l*ong," "*ra*nge," and "*n*avigation").

OMEGA is a new low-frequency variation of the Loran principle. It promises to be more accurate and easier to use than Loran.

Although the NAYRU rules for offshore yachts specifically permit the use of Loran, some sponsoring organizations do not. The feeling is that Loran is too expensive (about $900, plus installation). There are also those who feel that it somehow isn't "cricket," that navigators will forget how to take celestial observations if they have Loran. This is nonsense. No navigator worthy of the title would rely exclusively on a fragile electronic instrument with inherent errors. He would also take sights and use whatever other means were available to him to fix his position. There are many races that are (or could be) more interesting and challenging through the use of Loran.

Celestial observations are the backbone of offshore racing where reference to land, soundings, and radio transmitters is not available. To measure the angle ("altitude") of a star, the sun, or the

A Plath sextant. (Ted Jones)

moon, the navigator needs a sextant. Often a navigator will have his own sextant; he knows its errors and, of course, knows how to use it properly. Perhaps one of the most difficult tasks is to take an accurate sight on a bouncing deck when the horizon is obscured more than half the time by waves and when the star the navigator is shooting is moving in and out of the clouds. There are only certain short periods just after sunset and just before dawn when it is possible to see both the star and the horizon. Too bright and the star cannot be distinguished; too dark and the horizon cannot be distinguished. A noon sun sight is taken when the sun is on the meridian (north-south line) of the yacht or local apparent noon (LAN) and can be used to obtain a line of latitude. Other sun and moon sights can be taken at other hours to provide lines of position.

The navigator may ask one of the crew on deck to help him

record his sights. He will provide a pencil, pad, and stopwatch. When the navigator identifies the star he is shooting (or notes its bearing), his assistant should write down the name or bearing. Under this should be written the time in minutes and seconds from the moment the navigator calls "mark," and the angle in degrees, minutes, and tenths, which the navigator will read off. At least four observations should be taken of each star, and the assistant should indicate which time goes with which angle. At least three stars should be used if they are available.

When all the sights have been taken, the navigator gets out his pads, pencils, almanacs, and sight reduction tables. He will have a good hour's work ahead of him before he can come up with a fix.

The importance of the DR position becomes apparent when one realizes that at best, when navigating only by reference to celestial bodies, the navigator will have only a few periods during the twenty-four day when he can get a precise fix. In-between times he will have to make do with the DR.

You can readily see that under these conditions the navigator's job is most critical. Of course, he is not as busy as when inshore. His main concern will be to make sure that an accurate "deck log" is kept so that the DR position can be kept up.

The deck log is the responsibility of the navigator, but it must be kept by the watch captains. Each helmsman should either make his own entry or give the watch captain or navigator his information so that half-hourly log entries are kept. The navigator wants to know what course the helmsman made good, his average speed, or the log reading at the end of the trick. Also recorded should be the course ordered (by the navigator), the barometer reading, wind direction and velocity (estimated if there is no anemometer), sea conditions, general weather, and any other remarks the helmsman or watch captain wishes to make about the weather, the sails being carried, changes in sails set, other boats sighted, or events taking place outside the boat or on board. The log will become a permanent record of the voyage, and it should contain mention of anything that should become a part of that record.

Every experienced helmsman knows that he cannot always steer precisely what the navigator tells him to steer. He may find that, in spite of his best efforts, the yacht tries to sail high of his course. Under surfing conditions the helmsman may be going off below course to get the benefit of the wave action. The navigator is interested in what course was actually made good. He doesn't want the course ordered parroted back at him. He already knows it. Each helmsman, therefore, must keep careful track of his headings

THE NAVIGATOR   61

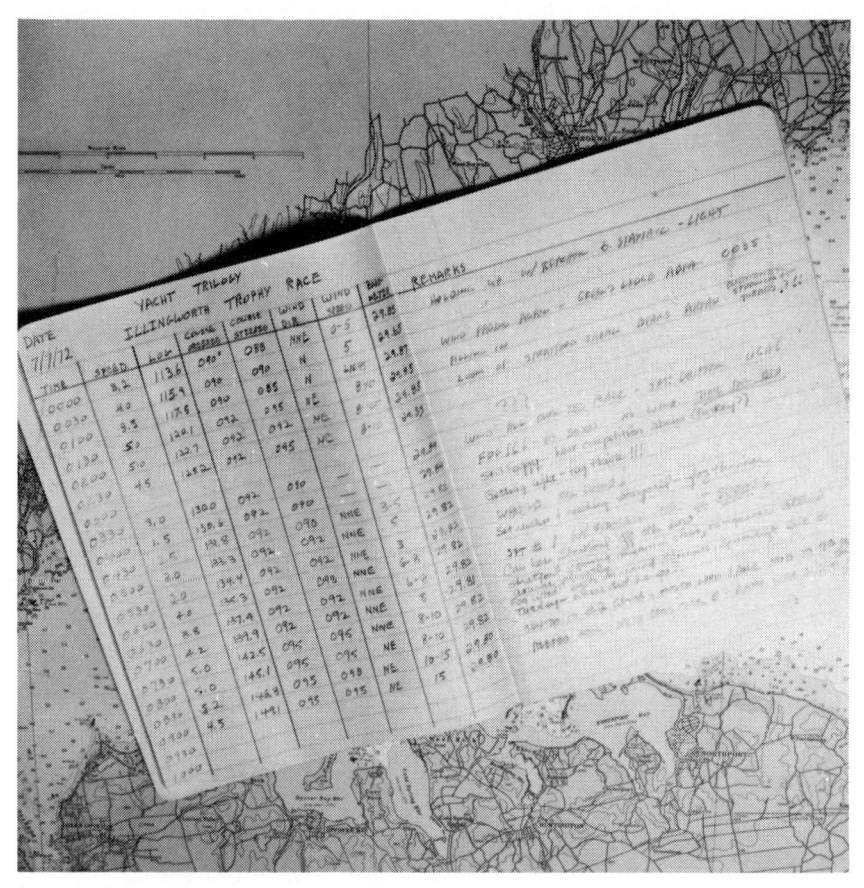

A typical page from a yacht log. (Ted Jones)

and constantly keep in mind what course he has been averaging. Don't fudge; don't lie to the navigator. He needs to know where you went to plot an accurate DR.

It should become second nature for each helmsman to calculate from minute to minute what course has been made good. In this way he can be continually correcting to get as close as possible to the course ordered, and he will have an accurate estimate of the course he actually steered to enter in the log. The importance of this cannot be emphasized enough. *Without accurate information in the log, the navigator cannot get you home first.*

A conscientious navigator will keep track of his helmsmen. He should have a compass at the chart table with which he can check the course. If he's on his toes, he will soon know if his helmsmen are reliable in the courses they report.

The things that throw navigation off most are currents and sets which the navigator cannot measure and which can displace his yacht far from where she would otherwise be. Without Loran, it is not possible to keep constant watch over currents and sets when offshore, but where Loran or visual observations can be made, it is absolutely imperative that the navigator constantly check his position against his DR to see that something unusual isn't happening. This is another reason why the navigator's job is a twenty-four-hour-a-day proposition. The ideal navigator is, therefore, one who can function with a minimum of sleep and short rest periods.

The conscientious navigator, as I see it, has to be extremely, painfully meticulous. He is constantly fiddling with the Loran until he must see wavy green lines in his sleep. He rarely sleeps more than two hours, but pity the poor watch captain who doesn't wake him in fifteen minutes if there's been a significant change in wind, sea, or weather. He can be irascible, irritable, and irritating (who wouldn't be on two hours' sleep?), but I have seen these navigators come up with the damnedest strategic suggestions. Almost without exception they are good ones.

Each experienced navigator develops his own special methods and shortcuts that help him get the job done more easily, more quickly, or more effectively. It is good for the soul to stay close to top navigators and to try to learn their secrets and innovations. The good ones work very hard at their craft, they are proud of their ability to do a superlative job, and most of them don't mind sharing their secrets with someone who shows an interest in their work and an appreciation of their ability.

Sometimes special circumstances will dictate special methods and expedients. For example, Patrick Ellam, who spent nearly twenty years in the yacht delivery business, told me of two things he finds useful when sailing strange boats and when shorthanded—two conditions a yacht deliverer finds constantly. Each time Pat leaves port under sail (almost always in a strange yacht), he takes a series of back bearings to determine the leeway angle and then uses this angle (separate readings are needed for beating and reaching) when plotting his DR position. The leeway angle becomes another factor (along with distance run, heading, and drift due to current) in determining dead reckoning. If one can be sure of drift and leeway angle, the DR will be dead accurate.

Another of Patrick Ellam's tricks could be useful in racing situations. When entering port (often shorthanded), rather than risk losing the chart overboard or having to dash below to check the chart, Pat studies the chart very carefully—memorizing each detail—so that he knows each light characteristic, each compass heading, each buoy. Although Pat claims to have a bad memory, he says he has been able to concentrate enough so that a photographic picture of the chart can be stored in his head for short periods. When safely docked, the memorized chart vanishes. Helmsmen and navigators, working along a tricky coastline or tacking up a narrow passage, could use a specially developed ability of this sort to great advantage. It could allow them to concentrate on sailing the boat faster without the distraction of wondering when to tack or what mark to look for next.

If you can't memorize all the details, make a pencil sketch of the chart and its paramount features.

Incidentally, Patrick Ellam and Colin Mudie sailed *Sopranino*, a just-under-20′ light displacement boat, across the Atlantic in 1952 —the first people ever to do so in a light displacement boat and one so small. Navigation was Patrick's responsibility, and he had never done any celestial navigation. After shoving off from Africa for the Canaries and Barbados, Pat got out his books and taught himself celestial navigation.

"Didn't you think that was a little risky?," I asked him many years later.

"Necessity is the mother of invention," was Pat's reply.

Although it obviously worked for Patrick Ellam to learn as he went, it won't do to go offshore racing and expect to win without a thorough understanding of every navigation problem likely to be encountered and every navigational device likely to be useful. Every possible bit of information that can help the navigator find his position must be gathered, evaluated, and plotted. Only when he is sure that he has used everything available to him can he relax a little and say, "We are *here*."

And at that point, he has done only half his job.

A start off Point Loma, San Diego, California.

Chapter 8 **Racing Strategy**

Position finding is but one of the navigator's duties. He must also have information about currents and weather, which—together with navigation—determine the strategy of the race. In addition to knowing the yacht's position, the navigator must also be involved in the decisions relating to where to go from "there" in order to finish the race in the shortest possible time. The skipper and watch captains will have something to say about which way they want to go because of various other considerations (they are most likely more familiar with the yacht's performance capabilities in the prevailing conditions), but it is the navigator who has the information about currents and wind patterns without which a meaningful strategy cannot be evolved. Therefore, in addition to being the yacht's position finder, the navigator should be chief strategist. Tactics—positioning the yacht in relation to competitors—ought to be left to the skipper, but strategy is properly the province of the navigator.

Tactics in sailboat racing consist of those maneuvers which keep you ahead of your near competitors *right now*. Tacking on the wind of a boat you have just crossed to slow him down; tacking ahead and to leeward of a boat you can't cross to give him a slowing dose of backwind; getting between another boat and the wind, cutting off his driving power and putting him behind you; luffing to keep your wind clear so you can keep a competitor from passing; staying between your nearest competitor and the next mark to be sure you get there ahead of him—all these are legitimate closed-course tactics. However, these same maneuvers are of little or no value in offshore racing.

Most offshore races prohibit luffing after a certain time or after passing a certain offshore mark. Instructions often specify that navigation rules of the road supplant the racing rules, taking away many of the tactics permitted in around-the-buoys racing.

When you are racing another boat through a handicap system, relative boat speed is not that important. Another boat may beat you across the finish line, but because of your handicap you may beat him for the prize. In this situation, staying ahead of another boat is of no importance. The important thing is to sail your own race, relying on your overall *strategy* for your boat to complete the course from start to finish in the fastest possible time.

Strategy in sailboat racing consists of those long-range plans which are calculated to make the boat sail faster or a shorter distance in stronger winds or with favorable currents. Strategic considerations ignore the presence of competitors. While current, wind patterns, and wind shifts play an important part in closed-course races, they are often disregarded for tactical considerations. In offshore racing, strategy—getting from start to finish in the fastest time—is all important.

Wind and current determine the overall strategy of a race. One is always seeking more wind or a more favorable slant, or less current or a more favorable boost from current. The crew that chooses its course well, assuming that the boat is kept moving at top efficiency, is the crew that has the best chance of winning.

Wind patterns fall into two categories: those associated with large weather systems and those generated by local temperature differentials. Local winds occur near land masses when the sun heats the land during the day to a temperature significantly greater than the nearby water temperature. Since warm air rises, the heated air over the land lifts and is replaced by the cooler air from over the water. This creates a flow toward the land or an "onshore breeze." The onshore breeze will blow from midmorning or early afternoon until early evening when the sun has gone down and the land area begins to cool. In the evening the land area will cool down, often becoming cooler than the nearby water, and the flow will be reversed—moving from the land to the water—creating an "offshore breeze."

The greater the temperature difference between the land and water areas the stronger the onshore and offshore breezes will be. These winds are generally stronger where the land and water meet —along the shoreline—and the daytime onshore breeze is generally stronger and more reliable than the evening offshore breeze.

These are general rules having to do with the theoretical development of local thermal winds. Each area also will have topographical features which will alter the theoretical wind pattern. Local racing skippers often spend many years learning the peculiarities of their area's winds.

RACING STRATEGY

The offshore racer cannot know every vagary of every place he will sail, but he should make it a habit to pick up bits and pieces of local knowledge whenever he sails in a new area or talks with a sailor from another area. A catalog of this knowledge, either mental or written down, can be a very useful strategic tool not only when sailing in or through these areas, but also as a means of guessing the local wind characteristics of areas with similar topography.

A good example of unusual local conditions is Long Island Sound, where many overnight races are sailed and where many other long-distance races start and/or finish. The local thermal winds along the northeast coast are usually quite strong in the summertime, blowing from a southwesterly direction. One would expect Long Island Sound to be blessed with strong afternoon breezes much as is the case along the New Jersey shore, the South Shore of Long Island, and along the coast of Massachusetts. Very often, however, there will be little or no wind in the Sound even on hot, sunny days when the onshore breeze is producing perfect sailing on Long Island's South Shore. While the greater continental land mass of Connecticut is heating and creating the onshore breeze which ought to be flowing on the Sound, Long Island, with its many housing developments and asphalt roads, is creating its own thermal, which lifts the onshore breeze so that it skips high above the sails of the Sound's becalmed sailors. Occasionally, the onshore breeze will overpower the Long Island thermal and blow steadily across the Sound (strongest near the Long Island shore). Sometimes the onshore breeze will skip the Long Island shoreline and come down along the Connecticut shore, and often the onshore breeze will have no effect at all on Long Island Sound.

The southwest coast of California presents a classic case of onshore breezes. They spring up regularly during the late morning

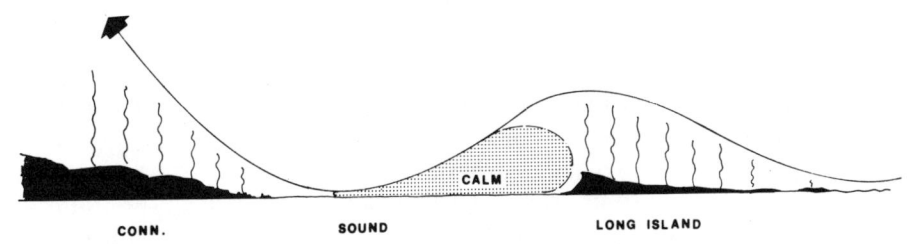

Hot air rising over Long Island elevates onshore breeze causing calm area on Long Island Sound. There will often be a light southwester close to the Connecticut shore when there is virtually no wind in the rest of the Sound.

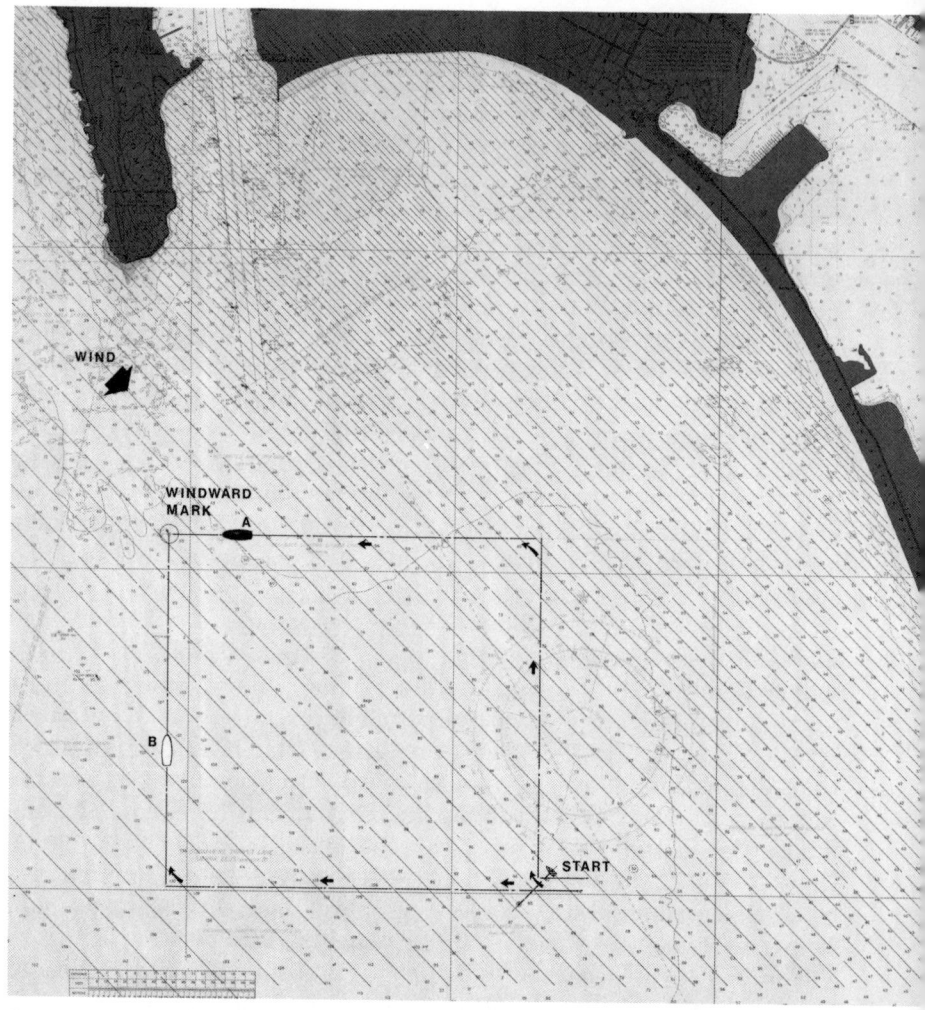

Stronger winds are generally found near the beach off the Southern California coast. Point Loma, off San Diego, tends to accelerate the onshore breeze favoring the inshore tack taken by yacht "A" in closed course races. (From C. & G.S. Chart 5107)

—blowing from the west to northwest—and blow fairly steadily into the late afternoon and early evening. Here the inshore tack is invariably favored because the onshore breeze is stronger near the beach. Off San Diego—where Point Loma sticks out from the coast—the onshore breeze is consistently stronger near the Point—
—perhaps 15 to 18 knots—while just a couple of miles to leeward, away from the Point's influence, the wind will be significantly lighter—8 to 12 knots. This is particularly noticeable on an Olympic

course where the windward/leeward marks are rounded several times. When the wind is always stronger at the windward mark and always weaker at the leeward mark, it is clear that the different strengths are not due to an overall building and subsiding of the wind but, rather, to the influence of the land, which is causing the wind to be stronger near the shore.

Small islands can either boost or retard thermal breezes. Block Island, off the coast of Rhode Island, has steep cliffs on its south side. These tend to block and lift the onshore breeze (southwest), leaving an area of calm which extends out several hundred yards *to windward* of the cliffs, while inside Great Salt Pond, further to leeward in the center of the island, the wind is accelerated considerably. It is common to leave Great Salt Pond in a strong breeze and find there is almost no wind a few miles off the island.

I have noticed this effect in the Coronado Islands just south of California. Anchored in the lee of South Coronado one night, we recorded winds of 20 knots even though we were within fifty yards of the extremely high and steep hills of the island. A few miles away, sailors reported light to drifting conditions.

Small variations in a shoreline can have a bending effect on wind as well, with the wind tending to flow parallel to the shore. If, for instance, a point of land juts out southward from an east/west shoreline, across which is blowing a southwest onshore breeze, the wind will be bent around the east side of the point so that it is blowing more nearly south than southwest.

Whatever information one can gather about local variations in wind should be cranked into the overall strategy of a race. If you know or can guess that the wind will be stronger near the shore, that's where you should be. If you can determine that an inshore

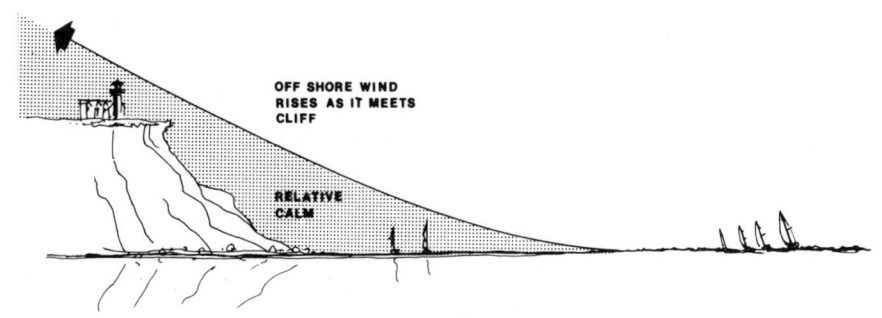

High cliffs such as those on the south side of Block Island often produce areas of relative calm extending out to windward of the cliffs.

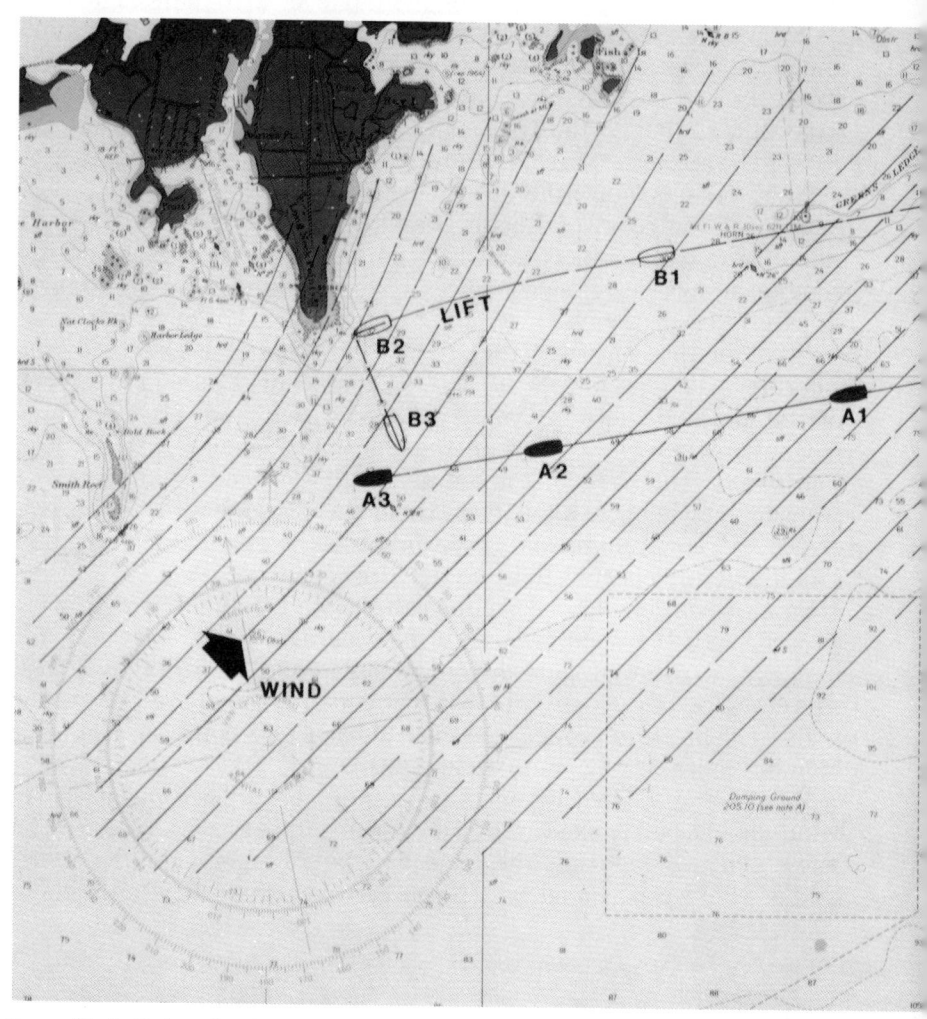

Long Neck Point, jutting out from the east/west Connecticut shore, bends the prevailing southwest onshore breeze giving "B" a lift at position "B2." If "A" and "B" were even at "A1" and "B1," "B" would pass astern of "A" when she tacks out to clear the point ("A3" and "B3"). (From C. & G.S. Chart 221)

tack will produce a lift on the opposite tack, by all means tack inshore. Use whatever wind information is available, weighing its relative reliability, to help you determine the course that will get you from start to finish the fastest. Wind information will form an important part, but not all, of your race strategy.

Currents

The effect of current is, perhaps the least well-understood factor in offshore racing. Some may think that currents are a factor only when one is close to shore in tidal water. However, those who have raced in the English Channel, in races through the Gulf Stream, or even Transoceanic will have discovered that the effects of currents should be considered carefully when planning offshore racing strategy. Many races have been won by carefully playing strong currents. Many more races have been lost because skippers and navigators were ignorant of significant currents, which slowed their yacht and set her off course.

There are three types of current. Tidal current is the horizontal movement of large bodies of water produced by the attraction of the moon and sun. There are tide and current tables available for most tidal areas which provide the time, direction, and velocity of tidal currents. (These should not be confused with "tide tables" which refer only to the vertical movement of the tide near shore.) Tidal current *charts* are available for some areas. These show the direction and velocity according both to one's location and to how the current varies with each hour after the specific point at which flood or ebb begins.

Non-tidal currents, such as the Gulf Stream, are those which flow more or less constantly in direction and velocity. While the general flow patterns of non-tidal currents are usually known, they may vary in speed and meander about considerably. These variations from the norm are not usually predictable over an extended period.

Wind-driven currents usually have low velocity, are restricted to relatively small areas, and are not predictable. Wind-driven currents are found only on the surface whereas tidal and non-tidal currents run from surface to bottom or many hundreds of fathoms deep. Wind can modify both tidal and non-tidal currents in either velocity or direction.

A race aboard Humphrey Simson's Bermuda 40 yawl *Kittiwake* provides an excellent example of the proper use of tidal current, and emphasizes the dramatic effect that such currents can have on the outcome of a race. *Kittiwake* was defending the Nantucket lightship Trophy having won the previous year's race. The course was from New London, Connecticut, around the lightship marking Nantucket Shoals—well offshore—and return to Newport, Rhode Island. We were naturally anxious to do well again.

At the start, the usually strong (four knot) current was running east out of The Race—one of two narrow gaps through which Long Island Sound's tidal water must flow. The rhumb-line course to the lightship was approximately SSE, and the wind was about SSW; we couldn't quite lay the rhumb line on the starboard tack.

We had a reasonably good start at the windward (west) end of the line, and instead of heading SE on starboard tack with the rest of the fleet, we tacked soon after crossing the line.

I suppose the others figured that the current would boost them best by taking it on their weather quarters so it would push them roughly in the rhumb-line direction. Sound strategy also would suggest that one should take the favored tack (starboard) toward the turning mark, which was about 100 miles away. If the wind came around to SW, which we had every expectation that it would, wouldn't *Kittiwake* have thrown away whatever distance she had made on the port tack?

I had figured differently. I thought that by crossing the current, taking it on our lee bow, we would be pushed more nearly toward the rhumb-line course and, because of our four-knot boost from the current, we would be sailing in a relatively stronger wind.

The results exceeded my wildest dreams. In less than an hour we had a commanding lead. While we moved across the current, our course made good was nearly due south. The rest of the fleet, which moved with the current, made good a course that was nearly due east. Furthermore, they had considerably less apparent wind as they were being pulled away from it, sagging along the Fishers Island shore.

Only a fool would figure himself to win a 200-mile race after sailing only five miles. So I couldn't imagine that something wouldn't happen to turn the tables on us, but as is so often the case, as lead boat, we got the breaks. After tacking to starboard we were able to sail into slack water and lay Block Island while the others had to make many tacks in fluky winds around the island. We were also the first to move into freshening winds. Our lead was so great that we were almost halfway around the course before the scratch boat—a 64′ yawl—caught and passed us. We finished second and easily saved our time on the scratch boat and the rest of the fleet, which straggled in hours after we had our victory celebration well under way.

Current had won the race for us only minutes after the start. After the first five miles, the final 195 miles was a matter of continuing to move and trying not to make mistakes.

Our situation was interesting because the great majority of the skippers failed to appreciate the full potential of the current. If

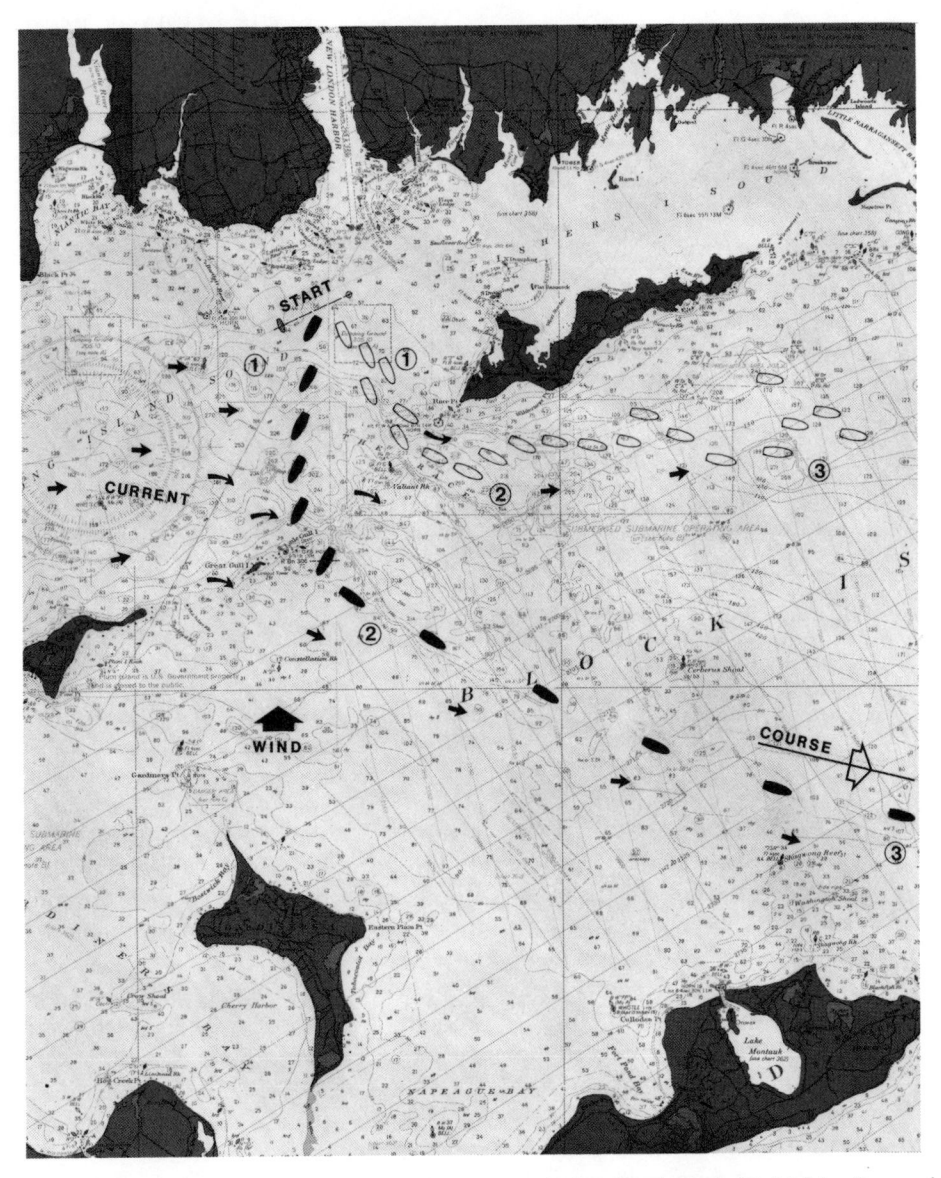

Kittiwake's track (black boat) at the start of the Nantucket Lightship Race. At position "1" *Kittiwake* tacked onto port, sailing across the substantial current while the rest of the fleet sailed with the current out past Race Rock. The current pushing *Kittiwake* to windward increased her apparent wind which increased her speed through the water relative to the other yachts whose apparent wind and speed through the water were reduced. When *Kittiwake* tacked back onto starboard, the current was more directly on her stern (position "2") still increasing her apparent wind while the rest of the fleet had the current on its quarter, pushing it to leeward. By the time position "3" was reached the race was all but won.

Vector diagrams are useful to explain the effect of current upon a yacht. If a current is flowing from the west (as in "A") the yacht will drift with the current to the eastward shown by its "actual position" to the right of its position with no current present. This can be plotted as in "B" where a yacht sailing six knots in one hour on a course of 045 degrees is displaced one nautical mile eastward. If the current was flowing one knot from the east, the yacht would be displaced one nautical mile west in one hour. These diagrams can be drawn on a chart (be sure to plot position in line with current flow) and projections of actual course lines will be valid as long as current is constant in direction and velocity.

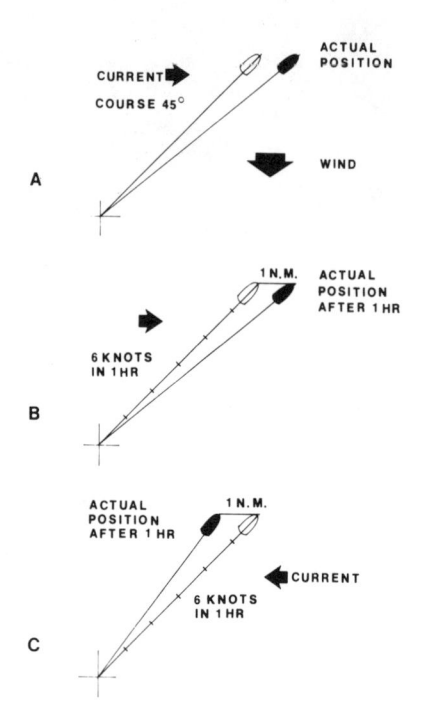

any of them had taken the trouble to work out vector diagrams of the current's effect, they would have seen clearly what it would be. I had merely sensed the advantage and tried it, and did not make a diagram until much later. If I had, I would not have been so surprised at the result.

No less an authority than Olympic Gold Medalist Peter Barrett has effectively and forever laid to rest the so-called lee bow effect. Pete has pointed out very clearly[1] that in a constant current it doesn't matter which tack a boat takes since, sooner or later, it must sail on the other tack for the same length of time with the same exposure to adverse current. No one can argue with the scientific proof of Peter Barrett's diagrams, but in offshore races, currents often are not constant and, during long races, they have time to change.

Consider a situation in which your boat is beating to windward across the English Channel from Le Havre to the Isle of Wight

---

[1] *One-Design & Offshore Yachtsman*, Vol. 8, No. 6 (June 1969), p 19.

RACING STRATEGY 75

on the last leg of the Channel Race. The current is flowing from the SW and has about three hours to go before it turns and flows from the NE. All other things being equal, it would pay to take the first hitch on the port tack and, after the current turned, take a hitch on the starboard tack. On each tack, the current would be pushing your yacht to windward. You would have had a stronger apparent wind velocity and a better angle on each tack while your competitor would have had a relatively weaker apparent wind on a less favorable angle. When racing offshore, a current will not usually be constant along your course line. You must decide, by vector diagrams if necessary, how you can best take advantage of the current to move you closer to the finish line.

When playing currents, the obvious strategy is not always the proper one. Again with *Kittiwake* in currents near The Race, we were finishing a race from up the Sound to Fishers Island. Ahead of us at dawn was our archrival Fred Lorentzen's Block Island 40′ *Seal*. We had come out on the short end of an upwind duel with *Seal* earlier in the race, and I knew we could not hold her to windward. With only a few miles to the finish, it looked as if we'd had it. Fred was covering us comfortably. As we approached The Race, the current was flooding and hitting us almost head on on port tack at between three and four knots, and *Seal* tacked to get out of it. In spite of the hopelessness of our situation we beat *Seal* by several country miles. When we got ashore, Fred kept scratching his head, saying, "I don't understand it. You sailed straight into that current and beat us."

If the race had finished at Race Rock, indeed it would have been all over; we would have had no chance to catch *Seal*. It seemed logical to tack and get out of the current—approaching Fishers Island in relatively slack water along the Connecticut shore, but the situation was desperate for us, and it called for a desperate gamble, which paid off. We were able, by pinching slightly, to take the current on our lee bow. While it was slowing us considerably, it was pushing us to windward gradually. The same vector that was slowing us was pushing *Seal* to leeward after she had tacked for the Connecticut shore, but she had no component to windward. The current was strong enough for us to get into the slack water behind Race Rock, where we tacked for the finish. *Seal*, meanwhile, had been swept far to the west, and still had a one- to two-knot current to buck as she approached the finish line.

Determining current can be just as tricky as determining wind. Current charts, which show the direction and velocity at various stages of the tide, are available for many areas, and these charts

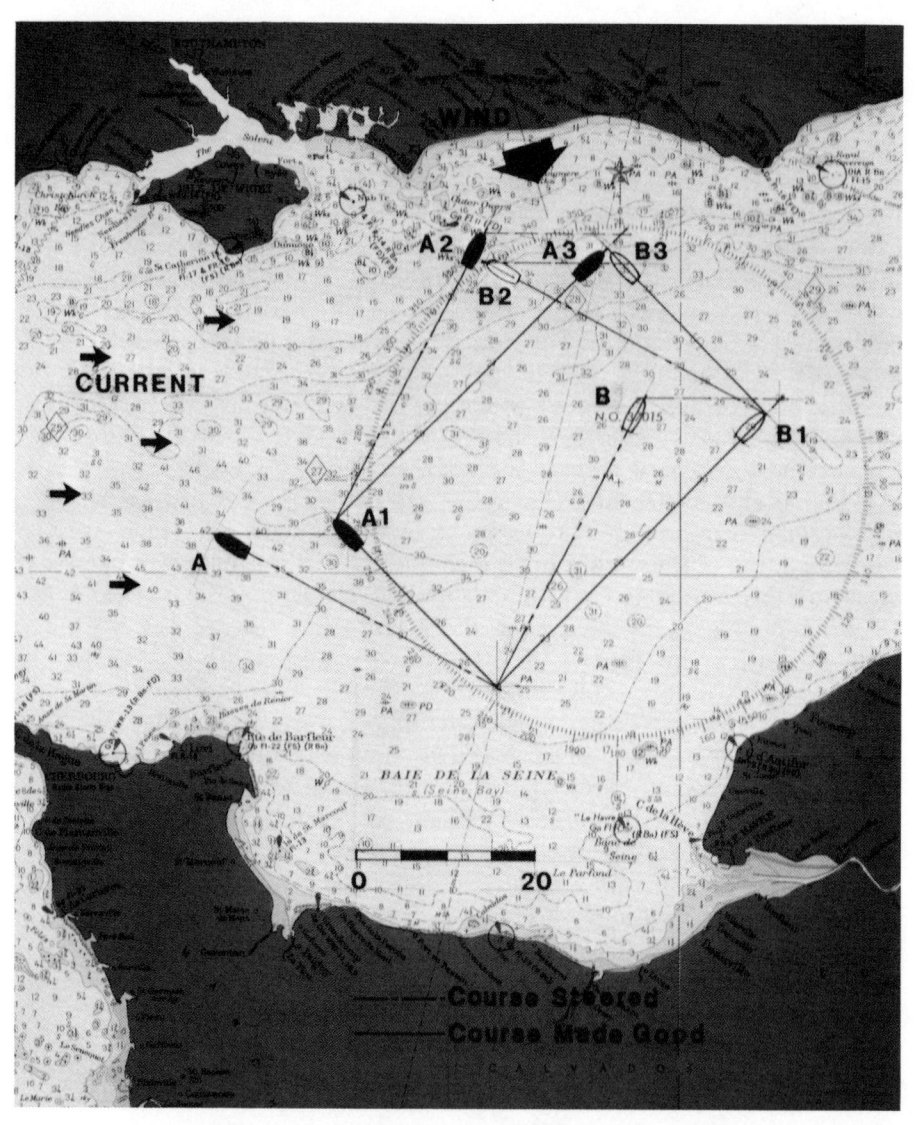

If current is constant in direction and velocity and all other factors are equal, it makes no difference if a yacht takes course "A" or course "B." While the yacht at position "A1" will be ahead of the one at "B1" they will be exactly even when they converge at "A3" and "B3." If the current had stopped when they were at "A1" and "B1" yacht "A" would be slightly ahead when both fetched positions "A2" and "B2" because "A" had a stronger apparent wind while lee bowing the current shown by the vector at "A"—"A1."

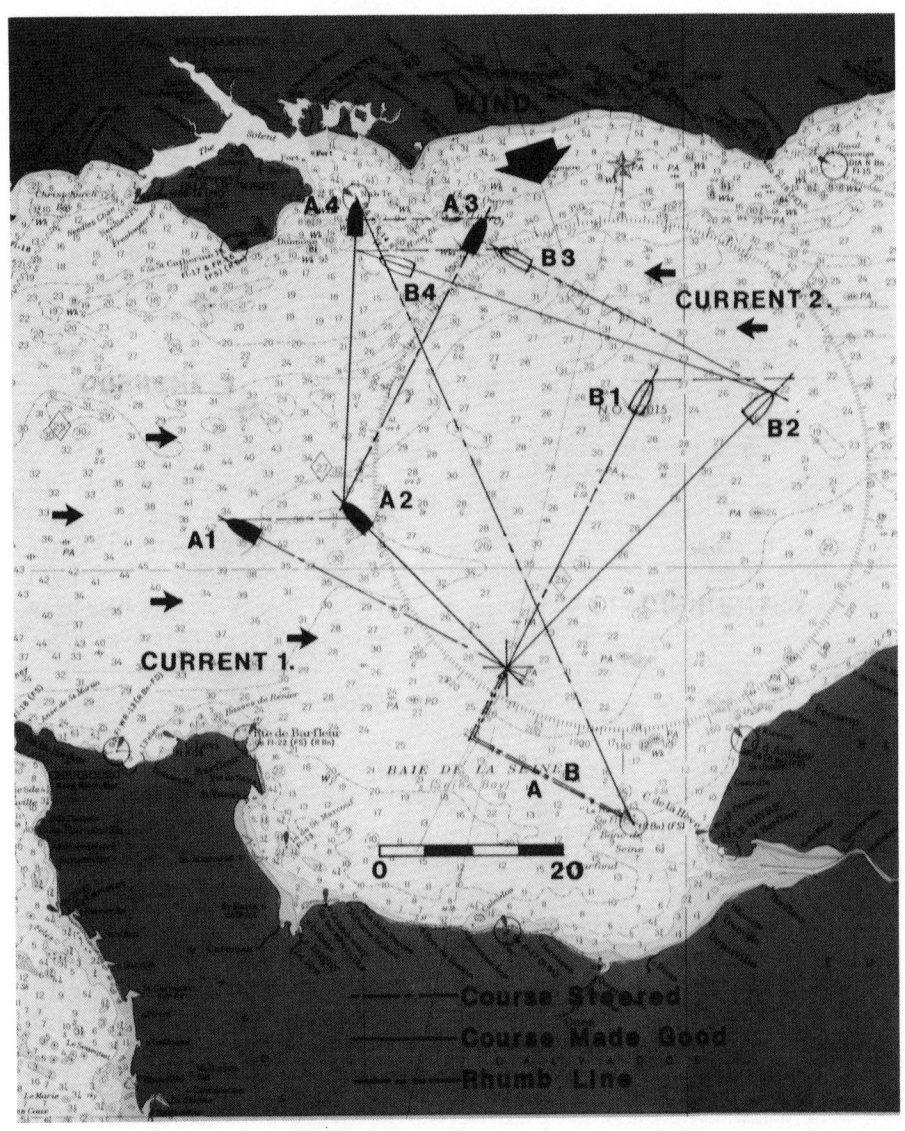

Beating across the English Channel from Le Havre, yachts "A" and "B" decide on different tacks. Yacht "A" tacks into the current for six hours toward "A1" but the current displaces her eastward to "A2." If she would normally make six knots, the effect of the current might be expected to increase her apparent wind and her speed through the water to as much as six-and-a-half knots. She would, therefore, find herself slightly ahead of her vectored position (dashed line) at "A2." Yacht "B" tacks with the current for six hours toward "B1" but the current displaces her eastward to "B2." Her apparent wind is decreased and her speed through the water might decrease to five-and-a-half knots. She would, therefore, find herself slightly behind her vectored position at "B2." When, after six hours, the current turns westward ("current 2"), yacht "A" will again have the advantage and arrive at Nab Tower at "A4" well ahead of "B4." If instead of turning west the current had stopped, the yachts would have fetched positions "A3" and "B3" with "A" slightly ahead. (From H.O. chart 36000)

are invaluable to the racing navigator, even though they are rarely 100 percent accurate. Even without current charts it is possible in tidal waters to figure out the general flow of current, although you will not necessarily know its velocity. Currents generally run stronger in deep water. They can form "back eddies," areas where the flow reverses the normal direction, around points of land and along shorelines. Studying water depths and bottom contours can help predict the course and relative velocities of currents, and when passing anchored objects such as channel markers and lobster pot buoys, the direction and velocity of a current can be estimated more accurately.

Offshore, where there are no current charts or buoys to observe, it is difficult to determine the direction and velocity of currents. The Gulf Stream, for instance, is constantly changing its course and its velocity. Charts show only the average axis, and in places where the velocity is frequently measured—such as off Miami—it has been know to flow north at nearly 10 knots and south at as much as two knots. These variations cannot be predicted with any degree of accuracy or consistency.

It is in these instances that the conscientious navigator earns his round of grog. If he is to have a clue as to the current's behavior, he must constantly refigure his yacht's position and plot this against the DR. If both are accurate, the difference is either current, leeway, or some combination of both. By calculating the leeway component (a thorough navigator will have various leeway components for various wind and sea conditions and points of sailing), the navigator can then determine the direction and velocity of the current.

If the race course takes the yacht out of sight of land or other visual references, the navigator will have to use Loran to calculate his yacht's position accurately. If Loran is not available or its use is prohibited, then he must rely upon celestial observations to tell him about currents. The conscientious navigator doesn't give up until all possibilities for determining current are exhausted.

The crew can be helpful to the navigator by watching other yachts carefully. If there is a competitor of the same size and speed nearby, the crew should log the magnetic bearings at frequent intervals (every five or ten minutes) to see if either yacht is gaining consistently on the other. If their speeds are different, it might be due to differences in current. The bearings must be magnetic—not relative—bearings. A wind shift will change the relative bearing of boats traveling the same speed, but it will not change the magnetic bearing.

Very often the Bermuda Race course crosses the Gulf Stream in the area of a meander—a wave in the axis of the stream. Sometimes the meander is positioned so that the flow is SE along the rhumb line to Bermuda. It could also be in a position where the flow was NW. If the navigator can't tell what the current is doing to his yacht, he will be in serious difficulty—not only as far as the race strategy is concerned, but also because his DR position will be next to useless. If, in a twenty-four-hour period, the navigator doesn't know whether the set is two knots SE, NW, or NE, he can find his yacht as much as ninety-six miles from where he thinks it should be according to his DR.

Suppose an overcast sky prevents celestial observations after a noon fix just before the yacht enters the Gulf Stream. Prerace predictions indicate that the yacht should be entering a southerly meander and should get a boost of two knots to the SE for the next twenty-four hours. Having no other information, the navigator would add forty-eight miles to his DR—assuming the yacht was making good a rhumb-line course of approximately SE—to find his estimated position at noon the next day. If, for some inexplicable reason, the axis of the Stream had shifted so that the yacht was actually sailing in a northerly meander with a two-knot current flowing NW, the yacht would have been set forty-eight miles to the NW and be ninety-six miles from where the navigator estimated it to be. This situation is not as absurd as it sounds. We got into a southerly meander and a small gale coming back from Bermuda in 1960, and at the end of three days we had made good four knots instead of our estimated seven. We started looking for our Montauk Point landfall when we were still actually about 200 miles away. Very discouraging! Yet in other situations a miscalculation could prove dangerous as well.

With Loran prohibited, the Bermuda Race can deteriorate into a contest of luck instead of skill if the weather is bad. It is for this reason that I have advocated the use of Loran in this race. As of this writing, my plea has been to no avail, although I'm sure it will happen sooner or later. When Loran is permitted and navigators may be able to get an accurate fix on the velocity and direction of the Gulf Stream, the Bermuda Race will finally justify its awesome reputation as one of the most competitive offshore races.

Even if there is no prerace prediction of the direction of flow of the axis of the Gulf Stream, without Loran it is still possible to draw a general picture of the Stream's flow pattern. The temperature of the water—when it rises rapidly from the middle 60s

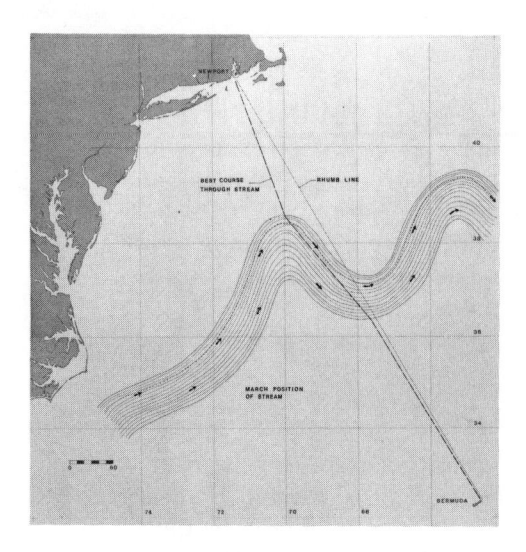

Actual plots of the Gulf Stream for the months of March and April 1966 show two meanders that might be encountered by yachts racing to Bermuda in June. In the March meander (above) a westerly course would have been best. In the April meander (below) an easterly course would have been best. Maximum current velocity is encountered along the 15-degree centigrade isotherm (dotted line) with velocity tapering off gradually southward. (From information supplied by Jan Hahn, Woods Hole Oceanographic Institute)

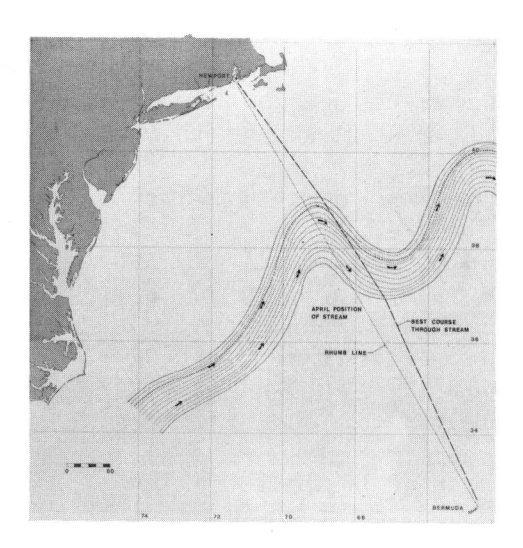

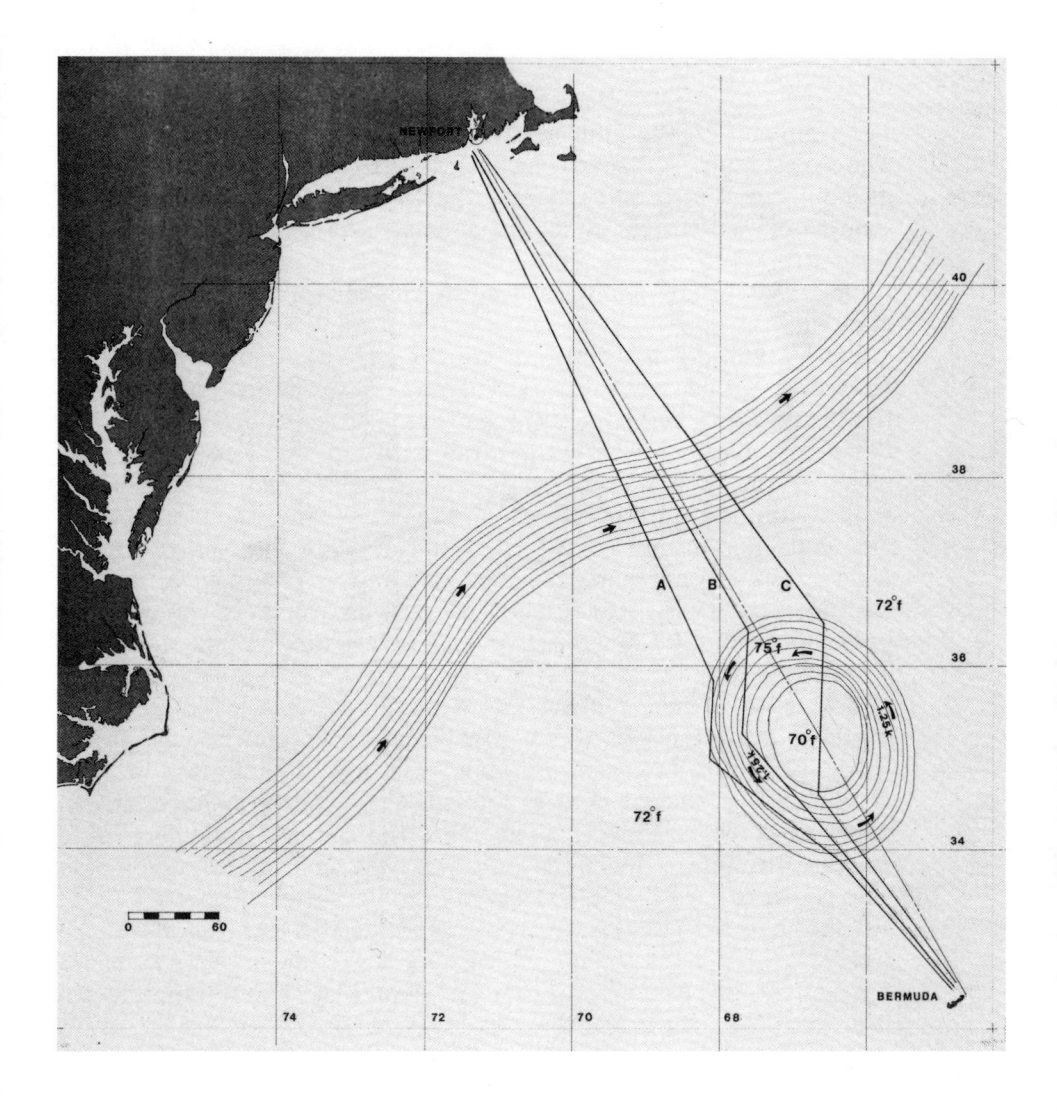

Occasionally Gulf Stream meanders break off and form revolving eddies along Bermuda Race rhumb line. If after passing through the Gulf Stream the water temperature again rises, presence of an eddy should be suspected. A 45-degree turn to starboard upon encountering a rise in temperature would take a yacht into areas of favorable current as shown by courses "A," "B," and "C." In course "A" an almost immediate return to water temperature found south of the Gulf Stream would indicate that the yacht had passed out of the eddy and should turn back to port to return to the eddy. A sustained rise in temperature as encountered by course "B" would indicate that the yacht was in the maximum current and should turn to port to stay in the eddy. A drop in temperature to below that found south of the Gulf Stream would indicate that the yacht had entered the eddy on an unfavorable course shown by "C." (From information supplied by Jan Hahn, Woods Hole Oceanographic Institute)

(Fahrenheit) to the middle 70s—indicates entry into the Stream. The water temperature will be hottest (76–78 degrees) at the axis, gradually diminishing as the southerly edge is approached. If, as soon as one enters the Stream, course is altered and the temperatures are taken at frequent intervals, it is possible to determine, roughly, at what point relative to meanders the Stream was entered.

For instance, if as soon as the temperature began to rise (suppose from 67 to 74 degrees), the yacht is turned to the east, after which the temperature begins to drop again, the axis of the Stream would be off to starboard. Chances are the yacht would be in a southerly meander and should alter course to starboard to get into the axis of the Stream flowing S or SE. If, on the other hand, the temperature had continued to rise rapidly, it would indicate that the yacht had entered either a northerly meander or no meander (normal west to east flow), and the best course would still be to turn to starboard to get away from the NW flow or to buck across the NE flow.

If a turn to the west is initiated as soon as the water temperature indicates entry into the Stream, a continued rise in temperature would indicate the axis was to starboard—keep going to starboard—and a drop in temperature would indicate the axis was to port. A sudden drop would tend to indicate a northerly meander—keep going to starboard to get away from the adverse current—and a gradual drop into the mid- or low 70s would indicate you had entered to the west of a southerly meander—turn back to port to get into the axis of the favorable current. If a turn to starboard indicates no change in temperature or a gradual rise to 76 or 78 degrees, there probably is no meander and the axis of the stream is flowing toward the NE.

With Loran to check current set againt DR added to the water temperature information, an extremely accurate picture of the Stream can be drawn. In terms of the Bermuda Race, this would allow navigators to work out the fastest courses to Bermuda. Much of the current guesswork would be replaced by knowledge and skill.

As important as currents can be, there are times when they should be disregarded or made subservient to other factors. Suppose, for example, you are able to determine that a northerly course will produce a one-knot current advantage over a southerly course, but you have good reason to suspect more wind on the southerly course. In light to medium conditions, it doesn't take much more wind to produce considerably more than a knot more speed through the water. In this case the current advantage should be disregarded in favor of the wind advantage.

In the St. Petersburg to Fort Lauderdale Race it is often advantageous to take a tack SE toward Cuba after passing Rebecca Shoal in order to get into the favorable Gulf Stream current. This is always a consideration and the strategy often works. On at least two occasions, however, the winning boats have completely disregarded the Stream, sailing close to the Florida Keys with no current boost until just south of Miami (where everyone gets it). The conditions must be carefully analyzed each time (vector diagrams may help) and appropriate weights given to each factor—current, wind, course, sea conditions—before chasing after a magic panacea.

Air Mass Weather

Weather is of primary importance when planning offshore racing strategy. We have already had a look at local effects and how they can be used to advantage. Yet local effects are limited mostly to areas near land and are affected drastically by the overall weather pattern or "air masses."

An air mass is a large portion of the atmosphere that has similar characteristics. That is, the air within it will be predominantly cold and wet (maritime polar), cold and dry (continental polar), warm and wet (maritime tropical), or warm and dry (continental tropical). The names in parentheses refer to the origin of the air mass, which determines its characteristics.

Air masses or weather systems produce the winds we sail with offshore, and they modify, dominate, or cancel the local thermal winds. Air mass winds flow from high pressure systems to low pressure systems. Anyone who looks at the morning paper to find the weather forecast knows that the prediction of weather is a "sometime thing," that very often the weatherman cannot give you as accurate prediction of the behavior of weather systems as either he or you would like. It should come as no great shock, therefore, to realize that weather system winds are not always predictable and that their character is the subject of considerable study by whole armies of scientists. It is not all a black art. It is possible for the offshore racer to learn enough about weather systems to be able to predict their winds with at least enough reliability for him to be able to formulate a good race strategy.

It is well beyond the scope of this book to delve into weather theory. While thorough understanding of weather theory may be of interest to navigators and seamen generally, what is more useful is the pragmatic approach to weather, the seaman's "weather eye" that tells him with a glance at the clouds how hard the wind will blow and from what direction. This type of weather wisdom is much more useful than theory. It is also harder to acquire, as it can be learned only through experience. Still, there are books and manuals that can provide basic understanding of weather and practical guides to local forecasting. Two of these are *Wind and Sailing Boats* and *Instant Weather Forecasting*, both written by Alan Watts, who is a sailor as well as a professional meteorologist. *Wind and Sailing Boats* is published by Quadrangle.

Low pressure systems and the fronts associated with them are areas of relative instability. There is a vertical movement of air, which, in turn, causes surface winds. The general flow will be counterclockwise toward the center of the "low," but it will be modified along the fronts, where it will be strongest. Winds will be generally from the east in front of an advancing low (east of it). In the area between the warm front and the cold front, winds will be from the south and southeast. Behind the cold front, winds will be from the west or northwest.

The difference in barometric pressure between the low pressure system and the surrounding areas of higher pressure ("highs") determines the severity of the storm in terms of the velocity of the surface winds. These pressure gradients will show on the weather map as isobars, lines of equal barometric pressure. When the isobars are close together, this indicates a *low* "low" with strong surface winds. Widespread isobars indicate that the pressure gradient between "low" and "high" is not so great and the surface winds will be less.

A strong cold front, where the cold air behind the front is underrunning the warm air in front of it rapidly and at a steep angle (as will be indicated by closely spaced isobars on the weather map), often will produce thunderstorms along the front. This is the "squall line" that sailors often speak of. A squall line is an advancing cold front with many thunderstorms spread along it. These can be quite awesome and can produce violent winds, up to hurricane force, for short periods of time. A squall line can be quite dangerous, but one can usually see them coming (from the west or northwest in the Northern Hemisphere) and be ready to take in sail, preferably before they hit.

High pressure indicates areas of relatively stable air. There is

RACING STRATEGY 85

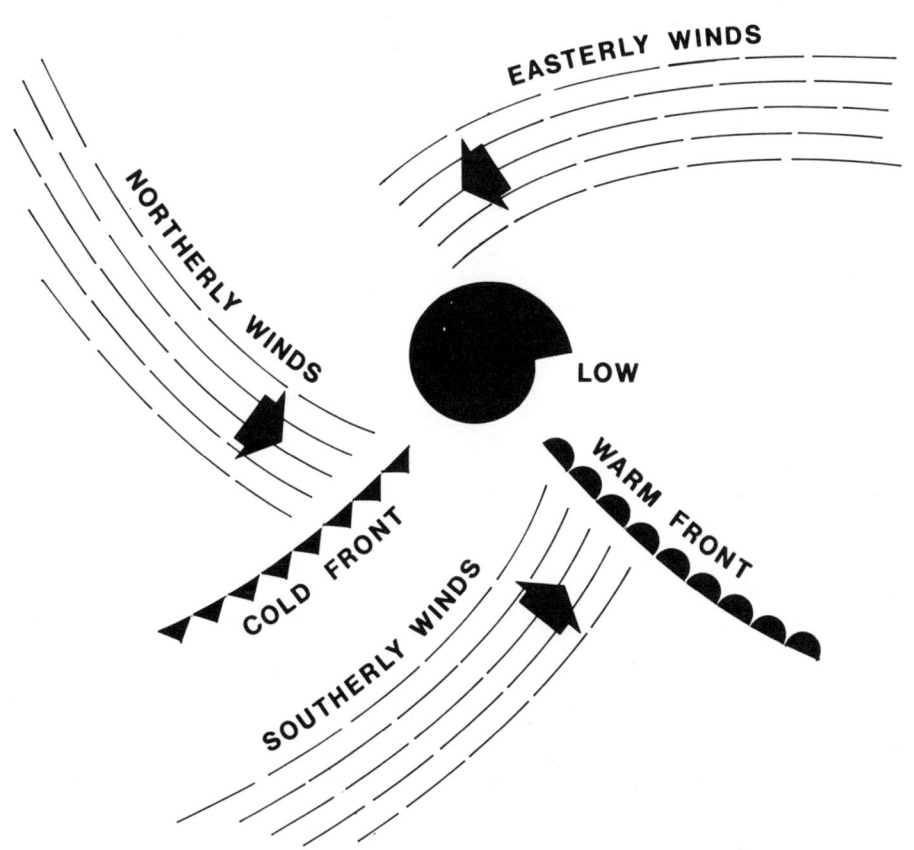

A top view of a typical storm or low pressure center showing how the counterclockwise cyclonic flow of air into the low produces surface winds from the east or northeast in advance of the low, from the south or southeast between the warm and cold fronts, and from the north or northwest behind the cold front.

not much vertical movement, therefore not much surface movement. When racing offshore, it is wise to avoid "highs" if possible, because there will be relatively little wind in them—sometimes none. In spite of a natural aversion to storms that we acquire as shorebound beings, when we go sailing offshore—and particularly when we go *racing* offshore—we want to head for the low pressure systems. Head for the stormy areas and go faster than your fair-weather competitors.

In the summer months, the hot sun bakes down through the clear air of a "high" and cooks things up a bit. Over land, the air is heated near the surface and tends to rise. Moisture in this

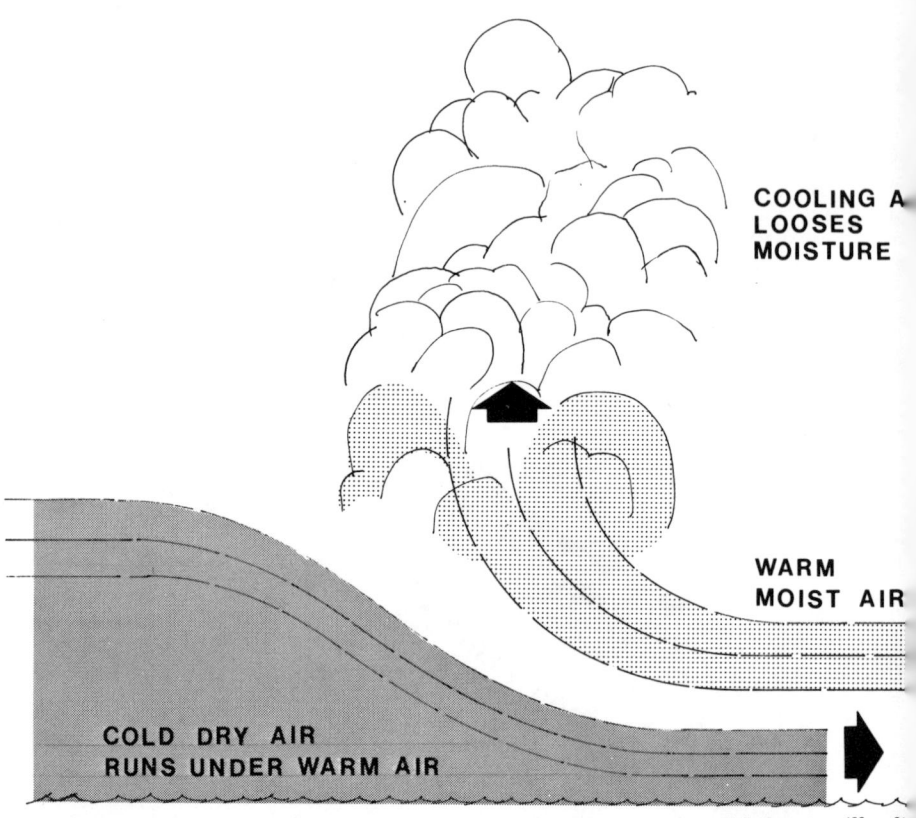

Warm moist air lifted rapidly by the cold dry air of a strong cold front will oft form a squall line of thunderstorms along the front. These can produce violent win for short periods.

rising air will be condensed as the air cools, taking the form of clouds. On very hot days, the air will rise rapidly and to great heights. Greater heights mean greater differences in temperature, which, in turn, mean more condensation to the point where rain begins to fall. Soon a miniature storm may develop with very unstable air and rapid vertical movement. There is a great clashing of warm and cold, moist and dry air. Black clouds form, lightning crashes, and the surface winds rush in under the storm to fill the vacuum created by the rising warm air. This, in very general terms, is how a thunderstorm—which some sailors call a squall—develops. The surface winds underneath a thunderstorm can be very violent, just as violent as in a squall line associated with an advancing cold front. They must be treated with extreme caution, as the wind may reach hurricane force.

Air mass thunderstorms occur frequently in the summer months along the East Coast of the United States. They usually do not reach far offshore but dissipate as soon as they get over water. They are a definite factor, however, in the many races whose courses follow shorelines.

Air mass thunderstorms can develop over water in the tropics. They are seen frequently, for example, in the Gulf of Mexico and in the Gulf Stream in the summer. In a general way, the same sort of vertical movement of air in otherwise stable air masses creates the massive tropical storms, known as "hurricanes," "cyclones," and "chubascos," which cause such great destruction both at sea and ashore in various parts of the world.

The offshore racer sailing in long races, such as the Transpac, Transatlantic, or Bermuda Races, where he has a wide choice of courses, wants to avoid high pressure areas and head for the lows. If the course is East, the yacht should be positioned (insofar as possible) so that the low pressure center passes to the north. As the low passes, therefore, the yacht will be sailing first in southeast winds, then southwest winds (between fronts), and finally, northwest winds. To the north of the low will be westerly headwinds, which should, naturally, be avoided. Obviously, if the course is west, the yacht should be positioned so that the low pressure center passes to the south.

Low pressure centers move over the surface of the earth. They can move slowly and sometimes even stop; or they can zip along at 20 knots. The speed at which the storm moves will affect the surface winds, adding to them south of the storm (assuming it moves in an easterly direction) and taking away from them to the north.

It is imperative to know the direction and speed a storm is traveling. If the surface winds near the center of a storm reach a peak of 40 knots and the storm is traveling northeast at 20 knots, surface winds south of the storm will reach 60 knots, while to the north they will be only 20 knots. This is, perhaps, an extreme example, but it illustrates the great difference in wind velocities that may be encountered in a storm system. Information about the storm is of vital importance, and all too often we are completely ignorant of the weather patterns surrounding us at sea.

Information about weather patterns is available from several broadcast sources (see Appendix). There is a high seas broadcast in plain language but the most complete is a Morse code broadcast each day from which the navigator can construct a complete weather map. It is necessary to be able to read Morse code numbers at the rate of five groups per minute, adding yet another necessary skill to the already prodigious list a navigator must master. However, if a two-speed portable tape recorder is available, the broadcast can be recorded at regular speed and played back at slow speed to make the code easier to read.

Facsimile recorders, which actually print a complete weather map, have been used aboard yachts, but they are not allowed on most races because of the cost and complexity of the installation.

Whatever the method the navigator uses to obtain it, weather information is absolutely essential to the formulation of an appropriate racing strategy. Without reliable weather information the navigator can only guess and take what comes. It is possible to win races without good weather information, but that method comes under the heading of luck, not skill.

Chapter 9 Helmsmanship Upwind

O. J. Young on the helm.

Carina is one of those boats that are always well manned. Each crew member is equally skilled in every department. When this is the case, it is easy to organize a watch so that everything runs smoothly and everyone pitches in with equal effort.

When I first started offshore racing, we would have four-hour watches and each of us would take an hour on the wheel. This works well when each watch member is a competent helmsman, but it is a rare crew that has eight members, each of whom can get the most out of the boat for an hour under all conditions. It is more usual, now, for tricks at the wheel to be limited to half an hour. Even the best helmsmen may wear down before an hour is up, and the boat is not moving at its best for the last fifteen minutes or so. Half-hour tricks allow more variety in helmsmen assignments. If, for instance, the watch consists of only three good helmsmen, they can be rotated more evenly at half-hour intervals. Obviously, one tends to get less tired in a half hour; the activity of changing helmsmen tends to keep the whole watch more alert, particularly at night, and the trick seems to move more quickly.

The ability to make the boat move fast and easily through the water differentiates a good helmsman from an indifferent one. This skill is not easily mastered, although some people could be called "natural" helmsmen because they seem to steer a sailboat effortlessly. Because helmsmanship is largely an art, it is hard to put in concrete terms just what one does to become a good helmsman.

The most important ingredient in good helmsmanship is concentration. No matter how good a "feel" a person has or how well he can sense a shift of wind, he will not be a good helmsman unless he can concentrate on the job at hand. This means disregarding unrelated activities that are going on around him but being the first to sense a wind shift, a change in velocity, or the need for a reef or a change of sail. He has his eyes on the headsails, the mainsail, the instruments, the compass, and the waves. The seat of his pants is attuned to the heel of the boat and its motion through the water. His ears pick up the sounds of wind and water. The skin on his face and the hairs on the back of his neck feel the direction of the wind. His hands feel the forces on the rudder.

The good helmsman cranks himself up to a hypersensitive state of alertness. When someone moves, talks, lights a cigarette, drops a winch handle, or turns on a light below, it's like firing a cannon in the effect it has on the helmsman's nerves. Yet a good helmsman must be able to overcome these common distractions. His brain has to be able to filter out the distractions from the signals he is receiving from sea, sky, and boat. If he loses his concentration, the boat wanders off course and slows down.

Some helmsmen lose concentration when they have suggested a change in sail trim or rigging. When ordering a change in jib lead or sail trim, they then watch transfixed while the crew tends to it. I suppose the helmsman is making sure that they do it right, but the net result is that he is not sailing the boat and it slows down. Very bad! Some very competitive skippers do this; it's as if they can't let go and trust their crew to do it right. One must force oneself not to be distracted in this way. If you can't help running the ship, then turn the helm over to someone who can and concentrate instead on sail trim, jib leads, and the fine adjustments.

When sailing on an offshore racer for the first time, anyone used to steering small boats will find himself quite surprised by the incredible slowness with which large boats respond. One must get over the idea that a flick of the wrist will move the bow to precisely the correct place to meet a wave or to correct a luff in the genoa. Some light midget ocean racers respond like dinghies, but they are rare. Anything that displaces much over 5,000 pounds has a mass that resists rapid accelerations (Newton's Second Law). The boat is not going to rotate about its vertical axis as rapidly as a dinghy would. One must, therefore, plan ahead and let the boat do most of the work—letting it seek its own line through the water—the helmsman acting more as an adviser or guiding agent than a commanding force.

Boats over forty feet in overall length are generally equipped with wheel steering. This device is very sensitive in modern offshore racers. The mechanical advantage multiplies the force the helmsman can exert against the rudder, but at the expense of greater movement of the wheel. While the wheel may move with a "flick of the wrist," the wrist must move considerably further than it did in the one-design to have a corresponding effect on the rudder. Most helmsmen who grew up in small one-designs prefer a tiller to a wheel, but tillers aren't really practical once the forces become so great that it is physically demanding to move the tiller/rudder combination.

Steering to Windward

Oddly enough, one often gets a better feel of a boat sailing on the wind by sitting on the weather rail near the shrouds rather than back aft at the wheel. On deck, you can see the waves and the sails much better, especially when there is no one else forward of you, than when you're aft with a row of bodies perched on the rail blocking your vision and disturbing the wind flow. For this reason it is helpful to have the relief helmsman on the weather rail before he takes his trick. This way he will have a better feel for what is going on when he goes aft to steer.

Only a few designs take advantage of this phenomenon by positioning the helmsman where he can best sense the needs of the boat. Center cockpits lend themselves well to this, but Bill Tripp's *Touché* (designed in 1957) was the first offshore racer to make special use of this technique. *Touché* has what amounts to a midships cockpit (she has very little actual cockpit—only the helmsman's footwells are let into the deck) with a wheel which can be positioned either to port or starboard or vertically on the centerline. Thus, the helmsman can get far to windward in the middle of the boat where he can best feel the action of wind and waves. When running downwind, he can stand up behind the wheel amidships.

Today, when sailing upwind, all good helmsmen steer from the windward side. The old-timers used to make their crew do all the ballast work (sitting to windward), while they would sit to leeward and squint knowingly up the slot at the genoa. That method may still work for narrow, heavy boats in smooth water, but it doesn't work in today's typical offshore racer. You can't see what's going on from down there!

When smart dinghy sailors started invading the offshore ranks, they taught us "big-boat guys" a lesson. They sailed their dinghies from the weather rail out of necessity—to hold the boats down—

Touche's midships cockpit is extremely modern in concept even though designed in 1957. The wheel pivots to either side to allow the helmsman to sit to windward when sailing on the wind. (Ted Jones)

and they showed us that they could sail better from up there on the high side, feeling the wind, watching the sails, and seeing the waves. They won races. It didn't take long for the competitive big-boat skipper to get the message. Get up to weather where the action is!

I can't tell just what it is that I look at when I sit to windward and steer a boat upwind, although I've tried to analyze it many times. I do know that I feel terribly uncomfortable whenever anyone changes his position in line with my vision or in any way obstructs my view forward. When it is necessary to ask him to move, I feel apologetic because it seems that I am being trivial and petty. I usually mumble something about not being able to see. I can see where the boat is headed, of course, but some vital piece of information which I must have in order to steer the boat well is being screened from my view.

Which brings up another important attribute of a good helmsman—the ability to know when he *isn't* getting the most out of the boat.

No one can operate in top form all the time. In the words of a song about a crap-shooter, ". . . When you're hot, you're hot and when you're not, you're not." So it is with helmsmen. The good helmsman will take himself off the wheel for the good of the ship when he's not hot and can't keep the boat in the groove.

However, the presence of an uninspired helmsman need not be considered a sign of bad luck for the outcome of the race. In fact, when handled properly, the situation can often become an opportunity for boosting the morale of the crew. Suppose the watch captain, a sage seaman long on both experience and reputation, says to one of the junior watchmates, "Jake, I don't seem to be able to keep her going as she should. How about giving it a try?"

Well, you know that Jake is going to jump at the chance to get more out of the boat than "Sage Seaman." He's going to concentrate for all he's worth; he is going to get more out of the boat and add to his experience at the same time. Everyone wins. Jake feels good because he has been complimented by his watch captain. The other watchmates benefit from the knowledge that in *our* watch aboard *our* boat ability counts more than rank. Sage Seaman, secure in the knowledge that he hasn't lost his magic touch forever, benefits from the rest and the knowledge that he has given a boost to a deserving fellow. The boat benefits because it is going faster, which it will with all those good vibrations among the crew. That, after all, is what racing is all about: going as fast as possible and having a good time doing it!

So now Jake is on the helm. The course is to windward. The wind is light—less than eight knots—and the sea is calm. What must he look for as helmsman, and what must he do?

The helmsman is in command as far as calling sail trim, stationing other crew members, and asking for sail changes. He may be overruled by the watch captain, who may have a better idea once he is informed of the problem, but the need for a change most likely will be noticed first by the helmsman. Since it is he who can feel the pulse of the boat, his suggestion will probably be the best one to make the boat sail faster.

In light air most of the crew will be sitting to leeward to help the boat heel, providing maximum draft for the sails. The helmsman should station himself to windward, however, so he can see what is going on. He may duck to leeward briefly to check the genoa or to look under it for obstructions and other boats or to check for wind shifts, but his *station* ought to be windward.

In light air and smooth water the helmsman should look for wind ripples on the surface. He will quickly learn that a certain darkening of the water's surface means either a lift or a header. With this knowledge he can anticipate the shift and adjust the

In light winds most of the crew should sit to leeward as in the top photo in order to reduce wetted surface and help the sails hold their draft. As the wind picks up the crew should move to windward to counteract the wind's heeling force. In heavy winds the crew should be as far to windward as the rules allow. Crew members below should switch berths as their weight is needed to windward or to leeward. (Howard Glass, above right and right)

boat's heading to take maximum advantage of it. Further to windward, 500 or 1,000 yards, the wind streaks on the water may tell him whether or not to continue on the present tack or to flip over to the other tack in search of more wind, hence, greater speed. The helmsman should not initiate a tack, however, without checking first with his watch captain or the navigator, who may have strategic reasons for not tacking.

The helmsman also looks at the jib luff, which he should be able to see from the windward side, to make sure the jib is trimmed in proper relation to the wind. Luff strings, short lengths of yarn attached to both sides of the sail about 10 percent of chord length aft of the luff, are indispensable for gauging proper jib trim. Both luff strings should lie straight along the chord of the sail, indicating a smooth flow of air along the leading edge. If the leeward one points up, down, out, or flutters randomly, there is turbulence along the leeward leading edge; the sail is overtrimmed or the boat's heading is too low (too far away from the wind). If the windward luff string does any of those peculiar things, there is turbulence along the windward leading edge; the sail is light (undertrimmed) or the boat's heading is too high (too close to the wind). One can usually see both luff strings—the shadow of the one to leeward (on the opposite side of the sail as viewed by the helmsman sitting to windward)—but most sailmakers provide a small transparent window to make it easier to see the one to leeward.

If the luff strings indicate that a change is in order, the helmsman must decide whether he should turn the boat to accommodate the shift or whether he should ask for a change in trim. This decision (and it is one that may have to be made scores of times in a half-hour trick on the helm) will depend on whether, in the helmsman's judgment, the boat will go faster with the sail trimmed or the heading adjusted. Is it a sustained shift and is the boat heading near the rhumb-line course? Ask for a change in trim. Is it a brief shift that may be gone by the time the crew can adjust the sail? Change the boat's heading.

Having adjusted to the indications of the luff strings, the helmsman turns his attention to the other telltales: the masthead fly, lengths of yarn on the windward shrouds, and the electronic apparent wind indicator (API). Are these indicators consistent with the information supplied by the luff strings? Usually they are, but occasionally—particularly in light air—the wind at the masthead may be different from the wind near the surface. The helmsman should try not to worry about trimming sails to these

These three photos show the windward side of a genoa and illustrate how the air flow affects luff strings. The upper string is to windward. In the first photo (top), the genoa is undertrimmed, or the yacht's heading is too close to the wind, causing turbulent flow over the windward side of the sail which is indicated by a drooped and fluttering windward luff string. The second photo (middle) shows a properly trimmed genoa. Both strings lie with the wind flow which is approximately equal (there appears to be less velocity over the windward side—a normal condition) and smooth. In the third photo (bottom), the genoa is overtrimmed, or the yacht's heading is too far off the wind, causing turbulent flow over the leeward side of the sail which is indicated by a drooped and fluttering leeward luff string. Note also that the windward luff string is raised even though the actual wind velocity has not increased. (Ted Jones)

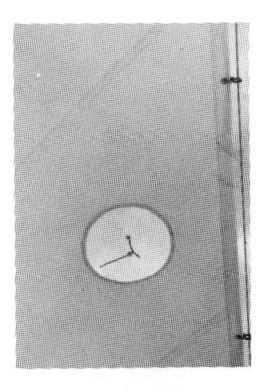

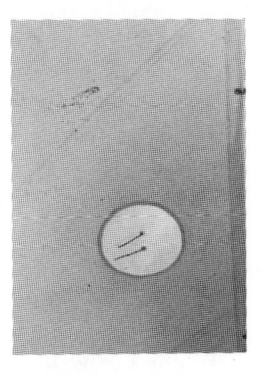

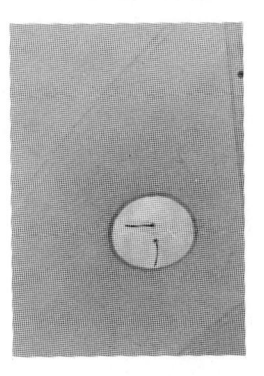

different wind directions, but he should call the attention of the sail trimmers to this fact. Perhaps a change of lead or an adjustment of the mainsheet traveler can take advantage of the situation.

The helmsman also must pay close attention to the speedometer. He isn't concerned with the actual speed (let the navigator worry about that), but the relative speed now versus the speed a moment ago.

Has the boat slowed down? Why? Maybe that last trim or heading change wasn't a good idea. Maybe the wind had lightened. Can the trim or heading be changed to get back up to speed?

Has the boat speeded up? Good! But why? Is it because the wind increased? If so, a change in trim may make the boat sail even faster. Can the genoa be trimmed so the boat can head a little higher? Or was the increase in speed due to the change just made in trim or heading? If so, leave everything alone.

In actual practice, the helmsman does not *focus* his attention on any one thing. He doesn't stare at the water hoping to gain some brilliant insight into steering faster. Nor does he stare at the luff strings trying to keep them always in line. He should merely glance at the water, the luff strings, the telltales, the API, and the speedometer long enough to record in his mind the information they give.

When I was in pilot training learning to fly by instruments, my flight instructor (who was also a boatman) told me to develop a pattern of eye movement to keep cross-checking all the instruments. Concentrating on only one or two instruments could lead to disorientation, causing a stall, a dive, or a spiral. While trying to pin down one instrument precisely, the others could get away from you. I had little difficulty developing this habit as I had been used to doing it when sailing. However, this was the first time I had to think consciously of regular eye movement, and I have found the *conscious* routine helpful in both sailing and flying. One without this experience will have to develop a pattern of eye movement to take in all the indicators of wind direction and boat speed. The information thus gathered is then fed to the helmsman's on-board computer (brain), where it is interpreted; commands are then initiated to make best use of the information. This happens in a split second, so dwelling on any one indicator cuts all the other inputs out of the circuit for a significant length of time.

The eyes are not the only sensory perceptors useful to the helmsman. The ears can pick up the sounds of the water going past the hull and the sound of the wind in the rigging. These sounds are important speed indicators. An increase in water noise means the boat is going faster; a decrease means slower. An increase in wind noise means more wind; a decrease means less wind. Your eye may be occupied looking somewhere other than the speedometer, but while your eyes sense the wind direction, your ears can sense boat speed and wind velocity. Your ears, sensing a speed change, can signal your eyes to check the speedometer, the wind direction, or the water's surface.

Your skin can tell you a great deal about wind velocity and direction if you develop the ability to interpret the sensation of the wind on your face and neck. Suppose your eyes are looking to windward for ripples on the water and your ears are tuned to the water gurgling past the hull. Now let the nerves in your skin tell you about wind shifts and changes in velocity.

Your tactile senses can also tell you, through your hands on the wheel, how the boat likes the sail trim you've given her. Does she have a neutral helm—flopping back and forth gently to indicate that she's in the groove—or does she have a heavy weather helm—tugging persistently against your grip to indicate that the mainsail is overtrimmed or the genoa is light.

Your sense of balance can tell you if the boat is heeling more or less than she has been. A greater angle of heel means more wind, indicating more potential speed, a change in trim, a change in heading. A reduced angle of heel means less wind (or maybe somebody below moved to windward).

Even your sense of smell may be useful. I've never been able to detect this, but different wind streaks may have different odors—one from the land (a lift?) smelling of grass and cow manure and from the sea (a header?) smelling of salt and seaweed. Farfetched? Perhaps, but why overlook anything that may help you make the boat sail faster?

The main thing to remember is to refine all your senses so that they can be feeding information to your brain simultaneously. The more information your brain has, the better it will be able to assess the situation. Suppose your eyes tell you that a puff has just arrived. Your skin tells you that the wind has increased. Your memory bank says that in light of experience it should be a lift. Your sense of balance tells you that the angle of heel has *decreased*. Your ears tell you that the boat has *slowed down*. Your hands tell you that the weather helm has disappeared. Something's wrong! "Tilt," says your brain, "we have contradictory information." The computer shuts down and spits out the "lift" card.

If you had been using only your eyes, your skin, and your memory circuit, you would have concluded that you had a lift and could head up, but it turned out that it wasn't a lift at all. You knew that right away because your other senses told you the boat straightened up (it should have heeled more), slowed down (it should have speeded up), and the weather helm disappeared (it should have increased). So, instead of heading up, you head off and gain a few important yards on your competitor, who is using only his eyes.

Assessing the "Groove"

Helmsmen are always talking about having the boat "in the groove," meaning that she is going at her optimum speed for the prevalent conditions. What does this mean?

The first keelboat I raced on was a narrow, deep, heavily ballasted Six-Meter named *Tidsfordriv*. *Tidsy* was an excellent teacher. She would go to windward faster than anything else around, and she'd tell you right away if she wasn't happy with the way she was being handled. If the helmsman was sailing her too full or too far off, she'd develop a lee helm and try to go further off. If the helmsman sailed her too fine or too close to the wind, she'd develop a weather helm and try to go further up. That wasn't all. She wouldn't get in the groove by herself; the helmsman had to coax her there by first driving her off—until he felt the lee helm begin—then gradually ease her up toward the wind until the helm disappeared.

Tidsy's large overlapping genoa, relatively high-aspect ratio mainsail, and narrow keel were responsible for these characteristics of her behavior. Her narrow beam and fast sailing ability accentuated them to a degree that made them hard to misinterpret.

Modern ocean racers (and many other keelboats) have some of the same features; hence, they have a similar feel. Their relatively wide beam and slower speed through the water tend to mask these characteristics so that one must be more sensitive to them than one needed to be with *Tidsy*.

On a boat where the rudder is attached to the keel (as was the six-meter's), the tiller or wheel will oscillate gently as she slips over the waves to indicate that she's in the groove. But this configuration is becoming rare in ocean racers, most now having separate rudders well aft—either balanced blades or preceded by a skeg—and short, high-aspect ratio keels.

The high-aspect ratio keel should be considered carefully, because it stalls more readily than the older, wider type. The helmsman can be fooled into thinking that the boat is moving well—the helm is neutral, the sails are full, the luff strings are parallel—but the speed is a shade lower than it ought to be with that particular weight of wind. What's wrong? The keel is stalled out. It has lost its grip on the water, and the boat is going sideways—making more leeway than it should, as well as not going fast.

The answer is to head off, easing sheets if necessary, until the speed builds up as fast as the helmsman thinks it should be for those conditions. Then he should head up gradually and call for trim. The keel has a good bite on the water, and the boat is in the groove.

Boats with separate rudders usually carry a slight weather helm when they are in the groove. It helps create the necessary lift. They usually do not indicate contentment by wagging their tillers gently as the attached-rudder boats often do.

As the Wind Picks Up

When the wind increases beyond the "light" classification, when it gets up around 12 or 15 knots, the helmsman gets a new set of data to watch. Waves enter the picture, and they must be gotten through with a minimum of fuss. At this wind speed, depending upon the particular boat, its size, and its sail inventory, one must also begin thinking about headsail changes and changes in mainsail trim and draft control to keep from overpowering the boat.

Waves need to be seen, which is why it is doubly important in medium conditions for the helmsman to be up to windward where he can see them. I think it is the inability to see all the waves—both the next one and the next five or six after that—that makes me fidget when someone sitting on the weather rail blocks my view.

There is a certain way that a boat must get through these small waves that is impossible to describe. It is easier to describe what one does in heavy weather, which will be gone into in detail subsequently. In heavy air one works the boat through each wave, while in medium air the small waves are treated as groups or patterns. The helmsman does not steer around, over, or through an individual wave. Each situation, each boat must be judged on its own. What you do that gets your boat to windward faster than the other boats is the right thing to do.

I recall sailing with Chuck Blair aboard his *Hotfoot,* a 32′ Alan Gurney design. It was a day race off Newport, Rhode Island, one of the runs of the New York Yacht Club Cruise, the wind was about 10 knots, and the seas were about two feet or less. From my perch on the weather rail, I watched Chuck work *Hotfoot* to windward.

Hotfoot would sail along for a dozen yards—three or four wave lengths—then she'd suddenly straighten up and appear to leap five or six feet to windward. She didn't slow down. Chuck would hold her there for a few seconds and then bear off again to *Hotfoot's* normal heading. It was truly phenomenal and a pleasure to watch Chuck work her to windward in this fashion. Although we were the smallest boat (not the lowest rated) in our class, we were first around the windward mark and won handily on corrected time.

What was Chuck doing? Specifically, what did he see or feel or hear to tell him how to work *Hotfoot* through the waves? Chuck couldn't say, except that he sensed a certain combination of wind, wave, and boat, and this allowed him to sneak those few extra feet to windward.

Chuck Blair and *Hotfoot* are not the only skipper/boat combination that can do this. I've watched others do it and I've been able, on occasion, to do it myself, but never have I seen a clearer and more consistent demonstration of working to windward in this fashion.

As the wind increases, so will the weather helm. This is fine as long as the helm is not difficult for the helmsman to hold and as long as it is not slowing the boat. Weather helm, particularly on boats with separate rudders, helps provide the hydrodynamic lift to move a boat to windward. Beyond a certain point, where the rudder approaches a stall, weather helm may be considered excessive. The boat slows and is on the verge of going out of control. When this point is approached, something must be done to reduce the helm.

Most often weather helm is caused by excessive heeling. The underwater lines of the hull are such that there is more curvature to the horizontal planes on the leeward side than on the windward side. The effect of this is to make the hull want to turn to windward. Also, as a boat heels considerably, the rudder is no longer operating in a vertical plane—trying to turn the hull—but in a more horizontal plane—trying to lift the stern as weather helm increases.

The obvious way to reduce heeling, and weather helm, is to reduce sail. One probably won't have to reef or change to a smaller headsail in a 10-knot wind, but a change in trim and/or draft control could help considerably. Easing the mainsheet traveler will move the leech of the mainsail to leeward with the effect of reducing weather helm. This usually should be accompanied by tensioning the Cunningham control and flattening the mainsail. Tightening the genoa halyard or increasing Cunningham tension will also be required where the genoa is fitted with a "stretchy luff." More will be said about these devices under the heading of "sail control," but it must be understood that the helmsman is the first to sense the need for trim and draft control. He may not pull the strings, but he must give the order and let the other crew members know when he is satisfied that the adjustments are correct.

More Wind

Wind speeds that exceed the 18- to 20-knot range call for more work by the crew (initially, at least) than by the helmsman. The helmsman is the "dirty guy" who orders the watch up forward to change the headsails or to reef the main, while he gets to sit aft—dry and secure—and watch his shipmates bouncing up and down, getting soaked, and wearing themselves out. As long as one is not overcome by feelings of guilt, the helm is the best place to be in moderately high wind situations.

This is not to say that the helmsman's tasks are any less demanding in moderately rough conditions than in light or medium going. He still needs to concentrate, he still needs to be experienced, and he will have to work harder than ever.

Waves are perhaps the first consideration. Waves slow a boat down. They crash into the bow, throwing spray aft at the crew. They lift the bow high into the air and let it drop with a crash. This expended energy must come from somewhere, and it is taken from the driving power of the sails. It is the helmsman's job to minimize the amount of energy expended making spray and lifting the bow so that more energy is available to drive the boat to windward.

There is another consideration. As a boat pitches in the waves, its sails are moving in an arc above the hull. As the bow lifts a few feet, the masthead—many feet above the hull—swings wildly aft at great speed through a large arc. When the bow falls a few feet, the masthead swings wildly forward. Anyone who doubts the magnitude of this movement should go aloft on a day when *gentle seas* are running. He will find it difficult to hang on and probably will return to the deck battered and bruised. (I would not suggest going aloft in rough weather except in the gravest of emergencies and even then only the strongest, lightest, most agile crew member should attempt it.)

This high-speed pitching causes drastic changes in the apparent wind velocity and angle of attack. One second the sails are operating in light air and are trimmed too flat (as the mast swings aft), and the next second the sails are operating in a full gale and are not trimmed enough (as the mast swings forward). Beyond a certain point, nothing can be done about this problem. It contributes to the reduced drive one can obtain from the sails at a time when one needs more drive to get through the waves. One must also consider reducing sail area as the boat becomes overpowered by the heeling force on the sails. It is, therefore, crucially important for the helmsman to minimize the expenditure of driving power on spray making and pitching and to reduce the pitching in order to preserve as much of the limited driving power available under these conditions.

The helmsman must concentrate on the waves, working the boat over each one. As a wave approaches, the boat should be moving at maximum speed. Don't try to pinch up; rather, drive the boat well off to obtain maximum power from the sails. Remember that when the mast is pitching forward, the sails will be undertrimmed (another way of looking at it is that the boat is being severely pinched—headed up too high). Heading off more than one would in lighter winds will compensate somewhat for this and will keep the sails driving more when the boat is pitching forward.

As the bow begins to rise to the approaching wave, head up slightly, taking the crest more nearly head on. Just before the crest passes the center of buoyancy (the point where the stern will begin to lift and the bow will fall into the trough of the next wave), head off sharply to prevent the bow from dropping out into the trough of the next wave. As the wave passes under the hull and the bow slips gently down the backside of the wave, head up to the mean heading so the boat can drive through the trough, keeping speed to meet the next wave in similar fashion. A corkscrewlike motion of this sort will minimize the expenditure of energy on both spray and pitching, with the result that the boat will get to windward faster than if she were left to her own devices.

Waves come in assorted sizes. Some are quite large, while others, in the same wind and body of water, are relatively small. Also, in a few yards along its length, a wave will vary considerably in

5 K SMOOTH WATER

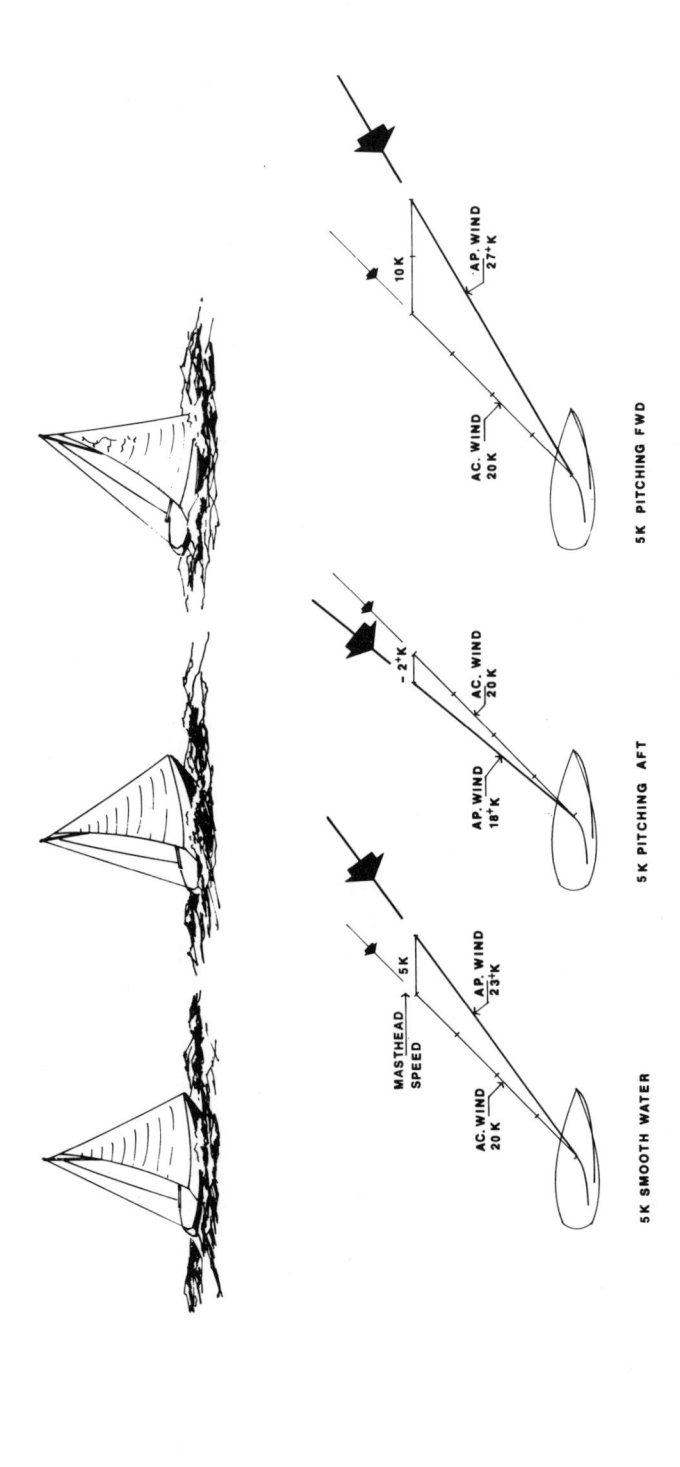

5 K PITCHING AFT

5 K PITCHING FWD

Pitching in large waves causes dramatic changes in the apparent wind acting upon a yacht's sails. In smooth water (left) with an actual wind speed of 20 knots producing a yacht speed of five knots, the speed at the masthead will also be five knots and produce an apparent wind both at the masthead and on deck of 23+ knots. As a wave is encountered the bow rises and the masthead moves aft rapidly (center). If the masthead speed is minus two-and-a-half knots, the apparent wind at the masthead shifts aft (lift) and is reduced to 18+ knots. As the wave passes under the stern the bow falls and the masthead moves forward rapidly (right). If the masthead speed is 10 knots the apparent wind at the masthead shifts forward (header) and is increased to 27+ knots.

size. Given the choice, one would prefer to sail in the small portions of the waves. The helmsman should keep an eye well ahead so he can assess the size of the approaching waves and adjust the boat's course, if possible, in order to sail through the smallest portions of the waves. This can be done by driving off (preferred) or pinching up (not so good) slightly to adjust the boat's track.

In moderately heavy weather as well as in medium going, the helmsman is in the best position to sense the need for changes in sail. Under these conditions the need will be for greater or less sail rather than for refinements in trim. The helmsman needs not only general experience with this type of weather, but specific experience with the particular boat he is steering. He must know the sail inventory and how she behaves with the various combinations available. Some boats can carry a number one genoa and a reefed mainsail more effectively than a number two genoa and no reef. Most sail systems are designed to use a number two (or even a number three) genoa under these conditions, with either no reef or a small reef in the mainsail. The helmsman must know what his particular boat likes best—what her sail system was designed to do. Then, when he senses that the boat is overpowered, he will know how to correct the problem and will ask for the right sail combination.

There is only one way to gain experience in moderately heavy weather. Go sail in it. Most of us get our experience racing—the wind comes up while we are racing, so we find out. This is the lazy man's way, and many a trophy will reside in another yacht's locker that could have been in yours if you and your crew had practiced in heavier weather. Sure, it's wet and sometimes cold and unpleasant out there, but you don't have to stay out forever. Think how good you'll feel when you get ashore to warm up and dry out while you recap the day's mistakes and triumphs.

Another round of grog for all hands!

Tacking

Sooner or later, when sailing to windward, the yacht must tack. This would seem a simple maneuver—certainly much easier and less anxiety provoking than jibing—yet a surprising number of otherwise well-informed helmsmen botch a tacking maneuver.

When attempting an ideal tack, the helmsman must try to preserve as much as possible of the speed made good to windward. This requires coordination and teamwork. Since the yacht is coasting and obviously not sailing through the tacking maneuver, its speed made good to windward will be diminishing. Therefore, the helmsman wants to maintain the driving force of the sails as long as possible on the old tack and regain the driving force of the sails as soon as possible on the new tack. One might think that the best way to do this would be to slam the boat around as quickly as possible and admonish the winching crew to get the sails trimmed as fast as they can. Unfortunately, this approach doesn't work because it ignores Newton's First Law of Motion: in effect, a yacht in motion tends to maintain that motion in the direction and speed it is traveling. An abrupt change in the direction the yacht is traveling will rapidly decrease its speed. Another law of physics is ignored by tacking quickly: that the helmsman can make any yacht tack more quickly than any crew can trim the sails. Furthermore, a quick tack causes the sails to lose their drive earlier.

The astute helmsman tacks gradually. He eases into the wind gently, but with enough way to carry the yacht's bow through the eye of the wind, and he holds the bow just off head to wind, keeping the genoa from filling while the crew gets the sail trimmed. Thus, he keeps the sails driving longer, he uses the momentum of the yacht to carry her to windward, and he positions the yacht in such a way that the crew can trim the sails to provide driving force as quickly as possible.

Exactly how the helmsman accomplishes his tack varies, depending upon both the characteristics of the yacht and the wind and sea conditions. A heavy-displacement yacht will coast or fetch quite far to windward in a smooth sea. Conversely, a light-displacement yacht will fetch almost not at all in a rough sea. A heavy-displacement yacht will naturally turn more slowly than a light-displacement yacht because of its greater mass and inertia, so the helmsman is helped to do what is natural by the laws of physics. Experience with different displacement types and with individual yachts will reveal the best way to tack in various conditions.

As a point of departure, here's how to tack a moderate-displacement boat in smooth water. After making sure that each crew member is at his station by giving the command, "Ready about," and after receiving assurances from the winching crew members that they are ready, the helmsman initiates the tack by gradually putting the helm down (tiller to leeward). As the bow begins to swing, the movement of the helm can be accelerated to match the accelerating rotation of the bow, and as the bow passes through head-to-wind, the helm should be gradually returned to center so that the bow stops with the genoa streaming along the leeward shrouds and just over the rail. Once the genoa is sheeted in (it should not be sheeted hard until the yacht is up to speed), the helmsman can bear off on course.

Part of the timing cycle is the proper letting go of the genoa sheet. If the sheet is cast off too soon, the yacht will lose drive and hesitate as she comes into the wind. If the sheet is held too long, the backwinded genoa will drag the bow of the boat away from the wind on the new tack, making it difficult for the winch grinders to get the sail trimmed. The sail should backwind just enough so that it blows through the foretriangle as the bow passes the eye of the wind. If the crew member casting off the sheet isn't sure of the precise moment to cast off, the helmsman can shout "Break!" or some other word when he wants the sheet cast off.

Here again is an excellent example of the type of coordination needed between the helmsman and the rest of the crew. If the helmsman merely throws the yacht about and lets the crew fend for themselves, he not only has slowed the boat, but he has injured crew morale. Working together as a team, the winch crew and the helmsman can help each other make smooth, maximum-speed tacks. This, in turn, helps the boat get where she is going faster, which is the reason you are out sailing together.

When tacking in heavy seas, the helmsman should try to pick a spot where the waves' action is the least so the waves will have a minimum effect on the speed. Crashing and diving into waves when tacking will stop a yacht. Use the same care in selecting a wave to tack on as you would in selecting a course through the waves when beating to windward.

Chapter 10 **Helmsmanship Downwind**

Ed Botterell in a St. Petersburg/Ft. Lauderdale Race. (Bruce Kirby)

One used to see skippers take their good helmsmen off the wheel once the windward mark had been reached and let the less experienced or less skilled aboard take the wheel. The belief was that anybody could steer a boat on a reach; all that was needed was someone to hold a compass course, and the boat would move as fast as it could no matter what. Somewhere along the line the more astute of these skippers realized that a few boats were sailing faster on reaches than they had any right to sail. Why? Because really good helmsmen were getting more speed out of their boats.

It is a demonstrated fact that a greater speed differential can be realized on a reach than on the wind if the helmsman understands how to get the most out of the boat and uses all his powers of concentration. This idea has developed not only because of increasing competition, but also because the design configurations of modern offshore racers tend to make them more difficult to steer off the wind. Thus, it is even more important that these yachts have skillful handling. Not only hulls have changed, but rigs now have more sophisticated controls which must be understood by the helmsman and the rest of the crew so that they may obtain the greatest speed from the boat. No longer does one set a compass course, trim the headsail and mainsail to the point "just before they luff," and sit back with the wheel in one hand and a beer in the other. The helmsman must concentrate on the speedometer, apparent wind indicator, wave action, rudder pressure, angle of heel, and a myriad other small indicators in addition to the compass, while the other crew members make adjustments to sheets, halyards, vang, Cunningham, outhaul, downhaul, and traveler controls. Each of these sail controls will be discussed in detail in a later chapter. At this point we will concentrate on steering the boat—beginning, again, with light air conditions.

Suppose the course to the next mark puts the boat on a reach that is too close to carry a spinnaker. The wind is light—about eight knots—and the apparent direction is around 50 degrees off the bow.

This is the easiest condition the helmsman will face. The boat is not overpowered; it does not tend to roll out and round up into the wind. The steering is not difficult. Once the sail controls are adjusted for maximum drive—as indicated by the speedometer—the helmsman's job is to see that the speed is maintained. He should be sure, for instance, that there is not too much weather helm. Weather helm will be readily apparent from the position of the tiller, which will be displaced far from the centerline, and from the considerable forces required to hold the boat on course. With a wheel, weather helm may go undetected; lacking the direct hookup of a tiller, one cannot see the relative position of the rudder. Also, the mechanical advantage of the wheel will reduce the forces required to hold it. To identify excessive weather helm at its onset, one must have the center position marked on the wheel and note how many turns, or partial turns, the wheel is deflected from center.

If, for instance, the wheel must be turned three-quarters of a turn in order to hold the boat on course, this could indicate excessive weather helm for these conditions. When the rudder must be deflected to such an extent simply to hold course, it causes increased drag and thus slows the boat.

In light air most boats will respond with reduced weather helm to easing of the traveler and a corresponding tightening of the mainsheet (if necessary). Easing the mainsheet and tightening the vang may also work, and it may be that the genoa (or reacher) is overtrimmed, requiring an easing of its sheet or a repositioning of its lead.

All this may not appear to be helmsmanship, but without the skill of the helmsman to detect weather helm, the sail-trimming crew members would not have a clue that their boat was not traveling at top speed.

In light going there is little else to bother the helmsman on a close reach, but he must constantly test the boat, suggesting changes in trim, perhaps ordering a staysail set, until he is positive that he has found the fastest combination of sails, sail trim, compass course, and helm.

Once the wind has come aft enough to allow setting of a spinnaker—possible even at 50 degrees with some specially cut reaching chutes—the helmsman's problems increase. It will be largely the helmsman's decision whether or not a spinnaker should be set; if it is not his decision, at least his reaction to the suggestion should be carefully considered.

Once again, knowing the boat is of key importance. The spinnaker is larger than any other headsail that can be set. Can the boat take the additional press of sail area without excessive heeling that would slow her down? The only person who can answer this question with certainty is the helmsman, who's "been there" before.

There will be a point—particularly on a close or beam reach—where additional sail area cannot be carried effectively. Rolling the leeward topsides into the water, creating an imbalance in the curve of the waterlines at the hull and increasing weather helm, will tend to slow the boat down. At eight knots of wind, this is unlikely, but you must know your boat to be able to tell for sure.

Once the spinnaker is set, the helmsman acquires yet another indicator to watch—the spinnaker luff. He has at his disposal the fastest and most reliable spinnaker-trimming device—faster than the spinnaker sheet—the helm. When close reaching in light air, the slightest movement of the rudder will have an immediate effect on the boat's course. The helmsman must watch for minute shifts in the wind and adjust the boat's heading to keep the spinnaker drawing at its optimum. Many crews try to make these adjustments with the spinnaker sheet, but most often they can be done more quickly and with less effort by the helmsman. The spinnaker sheet should still be hand-held, and the sheet trimmer must work in conjunction with the helmsman to make more permanent adjustments necessary to maintain course.

The helmsman is in the best position to know whether a staysail or double-slot (with a genoa or a reacher) would work. As before, his decision should be based upon his experience, the amount of weather helm (even though it is way forward, a spinnaker can induce weather helm), the angle of heel, and the speed through the water.

As the wind draws aft, the apparent wind velocity reduces and the helmsman's attention should focus on keeping the spinnaker drawing. In this case the prescribed course becomes subservient to the necessity for keeping the boat moving. As the apparent wind lightens, the spinnaker tends to collapse and may reach the point where it will not fill when headed dead downwind. Somewhere between the ideal course with the spinnaker not drawing and a broad reach with the spinnaker pulling vigorously lies the optimum heading for maximum speed made good downwind. This

HELMSMANSHIP DOWNWIND

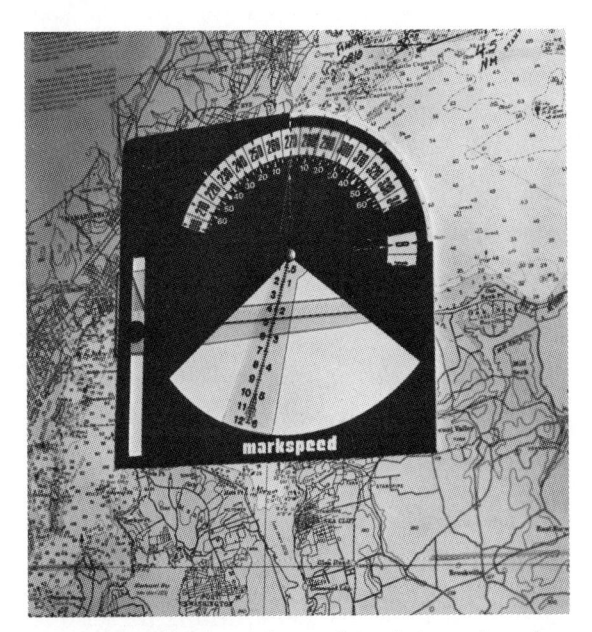

Markspeed plotter can be used to plot speed made good either downwind or upwind to show the optimum course to be sailed to reach the mark in the shortest possible time. (Markspeed courtesy of Lands End) (Ted Jones)

will involve "tacking downwind" on first one jibe, then the other. The angle of the tacks can be plotted mathematically, but one very seldom has the time or the mental dexterity to work out the best heading/speed combinations in his head. A couple of ingenious sailors have developed plotters, which one can use to work out the optimum headings for tacking downwind. A few gifted sailors can come very close by "feel." I invariably guess wrong and, not knowing the proper moment to jibe, come out either too high or too low, having wasted time and distance. Use of the plotter, preferably by the navigator with information from the helmsman as to different speeds at different headings, can prevent disastrous mistakes of this sort.

In really light going—drifting—a good helmsman can coax life out of a dead spinnaker by judicious selection of heading. The slower one goes, the less important the course to the next mark will be (sooner or later the wind will fill in or shift, creating a new set of course and speed problems), so you shouldn't be afraid to deviate considerably from the stated course to get the boat moving. Just be sure you keep the navigator informed! With a full spinnaker the boat may be traveling three feet obliquely for every foot toward the mark, but that is certainly better than a collapsed spinnaker and no movement. So what if your boat sails miles further than a competitor in the same time period if those miles will produce a net gain toward your destination while his idleness gains him nothing? The helmsman can produce those miles by adjusting the boat's heading to keep the spinnaker full and drawing.

As the Wind Picks Up . . .

Helmsmanship becomes more and more critical as the reaching wind increases. Once the wind velocity exceeds about 10 knots, the seas begin to build, adding yet another variable and another gauge for the helmsman to watch. As long as the seas are on the beam, they will not have too much effect on the heading of the boat; the helmsman will not have great difficulty maintaining directional control. Once the spinnaker is set on a close reach, its trim is critical, and small waves might spill a closely trimmed chute. Total spinnaker collapse must be avoided, and it is up to the helmsman to let the sheet trimmer know how much curl in the luff of the spinnaker is comfortable for the helmsman to handle.

Medium conditions, between 12 and 18 knots, will be critical when deciding whether or not to set the spinnaker. Experience will give the helmsman his best clues. He must be able to decide whether the added sail area of the spinnaker will drive the boat faster or merely heel her over. His indicators are weather helm, angle of heel, apparent wind angle, and speed through the water. If the boat has an anemometer, this may also be helpful, provided a log of apparent wind angles, wind speeds, and sail combinations is kept.

The tendency for weather helm will increase with more wind, and it may be impossible—depending on the particular boat—to reduce it. Weather helm may even become excessive in strong puffs; the rudder may eventually stall, and the helmsman may lose control of the boat temporarily. (More on this later.)

Broad reaching and quartering seas are more likely to disturb the boat's heading and create problems for the spinnaker. The luff will be easier to control on a broad reach, however, and the sail is not as likely to collapse.

As the wind velocity and seas increase, it becomes possible to gain boosts in speed from wave riding. A good helmsman can increase a boat's speed several knots by "surfing" down the face of even a small wave. The best helmsman can keep a boat wave riding for several seconds in moderate wind and seas.

To do this, one must learn to feel the motion of the boat. As a wave comes up astern, bear off slightly so that the boat rides down the face of the wave, the driving force of the sails being assisted by the force of gravity. As speed is picked up, it may be held by heading up again slightly—increasing the force of the wind on the sails—angling along the face of the wave. Normally, seas in 12- to 18-knot winds will not be large, so surfing or wave riding will be minimal under these conditions. It may be worth working quite hard to get just a few boosts, particularly in a small boat, which will surf sooner than a large boat. This is where the really sharp helmsman is worth his weight in beer because he will be getting those precious extra feet with each wave, while your competitor slips slowly but inexorably behind.

Running in moderate air brings us once again to decisions about tacking downwind. It depends largely upon the individual characteristics of the boat, but usually tacking downwind under these conditions is not effective. Helmsman and navigator should work together and try it out on the plotter just to be sure, but more likely the helmsman will be busy steering dead downwind, watching the spinnaker, feeling the wind direction on the back of his neck, checking the apparent wind indicator, the speedometer, the compass, and so on. Undivided attention to all the indicators can produce a significant increase in speed, although not as dramatic an increase as that obtained on a reach or on a run in light air.

This brings us to consider moderately heavy weather in winds of over 20 knots. In this situation many boats become difficult to manage on reaches, and many crews begin to settle for survival instead of victory.

Not Quite Storm Conditions

In an article in *Yacht Racing*,[1] Bruce Kirby advises, "Stop surviving and race." His thesis is concerned primarily with one-

---

[1] Bruce Kirby, "Stop Surviving and Race," *Yacht Racing*, vol. 11, no. 4 (April 1972), pp. 44–47.

design racers, but it applies equally well to offshore racers. This is where the boys get separated from the men, the timid separated from the brave, and the inexperienced separated from the knowledgeable. The gains one can make in higher winds are proportionately greater than those available in light-to-medium air. Also, more of your competitors (the timid and inexperienced) will be trying less hard to beat you. When you have less competition, work harder, don't slack off!

The conditions discussed here are not yet in the storm category—survival conditions will be dealt with in a separate chapter—but are marked by winds that exceed the force for which most boats are designed to carry full sail.

The decision to carry a spinnaker in winds over 20 knots will be delayed until the wind is well abaft the beam. Most boats, in beam winds, simply bury their leeward rails under spinnaker and go no faster—even slow down. As the wind picks up, the center of effort of the sail plan should be as low as possible to reduce the heeling moment to a minimum. For close reaching, beam reaching, and sometimes even broad reaching, a special, high-cut overlapping jib called a "reacher" is more effective than a spinnaker—even one especially cut for reaching. The reacher is normally the same size as a number one genoa, but cut fuller. Its high clew keeps the foot of the sail out of the bow wave. Many reachers also have a grommet midway along the foot where a halyard or lift can be attached to lift the foot farther out of the bow wave if necessary.

With the reacher set instead of the spinnaker, the helmsman's problems are no greater than close reaching in light to medium winds. In fact, since the sails are driving the boat near her hull speed most of the time, small changes in weather helm—it may be considerable—or in sail trim will have a relatively small effect on speed.

The helmsman must keep the weather helm within manageable limits by ordering the vang set up really tight, with the mainsheet eased well out to free the leech and reduce heeling.

Heeling is the major cause of trouble when reaching in moderately heavy winds. The more a boat heels, the more imbalance there is in the underwater planes, tending to force the boat to turn toward the high (usually windward) side. Also, the more a boat heels, the less the turning effect of the rudder, which, as it rotates through its horizontal axis, becomes more of an elevator—lifting the stern instead of turning it. These two forces, plus the forces acting through the sails, combine to make a boat difficult to steer when it is heeled excessively.

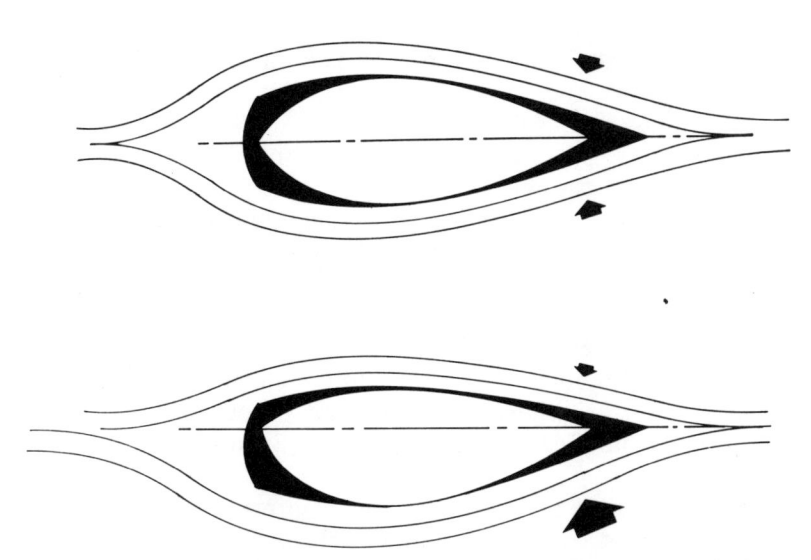

The shape of a yacht's underbody when heeled becomes asymmetrical, creating an imbalance in the hydrodynamic forces acting on the hull tending to force the yacht to turn toward the high (usually windward) side.

Reaching in 20-knot-plus winds, the modern ocean racer, with its cutaway keel and spade rudder, has garnered a dubious reputation for controllability. In many cases, the reputation is deserved, although ultimate seaworthiness of a well-built boat rarely has been a problem. When pressed hard under spinnakers, these boats quickly developed the alarming tendency to round up or broach. In the days of wooden spars, cotton sails, and Manila sheets, this could not be tolerated. Something would very likely break in the wild broaches that our modern offshore racers can usually take without damage. What's going on?

Imagine a boat broad reaching in winds between 20 and 30 knots. The spinnaker is set, and the boat is providing a wildly exhilarating ride for its crew, surfing down the face of the quartering waves. The aggregate helm forces produce a weather helm, but because the waves are constantly changing their influence on the hull, the forces the helmsman feels and the corrections he has to make to maintain his heading are continually changing. As the boat rolls and yaws, the forces on the sails change also, further aggravating the steering problems.

Suddenly, the boat heels sharply to leeward. The helmsman feels a violent weather helm—or tendency for the boat to head up—

and he makes a large correction by cranking many turns on the wheel. His correction may be enough and in time, but possibly it will be too late or he may have corrected too much, and the rudder will stall out—losing its ability to control the boat's direction. When this happens, the sail forces and hull forces combine to round the boat up toward the wind. If the gust is a particularly strong one, she may come to a stop lying on her side, coming up only when the pressures on the sails are relieved. Very often the spinnaker will collapse, letting the boat come more upright; then the spinnaker will refill with a bang and the boat will be slammed down on her beam ends once again. For the inexperienced, this can be truly frightening. An experienced helmsman can prevent many, but not all, broaches, and when they do occur, they usually can be routinely handled and the boat brought quickly back under control.

In the 1970 Southern Ocean Racing Conference I sailed with Bruce Kirby aboard the prototype C&C 35, *Redhead*. In the second race, from St. Petersburg to Fort Lauderdale, the winds were around 30 knots. Once outside Tampa Bay we had a broad reach under spinnaker for 100 miles. The seas were moderate and gave us excellent surfing, with the speedometer often pegged at 10 knots.

The week before we had had similar conditions but more of a dead run to the Boca Grande Sea Buoy. When running, we had had no problems broaching—although many other boats did. But in the Lauderdale Race, with the wind and seas more on the quarter, we were continually broaching. We soon got quite used to it. The boat would round up uncontrollably, the spinnaker would collapse, the boat would straighten up, the helmsman would head off, the spinnaker would refill with a bang, and the boat would either take off on a wild 10-knot-plus surfing ride or broach again.

As each helmsman became more familiar with the boat (this was the first sail for some and only the second time any of us had sailed her), he would discover how to avoid some broaches and to ride with the unavoidable ones. He got to know the feel of the wheel when all hope was lost, when no recovery was possible. Dr. Fred Anfossie was the first to discover that if, when he felt that a broach was unavoidable, the helmsman steered into the broach, control could be regained more quickly. Fred found that by neutralizing the helm at the onset of the broach, the boat kept its speed, and as soon as the spinnaker collapsed, the rudder was still very effective in heading the boat off, back on course. It was not necessary to ease the spinnaker sheet or mainsheet. The spinnaker would refill by itself, and we'd fly away on course.

The 57-foot *Enzian* rolls heavily to windward then...

jibes and almost broaches while...

a sister ship does a full "wipe-out" broach astern.

Rather than reduce sail, we set a spinnaker staysail to help drive the boat through the broaches. They became so routine that we got quite nonchalant about them. At one point Ed Botterell was to leeward adjusting the staysail sheet when Fred shouted, "I lost it" (meaning that we were about to broach). Ed calmly grasped the handrail on the cabin top, remaining on the leeward side, and waited for Fred to steer us through the broach. Then Ed went about trimming the staysail sheet. He didn't even get his feet wet. A few hours earlier we all would have been scrambling for the weather side.

A more cautious crew might have taken in the spinnaker under such conditions. Many did, but we sailed faster. As it turned out, the rudder post broke under the strain many hours later—a structural fault soon corrected in *Redhead* (and subsequent C&C 35s) but not, of course, before it cost us the race—but that's another tale!

Aboard *Kittiwake* in the 1966 Transatlantic Race we surfed for days before 35-knot winds under spinnaker. We had a contest among the helmsmen of our watch to see who could go a full half-hour trick at the wheel without rounding up and dumping the spinnaker. It took several watches before any of us earned the right to wear "No Flop Club," in embossed tape, on our foul-weather jackets, but before many days had passed, we all had our badges with fifteen or twenty "clusters."

Lately, new designs have been overcoming the early tendency to broach. Skegs and long-veed after-sections are improving boats' directional stability. Nevertheless, with every boat there is a point where the helmsman will lose control. If he knows what's going on and doesn't panic, all should be well.

You need not fear broaching, provided your boat is strongly built and rigged. It is best to avoid it if possible, but if the only way to avoid an occasional broach is to take down the spinnaker, then one must live either with broaching or with defeat.

I'm not sure it is possible to describe fully the many factors that combine to control a boat and give it super driving power. Each boat, each wave, the way in which boat and wave meet, and the action of wind on sails at any given moment differ so drastically that it is difficult to make generalizations. One simply has to go "out there" and try to learn how to do it.

Then one learns to his dismay that the next time, under slightly different conditions, the same techniques might not work at all.

I'm reminded of a trip back from Bermuda. After a couple of days of pleasant spinnaker runs, the wind came on the beam and freshened to 40 knots. A friend who was along on his first ocean passage, and very nearly his first sail, took his trick at the wheel at the height of wind and sea.

After wincing for several minutes, as he let the boat smash into seemingly every wake, I lost patience. "For heaven's sake, Don," I shouted above the wind's roar, "try to steer around the waves instead of smashing through them." To which he replied, "Damn, just when I was beginning to get the compass settled down, you tell me to look at something else." He'd had his nose in the binnacle, disregarding wind and wave.

It is the sea that counts most when reaching in moderately heavy weather. The compass is still the primary instrument, but you will find it difficult to hold a course within 15 or even 20 degrees. You must mentally average the swings of the compass in order to maintain the course ordered.

If there is one secret of steering downwind, it is anticipation. Learn to anticipate the way the bow will be trying to turn next and make a correction with tiller or wheel before the bow begins to swing. Corrections should be rapid but small. Learn how to find the critical rudder angle—beyond which it becomes more of a brake than a steering device—and never exceed that angle, which probably will be no greater than 20 degrees. The temptation, when the bow slews wildly off to windward, is to crank in as much rudder as fast as one can, but this will invariably lead to overcontrolling. Too much correction will cause a more violent reaction, with the bow swinging wildly in the other direction. Overcontrolling is self-defeating in that it makes the boat less manageable, slows it down, and wears out the helmsman.

The art of catching a wave is not difficult to master with practice, and it is of utmost importance in any kind of sailboat racing, not just offshore. Some sailors who are well versed in small-boat racing don't realize that those great big lumps of fiberglass, aluminum, steel, and Dacron we race offshore can surf and wave-ride just as effectively (although not with a proportional increase in speed) as a planing dinghy. Even 50- and 60-footers surf, sometimes with alarming speed.

A planing dinghy is urged onto a plane and down the face of a wave by heading off just before the crest of the wave, pumping the sheets vigorously, shifting crew weight first forward and then aft, then heading up across the face of the wave to keep from overriding it into the trough and increasing the apparent wind across the sails. The same principles apply to surfing an offshore racer, although it is not possible to shift crew weight, and it is

Carina gets a surfing boost from a relatively small wave (above). *Tara* plunges down face of a large wave off Nassau (below).

usually not practical to make rapid adjustments in the trim of the sails. Small offshore racers, however, can be made to surf more readily by pumping the main and spinnaker sheets, so don't overlook this possibility. I've done it effectively on a 35-footer!

Head off just before the crest of the wave reaches the stern, then head up as speed increases to keep from dropping back down into the trough. Practice the action any time you are in a boat—any boat—when there is a following sea. I have learned quite a bit about surfing by running small outboards and large power cruisers in following seas. Don't let any opportunity pass. (The best training of all is a surfboard at the beach.) In offshore racing, *the ability of a helmsman to surf a boat well is more important than his ability to steer upwind!*

Close quarters at Cowes—a "string puller's" nightmare. (Jack Knights)

Chapter 11 **Sail Handling**

One of the keys to making a boat perform at its optimum involves the proper selection and set of the sails. Particularly when sailing to windward, sails must be set so that they provide not only maximum drive but also minimum heeling force. Much can be done with proper trim of the sails that are set at any particular time, but the wind velocity or sea condition might change enough that changes in trim, Cunningham tackle, vang, traveler, etc., will not improve the drive of the sails that you have up. It is then necessary to consider making a change.

The steps outlined in this chapter are general in nature because of the differences in rig between boats. They will provide, however, a general procedural outline that can be modified to suit most boats. Small boats will have fewer crew to handle the various tasks, but will also make fewer physical demands on the crew. Nevertheless, there are a certain minimum number of steps that must be accomplished with each procedure, and in some cases it will take longer, or the crew must be considerably more agile, to perform the procedures rapidly and precisely. Very large boats need considerably more brute force. They have a larger crew to handle the same number of specific duties, but often two or three people will be required to perform one function. Perhaps the medium-size boats with eight or nine in the crew have the best of it. There are enough crew members so that each person can handle a specific duty, and the physical forces are small enough so that he can cope with them alone.

Reefing

At some point in an increasing wind, a boat will sail faster with less sail. Reducing sail allows the boat to stand up straighter, presenting her designed shape to the waves and keeping the keel more nearly vertical to resist leeway. When it becomes necessary to reduce sail, first ease the mainsheet traveler and carry a large luff in the mainsail. Beyond this, it will be necessary to change headsails or reef.

To reef with a roller reefing boom, proceed as follows:

1. Remove the vang tackle and move the vang claw or strap to the outboard end of the boom, or remove it.

2. Release the lacing that holds the lower slides to the luff of the sail, and remove the Cunningham line.

3. Slack the mainsheet.

4. Have one person ease the halyard as another cranks the reefing handle, taking up the slack as the sail is eased. Be sure the luff does not jam on the reefing gear.

5. When sufficient reef is rolled in, take up taut on the halyard and ease the topping lift.

The "old-fashioned" method of reefing with "reef points" (a line of grommets or several lines of grommets sewn into the sail partway up the luff and parallel to the boom) is coming back into popularity with several new wrinkles.

"Slab reefing," as it is now popularly known, involves pulling grommets in the luff and leach down to the boom. A few reef points are usually provided to hold the middle part of the sail and to furl the unused cloth between boom and reef. The proper method of tying in reef points is to lace from grommet around the bolt rope of the foot of the sail. If the foot of the sail slides in a groove, it will be necessary to tie the reefing lines around the boom, but care must be taken to avoid tying in outhauls, topping lifts, and other lines which may have to be used later.

To reef with slab reefing, proceed as follows:

1. Slack the mainsheet (it is unnecessary to remove the vang tackle or release the lacing on the luff or Cunningham line).

2. One person should ease the main halyard while another takes up on the luff-reefing line through the luff grommet.

3. Take up on the leach grommet until the sail is down to the boom and stretched tight along the reef points.

4. Lace in the reef points with either a continuous light line or short lengths of line specially designated for reefing.

Some boats are rigged with a continuous line through both the leach and luff grommets. This rig eliminates a step, but there is considerably more friction in this, necessitating a winch on even the smallest boats.

Slab reefing is much quicker than roller reefing but has a disadvantage in that reefing can be accomplished only where there are reef points. With roller reefing, the amount of reef is infinitely variable.

For short legs, the reef points need not be tied in at all. Some mainsails eliminate reef points altogether by providing a wire in a sleeve to keep tension along the boom. This, in turn, has the disadvantage that the excess cloth cannot be gotten rid of.

Changing Headsails

When wind strength increases to the point that the boat is overpowered even with a reef, or the headsail stretches out of its proper shape, a smaller headsail of heavier fabric must be substituted. Conversely, if a small genoa is set and the wind strength decreases, a larger sail must be set in its place.

Before making a headsail change, it must be determined how long the new headsail will be required. If there is only a mile to go and the boat is not drastically overpowered, it may be best to hang on to what is set—the act of changing will very likely result in more lost ground than would be recovered by the increase in speed a different headsail would provide. It doesn't take too many minutes at less than optimum speed, however, before one reaches the point where a headsail change will result in a net gain.

If, for instance, it takes one minute to change from a number one to a number two genoa, by experience you know that the boat will slow from six knots to almost zero knots while changing, and you can expect to go six and one-half knots after the change, you can estimate whether or not the change is worthwhile. A bit of calculation will show that it would take twelve minutes to make up the lost ground.

A simple formula for determining the time it will take to make up the time lost while changing will give you something a little bit better than a rough guess. You cannot know for sure in advance if a headsail change will result in an increase in speed of one-half, or one-quarter, or zero, so at best this is a rough guide:

$$t_2 = \frac{v_1 t_1}{v_2 - v_1}$$ where: $v_1 =$ velocity before sail change
$v_2 =$ velocity after sail change (estimate)
$t_1 =$ time in minutes required for sail change
$t_2 =$ time in minutes required to gain lost ground

When preparing for headsail change, the new sail is hanked on to leeward of the sail that is set.

The old sail is unhanked as it is lowered and is allowed to fall on top of the new sail.

As the new sail is hoisted (when all the hanks of the old sail have been removed from the stay) it spills the old sail to windward, keeping it on deck instead of dumping it to leeward and into the water as would happen if the new sail had been hanked on to windward. (Ted Jones)

SAIL HANDLING

The key to headsail changes, therefore, is speed. Speed can be developed only by practicing a set routine. A suggested routine for changing headsails follows:

Foredeck
1. Hanks on new sail.
2. Pulls down old sail.
3. Unhanks old sail.
4. Switches halyard from old to new sail.
5. Cranks halyard winch.

Halyard
1. Ties on new sheets.
2. Casts off halyard.
3. Changes sheets and lead if necessary.
4. Hoists new sail.

Cockpit
1. Casts off sheet (waits until sail is almost down).
2. Trims new sheet (waits until sail is almost up).

Helm
1. Luffs as old sail comes down.
2. Bears off to keep boat footing under mainsail.
3. Heads up as sail is sheeted home.

Under no circumstances should the tack of the old jib be detached before one is ready to stow the sail below. Without the tack attached, the sail can be washed overboard. At best, it will be difficult to recover, trailing aft attached by the sheet. If the sheet has been untied, too, the sail will be lost!

On most boats there is no reason why a practiced crew cannot make a change from a number one genoa to a number two in thirty seconds in normal sea conditions. In rough weather it will take longer because of the increased difficulty of working on a bouncing, wet deck.

Many boats are now equipped with a special interim jib or have adapted other staysails to keep the boat driving to windward during a headsail change. This is more work for the crew (and more expense for the owner), but will take some of the sweat out of rapid headsail changes. The procedure for using an interim jib is the same as for a normal headsail change except that between steps one and two, foredeck sets the interim jib and after the change is complete, he takes the interim jib down.

The interim jib will provide significant drive, particularly in boats with large foretriangles relative to the mainsail area. It is often possible to lose as little as 15 or 20 percent of speed made good to windward while the interim jib is set. When the speed made good goes to zero while the foretriangle is bare, the addition of an interim jib is truly worthwhile.

Slotted Stays

Marblehead sailmaker Ted Hood has developed a rod headstay which incorporates a luff groove similar to those found in spars for mainsail luff and foot. With the C-stay, as it is called, one does not have conventional hanks that wrap around the stay (although these may be used). Instead, the luff of the sail slides in the groove. The main advantage of the C-stay is that it improves the aerodynamic flow around the luff of the jib.

In theory, it is easier to make a headsail change with a C-stay as there are no hanks to clip on or take off. Crews I have sailed with have had some difficulty feeding the luff rope into the groove, and the sails have tended to get away from the foredeck man with neither attached except at the tack. I have watched more practiced crews, however, who had no difficulty and could, in fact, make more rapid sail changes with a C-stay than with conventional hanks. While my experience with the C-stay has been minimal and not particularly successful, I would conclude that it has no sail-handling disadvantages when compared with conventional headstays and hanks once a crew has had the time to practice using it.

In addition to the C-stay, several other similar devices, consisting of a plastic or metal sleeve fitting over the headstay, have been developed. Procedures for the use of the C-stay and these similar devices will be the same as when changing headsails with hanks except that the steps that call for hanking on the new sail and removing the hanks on the old sail are eliminated.

Two devices that allow changing headsails without first taking down the sail to be replaced were perfected in 1973. Bob Barton, of Murphy & Nye Sailmakers, assembled a luff sleeve that clips to a yacht's existing headstay. With this he uses small luff tapes that will fit two-at-a-time in the sleeve. Thus, a crew can hoist the new sail in the sleeve alongside the sail it will replace. When the new sail is properly set, the old sail is taken down.

Tim Stearn has a patent pending on an aluminum rod headstay called a Twin Stay. This is similar to Hood's C-Stay except there are two grooves for the luff tape. By rotating the Twin Stay in

SAIL HANDLING

The "Twin Stay" has double luff grooves to allow setting of replacement sail before taking in the sail it is to replace thereby eliminating prolonged reduced speed during headsail changes. Luff tape of sail is led through crescent-shaped casting (suspended from stay) which feeds tape between plates (bolted either side of stay) thence into groove. Swivels at top and bottom of Twin Stay allow it to rotate. Two genoa halyards are required. (Ted Jones)

special bearings at each end, a crew can set a new sail in the forward groove, get it all set, rotate the stay again, and then lower the old sail—much the same way as with Barton's system.

Both of these systems promise to revolutionize the art of headsail changing. Not only do they provide the capability of changing headsails without slowing the yacht, but sails can be changed with fewer crew members on deck.

Sail Controls

The recent history of yacht racing has seen many developments in sail controls as we have first found the need for, and then thought of, ways to change the shape of sails made of synthetic fibers. Briggs Cunningham is credited with the invention of the luff tension control which bears his name, when he shortened the luff of a sail by lashing a light line between the tack fitting and the first sail slide. Soon this device became more sophisticated; a grommet in the sail and a proper line made the "Cunningham" adjustable.

The use of a tackle called a "boom vang" was described by Robert N. Bavier in 1947.[1] Its purpose was to tighten the leech of the mainsail when reaching, removing the twist from the top of the sail.

Travelers, first used simply as devices to allow the mainsheet to slide above the tiller, were found to be effective in controlling mainsail drive when the position of the slide was adjustable.

With the universal use of sails made of synthetic fibers (particularly Dacron and Terylene), sails that do not change their shape in different winds or when wet, racing sailors have found it necessary and advantageous to develop the means to alter sail shape and thereby control a sail's driving power.

Most of these developments took place in small boats. As competition has become more fierce in each class, however, top-ranking sailors have found more and more ways to control the shape of their sails with more and more complex assemblages of equipment. It is common to see a Finn, Flying Dutchman, Fireball, or 470 with so many controls that each is labeled. The uninitiated observer requires a road map to follow the intricate paths that the lines for each device take—and a degree in mechanical engineering to understand their functions. Gone are the days when the halyard was taken up as tight as possible; ditto the outhaul. I can remember also when my crew stood on the sliding gooseneck (a new gadget that some of my less fortunate competitors didn't have) while I cleated the downhaul before we cast off the race—never to touch halyard or outhaul again until putting the boat to bed. Now one must know the subtle intricacies of Cunninghams, boom vangs, Barber hauls, Marshall hauls, J.C. straps, traveler controls, backstay adjusters, mast jacks, downhauls, uphauls, inhauls, and outhauls.

More recently, those dinghy devices not specifically prohibited in offshore-racing rules have found their way aboard offshore racers. One thinks of a mainsail, for instance, as having a halyard

---

[1] Robert N. Bavier, *Sailing to Win* (New York: Dodd, Mead, 1947), pp. 92–94.

These photographs of a test model developed by Hathaway, Reiser and Raymond, sailmakers, demonstrate the changes in shape and position, relative to the mainsail, possible with adjustments in sheet lead (fore-and-aft or athwartships), halyard tension or Cunningham tension. (Ted Jones)

The first series of model photographs shows what happens to the genoa when the sheet lead is adjusted fore-and-aft.

Here the lead is too far forward, pulling the leech too tight, closing up the slot, and constricting the flow of air between the leech of the genoa and the mainsail. The lower portion of the sail is undertrimmed and too full, while the upper portion is overtrimmed and too flat.

Here the lead is positioned about right. The leech of the genoa is close enough to the mainsail to produce a good "slot"— accelerating the air between them. Both the lower and upper portions of the genoa are trimmed to the same angle to the apparent wind, and the draft is uniform from top to bottom.

Here the lead is too far aft, allowing the leech to fall off aloft and opening the slot between the genoa and mainsail excessively. The lower portion of the sail is overtrimmed and too full (excessive draft), while the upper portion is overtrimmed and too flat (insufficient draft).

The second series of model photographs shows what happens when the genoa halyard and Cunningham are adjusted to increase luff tension.

Here the Cunningham line and halyard are eased to produce a gentle curve in the chord line (black band) with the point of maximum draft just forward of the mid-chord point. Shape and leech position are similar to that shown in center photo on page 133.

Here the Cunningham line has been tightened, moving the point of maximum draft forward. Note that this also eases the leech (moving it away from the mainsail) having somewhat the same effect as moving the sheet lead aft.

Here the Cunningham line has been made very tight, moving the point of maximum draft even further forward and easing the leech excessively. This condition is accentuated by some stretch in the rope halyard on the model. Note similarity to photo where lead is too far aft on page 133.

The third series of model photographs shows what happens to the genoa when the sheet lead is moved athwartships.

Here the sheet lead is set at a 10-degree angle to the centerline. This is a common position for yachts with the sheet led to the rail although most modern offshore racers can set their genoa lead effectively at 8 degrees in some conditions.

Here the sheet lead is moved inboard to 5 degrees, and the sheet is eased to open the slot. Note that the chord shape is not changed but the leech tends to fall off slightly at the top approaching the extreme shown in photo where lead is too far aft on page 133.

Here the sheet lead is moved outboard to 15 degrees and the sheet is trimmed to keep the slot closed. Again, the chord shape is not changed but the leech is tighter at the top approaching the extreme shown in photo on page 133 where lead is too far forward.

and a sheet. Aboard our 26-footer *Trilogy*, which we raced from 1970 to 1972, there were no less than nine distinct controls for the mainsail. In addition to the halyard and sheet, there was a Cunningham for adjusting luff tension; a "Marshall haul,"[2] which controlled a draft-control wire in the foot; a zipper, which further controlled draft along the foot; a continuous reefing line laced between the boom and the leech and luff-reefing grommets; an outhaul tackle rigged inside the boom; a semipermanent boom vang, which led to the deck; two traveler controls, rigged to either side of the traveler (count them as one control); and a leech line to control leech flutter.

Yes, we were busy tweaking and hauling on all those "strings," but the mainsail could be made to assume almost any shape, size, and position we wished. Being able to control it completely, *Trilogy*'s crew could derive the maximum power from the mainsail in virtually any wind condition.

There is no text that will tell you how much to pull on what line in what wind condition to make your sail adjust to its optimum shape. Each crew must determine for itself the combination of adjustments that will make their boat sail the fastest. One used to hear a great deal about the mystique of "tuning" a boat. Eager novices used to spy surreptitiously on the hotshots' boats to try to discover the secrets of their tuning. Imagine their bewilderment when they found that each hotshot had a different secret. "Tuning" went out with Manila sheets and Egyptian duck. There are few hard-and-fast rules on setting up a rig even among strict one-design classes, where boats are identical. What works for one may not work for another. What works for you—the adjustments that make your boat sail faster—is what you should do.

Some generalizations can be made, however, about the overall effect that a specific change in sail shape will have. The *amount* of control, the tension on a line, and the interaction of mainsail and headsail can be determined only by trial and error and the keenness of an experienced sailor's eye. Once again, the need for practice and the experience of doing becomes apparent.

A full sail, with the point of maximum draft not quite halfway between luff and leech, is best for light winds and smooth seas. In light winds and moderately rough or sloppy seas, a slightly flatter sail usually works better. As the wind increases, the draft should be reduced, and the point of maximum draft should move

---

[2] Named after sailmaker John Marshall, who made it for *Trilogy*.

Without a vang (above) the wind forces in the mainsail cause the main boom to lift which, in turn, causes the upper part of the sail to fall off to leeward. If the sail is trimmed so that the upper part is most efficient, the lower part will be trimmed too tight. If trimmed to the lower part, the upper part will luff or be undertrimmed.
Setting the vang (below) pulls the main boom down and takes the twist out of the sail. The vang may be adjusted so that most of the sail is in the same plane and can be trimmed to the proper angle to the wind. (Ted Jones)

forward. As the wind approaches the point where reefing becomes necessary, the sail should be as flat as possible and should remain fairly flat when reefed. In rough seas the mainsail should be full again to provide drive while heading off to get through the waves (see Chapter 9).

Mainsails have several controls by which the shape of the sail can be altered: the halyard, the sliding gooseneck, and the Cunningham control luff tension. The halyard should be set so the headboard is at its maximum height (controlled by the measurement point). The sliding gooseneck (if one is provided) can be used to adjust the luff tension. However, moving the boom affects all the cloth in the sail—stretching or relaxing it more or less equally but causing little change in shape. By adjusting the Cunningham, the tension in just the luff area can be varied, and as Cunningham tension is increased, the mainsail tends to flatten and the point of maximum draft tends to move forward.

Outhaul tension likewise tends to flatten the lower portion of the sail. In addition to the outhaul, some sails have zippers or Marshall hauls to remove large fullnesses that may be built into the foot of the sail for light winds.

Mast bending, a device used very effectively by most one-design classes, is not used to any great extent in most offshore races. The masthead rig is not designed to bend because it depends upon the columnar support of the mast for headstay/backstay tension (which reaches thousands of pounds even in quite small boats and over 10,000 pounds in the larger ones). Bending the mast out of column endangers the rig because the high compression forces could cause the mast to fail.

There is some ambiguity in rules designed to prohibit deliberate bending of masts. Some natural bending cannot be avoided, however. The intent of the rules is to allow natural bends but to prohibit devices (other than rigging) designed solely to promote bending.

Some bending can be achieved through permanent or semi-permanent shroud adjustments. It may be necessary to induce a slightly forward bow to keep a mast standing straight in strong winds (the tension of the sailcloth will tend to cause the mast to bow aft), so it is possible to induce slight—more or less permanent—bends in masthead rigs. However, most mainsails are cut without regard to mast bending as a means of drastically controlling mainsail shape, as is done in dinghies.

On yachts with their foretriangles terminating below the masthead, it may be possible to induce bending without endangering

SAIL HANDLING 139

the rig by increasing tension on the permanent backstay—running backstays usually being relied upon to provide sufficient headstay tension. I had this rig on *Teazer*, a modified 24' Shark. Even though the mast section was quite stiff, I could induce a large bend in the mast that flattened the mainsail to the point where vertical ridges appeared in the sail—more than enough.

In the long run, the rig proved incapable of standing the strain without running backstays (which I had fitted, but a subsequent owner did away with) and collapsed while racing.

Genoa shape is controlled in much the same way as mainsail shape. The halyard, and sometimes a Cunningham (less common in headsails than in mainsails), controls luff tension by stretching the cloth of the luff, which is sewn to a rope or loosely around a wire that limits ultimate stretch. Increasing the tension of the halyard, Cunningham, or both tends to flatten the sail and to move the draft forward.

Headstay tension is important to limit both the fore-and-aft and athwartships sag of the genoa luff. Sagging aft, due to tension in the cloth, will increase draft and move the point of maximum draft aft, while sagging to leeward will reduce the ability of the boat to point close to the wind.

With a headsail there is no outhaul, but the position of the sheet contributes to the shape of the sail. If the sheet lead is far aft, the foot of the sail will be full, the leech will be tight, and the draft will be higher in the sail. If the sheet lead is far forward, the foot of the sail will be full, the leech will be tight, and the draft will be low. The sheet lead is moved forward and aft until the shape is uniform and the draft is centered. The lead position to achieve this can usually be located by luffing the boat and observing how the genoa breaks. If the top of the sail breaks first, it is too far forward. If the whole luff of the sail breaks at once, the lead is probably just right.

The interaction of mainsail and genoa is important and must be adjusted in small increments until it is right. Much depends upon the fullness of the mainsail, the cut of the genoa, the distance between the two, and the placement of deck fittings. One should try to avoid backwinding the mainsail. On the other hand, some boats sail well with the main slightly aback. Each crew must fiddle with the adjustments of genoa sheets and leads and mainsail controls until they hit upon a combination that makes the boat sail fast.

The function of the crew members who are sail trimmers is to make continual adjustments to the various sail-control devices in

These photos show how tensioning the Cunningham tackle (outside of photos, past the lower left corner) tensions the luff and moves the draft of the sail forward. Luff tension must be increased as the wind increases to counteract the tendency of the draft to migrate aft as the sailcloth stretches. The tension is about right in the top photo and too tight—causing wrinkles in the luff—in the bottom photo. Both photographs were taken in the same wind conditions. (Ted Jones)

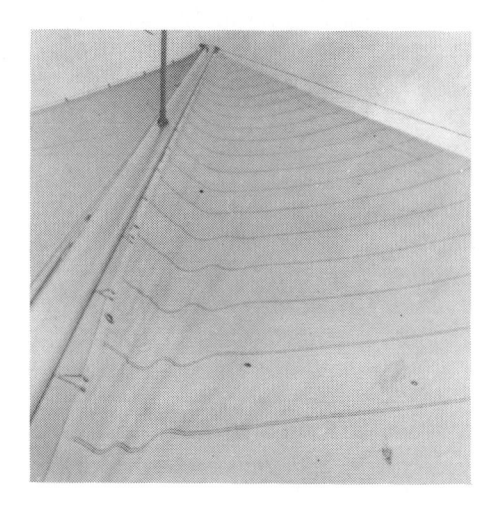

order to keep the boat moving at her optimum speed. This is one of the most important aspects of racing, possibly second only to helmsmanship and strategy, but sometimes just as important. To be a good sail trimmer, you must understand the function of each sail control, know the sails and how they should look under a variety of conditions, and know the boat and how she behaves under different conditions with different sail combinations and shapes.

Not only is the number of variables almost infinite, but the conditions are infinitely variable. The steadiest of winds varies sufficiently so that constant adjustment must be made. If you watch the well-sailed boat sailing to windward, you will very likely see someone sitting by the genoa winch. He will be making continuous adjustments with the sheet and the halyard or Cunningham. He also may be calling changes in mainsail trim or making them himself.

Having a good sail trimmer aboard will relieve the helmsman of worrisome thoughts of trim and allow him to concentrate on steering the boat instead. Of course, there must be a great deal of understanding between the sail trimmer and the helmsman. Each must know what to expect from the other, and each must have complete confidence in the other. They must work well together as a team and practice their teamwork.

How to Use a Winch

Sheet winches come in a variety of sizes and gear ratios. However, their operation is similar so that basic procedures will apply to all types.

The most demanding winching operation involves tacking a genoa. Two or more crew members are usually required to operate a genoa winch. One will "tail"—pull in the slack of the sheet around the winch drum—while one or two will crank the winch drum with the winch handle.

To tail a genoa winch, the "tailer" takes three or four turns clockwise around the winch drum. When the old leeward sheet is released, the tailer pulls in the slack, hand over hand. He must keep tension on the tail to prevent overriding turns from jamming the winch. This technique is quite important and requires some practice to learn. The tailer should move as fast as he can, gathering in the tail of the sheet. At first there will be very little

When making fine adjustments to the genoa sheet, do not take the time to uncleat the line but grasp it between the winch and the cleat to hold the slack while cranking. Uncleat and recleat the line after the adjustment has been made. (Ted Jones)

resistance, but it will gradually increase until the tailer can no longer pull. At this point, the cranker takes over.

With the tailer maintaining tension on the tail of the sheet, the cranker—having inserted the winch handle either while the tail was being gotten in or when the tailer stopped (depending upon the type of winch)—rotates the winch handle until the sail is sheeted home. Again, the resistance will increase as tension on the sheet increases until, in moderate to heavy winds, the cranker must use nearly all his strength to turn the winch. It is sometimes necessary to have a relief cranker to take over midway or when the first cranker tires. Proper cranking also requires practice and learning coordination with the tailer.

Some winches are geared with two speeds. These are used in the same way at first, with the handle being rotated in the high-speed direction until sheet tension builds to the point where low-speed gearing is needed. To engage low gear, the rotation of the handle is simply reversed.

Three-speed winches operate with a direct motion for high speed and reverse rotation for intermediate and low speeds. Some three-speed winches change speed automatically, while others require switching as well as changing rotation direction to engage the third speed.

"Coffee-grinder," or pedestal, winches have the handle offset from the winch drum and can be cranked by two crew members who stand facing each other. Greater power and speed can be developed in this way. These winches have two or three speeds. Their drums are usually larger and have a cleat on top. Usually two or three wraps are sufficient for initial tailing as additional turns may be put on while the winch is being cranked.

The use of winches for sheets other than genoas and for halyards and lifts is the same, but there usually is not the same need for speed and coordination. One person can often operate both the tail and crank for mainsheet, topping lift, and foreguy winches, although it is better to have two people for genoa and spinnaker halyard winches.

Reel winches for halyards and some other specialized uses store the wire on a drum. Backing off is prevented by a brake system which allows rotation of the drum in only one direction. When the brake is released, the drum unreels the wire and (in the case of a mainsail halyard) lowers the sail.

Extreme care must be exercised when lowering sail using a reel halyard winch. It is best to release the brake without a handle in the winch. This is not always possible. There are times (as when reefing) when the halyard must be released under control. With many types of reel winches this can be done only by holding the drum with the handle once the brake is released. If the crew member holding the handle loses his grip, the drum will spin with the handle in it. The spinning handle can cause serious injury to those operating the winch, or it may fly out and hit someone well away from the winch.

There are types of reel winches that have proportional braking which controls the drum with or without having the handle in place. These are much safer than those without proportional braking whose brakes must be either engaged or disengaged.

There is no great mystery about operating winches. Basically, they are simple, logical machines whose purpose is to multiply the muscle power of the crew by sacrificing speed. The cranker should stand so that he can put his back into cranking. This position will vary with different winch placements. A certain amount of practice will be necessary to discover the most convenient and most powerful position. The tailer must find a position that is out of the way of the cranker. His position also should allow him to get his back into the tailing job, especially as the sheet tension increases. This may mean tailing between the cranker's legs or some other seemingly ridiculous position. No matter; the positions that result in the fastest sheet trimming are the best positions to use.

There are as many cockpit winch arrangements, including linked winches and crisscrossed leads (to allow the crew to be on the windward side for the genoa winching), as there are custom yachts. Each has its advantages, disadvantages, and peculiarities, and the crew must learn by practice how to use them effectively.

Chapter 12 **Spinnaker Handling**

Don McNamarra, Alan MacDonald, and Randy Tankoos hold down the foredeck aboard Bill Luders' *Storm* and try to keep Bob McCullough's *Inverness* from getting by to windward. (Morris Rosenfeld)

One of the great secrets of good yacht racing involves the spinnaker. The spinnaker sometimes may be uncontrollable, unseamanlike, and dangerous—but it is damned effective when properly set. From an aesthetic point of view, the spinnaker is the most beautiful sail a yacht can set.

Since the spinnaker is not hanked to a stay or pulled taut between head and tack like all the other sails, it tends to sway around and often becomes difficult to control. When things start to get out of hand in heavy weather, it may help to remember the following technique. The simple act of tightening the luff and leech of the spinnaker—pulling them down, the pole and the clew closer to the deck—can limit the spinnaker's arc of gyration, thereby making it and the yacht easier to control.

As a general rule, spinnakers can be set to good advantage on a close reach. There is an old rule of thumb that says, "When in doubt, set," and this is not bad advice. What should be added, however, is that if it doesn't work right away, if the boat obviously slows down, get rid of it! The boat definitely will lose ground every time the spinnaker collapses. Three or four collapses on a short reach will cancel any advantage that may have been gained by setting, but if your crew can keep the spinnaker flying while the other crews can't, you will have a decided advantage. As with any other maneuver, practice and knowledge of the capability of boat and crew are essential.

On long legs, it may pay to reach off enough so that the spinnaker can be carried effectively in the hope that a wind shift will allow you to resume your course later on in the leg.

Spinnakers should be properly bagged and sheets led before the start of the race and preferably before leaving the dock. The sail should be arranged in the bag so that it will set without a twist. Starting with the head, follow down each luff, holding the luff

SPINNAKER HANDLING   147

tapes together until each clew is located. Then, starting with the foot of the sail, stuff the sail into the bag (or turtle), keeping the luff tapes until last. When most of the sail is in the bag, arrange each luff on top of the bag so that one luff is on each side of the bag with the head in the middle. Tie the three corners together outside the bag—or arrange them around the outside of the turtle—so that they are readily at hand when it is time to set.

This procedure must be repeated when a sail is taken down. Rebag the sail as soon as you can spare a hand from trimming sail and cleaning up on deck. Remember, you may want to use the sail again—sometimes in a matter of minutes.

As with so many techniques, an old-fashioned idea has found a new twist with spinnaker sets. Stopping the spinnaker with rotten twine so that it could be hoisted in a long tube without filling used to be standard procedure on virtually all boats. However, differences in breaking strengths and inconsistent tying accounted for many delayed sets because of the difficulty in breaking out the stops. Gradually, turtles and other devices to allow spinnakers to be set flying proved faster and more reliable, and over the years flying sets have taken over almost exclusively on all but the largest boats and the hairiest storm chute sets.

Recently, however, crews have been reverting to stopping with rubber bands instead of rotten twine. The rubber band method works with excellent reliability. The spinnaker must be furled by stretching out the two leeches to keep them from twisting (as when making up in a bag) and then bunched together in a loose roll all along the length of the sail. In practice, the cloth is bunched to the leeches as one applies the stops from head to foot. Since a rubber band forms a continuous line, the sail must be passed through the band. This is best done by placing a number of rubber bands on the outside of a large coffee can that has its top and bottom cut out. The spinnaker is then drawn through the can and the rubber bands are slipped off at suitable intervals as the sail is furled.

Using regular number 16 rubber bands (available at most stationery stores) for medium-size boats, this system is completely reliable. The sail remains stopped until it is needed, and all the stops break cleanly with a tug on sheet and guy.

Sheets must be led so as to be outside of everything on deck. Be careful not to twist them around the genoa sheets or loop them underneath the lifelines or bow pulpit. (Visualize how the sail will look when it is set, well above the deck and forward of the headstay.) Clip the two sheets together, leading one completely

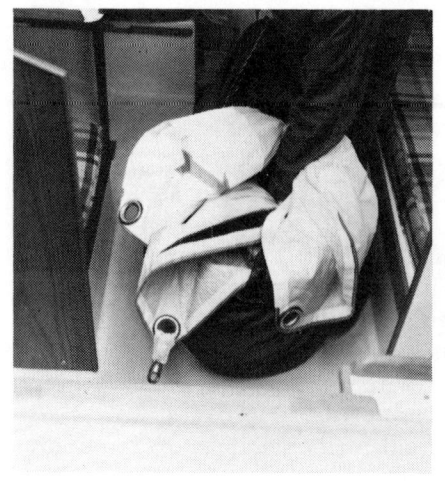

The spinnaker should be bagged with each luff to different sides so they don't get twisted. As the corners of the sail are reached, they should be kept separated and orientated with their respective luffs. Either tie the corners together with the sailbag draw string or leave them hanging out of the top of the bag. (Ted Jones)

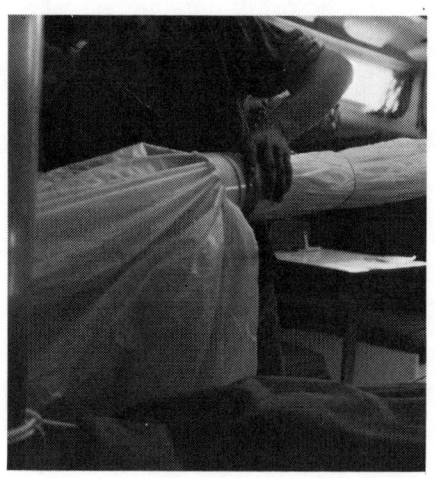

Stopping with rubber bands is done by drawing the spinnaker through a plastic bucket (with the bottom cut out) and slipping the bands onto the bunched sail every two or three feet. Keep the luffs straight and use more or fewer bands depending upon the wind strength. (Ted Jones)

SPINNAKER HANDLING

around the bow, or fasten them to pulpit or stanchion bases on either side. Setting the spinnaker takes a minimum of three crew members. On really small boats the skipper may be able to handle both sheet and guy while steering with the tiller between his legs, but this method is not recommended for maximum efficiency.

The helmsman is the key man in any spinnaker work. He alone can position the boat to ease the problems of his foredeck crew. Too many skippers, unfamiliar with what goes on "up front," steadfastly maintain their course while screaming curses at their struggling foredeck man for not filling the spinnaker. The skipper who knows what's going on up there heads off or heads up to get the sail filled as quickly as possible.

The helmsman is the most important "foredeck man" on the boat!

Setting the Spinnaker

When setting the spinnaker from a windward mark rounding, get as much setting up done in advance as possible. You will first have to determine the side the pole will be carried on the next leg. You will then have to decide whether you will make a round-jibe-set maneuver or a round-set (without jibing first). Assuming you will be approaching on the starboard tack and will be carrying the pole on the starboard side (round-set), you can get the pole up as soon as you are sure you can fetch the mark on starboard. On a round-jibe-set maneuver you will have to wait until the jibe is completed before hoisting the pole, although it can be ready to hoist with the inboard end on the mast and with the lift under the jibsheets before the jibe. With that one difference, round-set and round-jibe-set will be carried out the same way. A Spinnaker Drill (setting the spinnaker flying out of a bag) follows:

The three crew members will be called Foredeck, Sheet, and Guy in describing the sequences of setting, jibing, and taking down. The helmsman may double as either Sheet or Guy, but it is better if he doesn't have to.

Foredeck
1. Takes spinnaker forward and attaches bag onto lifelines.
2. Hooks up sheets and foreguys.
3. Checks halyard for proper lead and hooks onto head.
4. Sets up pole (genoa sheet over lift, if tack is a possibility).
5. Hoists spinnaker.

The foredeck above is set up for a round-set maneuver. The spinnaker is ready to be hoisted out of its bag, and the halyard, sheets, and guys are hooked to the sail. If a tack is necessary, the pole should be lowered at its forward (outboard) end and the genoa sheet (crossing the halyard winches in the foreground) should be led over the spinnaker pole forward of the topping lift. (Ted Jones)

This photo shows the foredeck set up for a round-jibe-set maneuver. The spinnaker is on the windward side with the lines attached ready for hoisting. The spinnaker pole is down forward, ready to be hoisted on the port side, and the jib sheet is led over the top of the pole forward of the lift. Hoisting can begin as soon as the helmsman alters course to round the mark. (Ted Jones)

SPINNAKER HANDLING

    6. Casts off jib halyard (if not double-slotting).
    7. Gathers jib on deck and lashes down if necessary.

Sheet
1. Makes sure lead is clear.
2. Adjusts genoa sheet when rounding.
3. Trims spinnaker sheet to fill sail when hoisted.
4. Assumes a position where luff of sail can be seen and hand trims spinnaker for maximum drive.

Guy
1. Makes sure lead is clear.
2. Trims guy as sail is hoisted.
3. Adjusts guy, foreguy, and lift as necessary.

Helm
1. Bears away around mark and calls "hoist" when clear of mark.
2. Turns to heading of next mark.
3. Steers boat to help fill spinnaker.
4. Coordinates heading and spinnaker set with sheet tender.

Close coordination between the sheet tender and the helmsman is needed. Sometimes it is easier to turn the boat to keep the spinnaker full than to try to make quick trim adjustments. Practice will develop teamwork and give each person a good sense of which to do when.

The foredeck position is usually filled by the most experienced crew member. He will often take over on the spinnaker sheet when the foredeck is cleaned up. The crew member on the spinnaker sheet calls the set of the pole. If the helmsman changes course, he should tell the sheet tender.

Jibing

On small boats (under 25′ IOR rating), I recommend double foreguys to facilitate safer jibes while using either the "dip-pole" or "end-for-end" jibing methods. The foreguys should always be attached to the clews of the spinnaker through one of the rings in the spinnaker sheets. This assures complete control of the clews at all times. The foreguy on the sheet end may also be used as a "twitching line" to refill a collapsed spinnaker when close reaching. An additional foreguy or downhaul on the pole may be needed to control the pole when jibing.

To dip-pole jibe, the spinnaker pole is first run to the top of its track on the mast. The genoa and staysail must be down and stowed so as to allow room for the outboard end of the pole to *dip* between the deck and the headstay. This is done by first tripping the afterguy out of the pole end and slacking the pole lift until the pole can dip. The sheet must be eased—the strain is taken by the leeward foreguy—until a bight of the sheet can be clipped into the pole end to become the new guy. When this is complete, the mainsail is jibed, the pole is lifted, and the new guy trimmed to position the end of the pole where it is wanted.

The specific duties of each crew member are as follows:

Foredeck

(This person is in command of the operation—he can always be overridden by the helmsman if the mark or another boat dictates a specific course, but in open water Foredeck should control the entire procedure.)
1. Take down staysail if set.
2. Stow unused sails so that they are out of the way.
3. Trip old afterguy out of pole.
4. Lower pole, making sure pole goes forward as it is lowered.
5. Attach new afterguy to pole.
6. Raise pole.
7. Call trim of pole and clew.

Sheet (to be new guy)
1. Take strain on leeward foreguy.
2. Ease sheet as pole is dipped, watching Foredeck for instructions. Sheet is now the new guy.
3. Trim new afterguy to optimum position while also easing new foreguy (if help is available for this, ask for it).

Guy (to be new sheet)
1. Trim slightly and gradually after pole is tripped.
2. Cast off old foreguy, making sure it is clear to run.
3. Trim sheet to optimum position when pole is set.

Helm
1. Bear off dead downwind when foredeck is ready.
2. Hold dead downwind while pole is dipping.
3. Head up slightly (or to new course) as soon as pole is raised. *Do not head up too far too soon!* Tell Mainsheet that you have altered course so he can ease mainsheet.
4. Watch spinnaker to keep it full and listen for instructions from Foredeck.

The dip-pole jibing sequence is begun by tripping the afterguy out of the pole (which may also be done by the foredeck man in the pulpit with a longer trip line). Note that the foredeck man has the new afterguy in his hand ready to snap it into the pole.

The pole is lowered and let forward to dip under the headstay, and as it swings through the foredeck man hooks the new afterguy into the pole. He must make sure that the lead will be straight through the end fitting when the pole is trimmed aft.

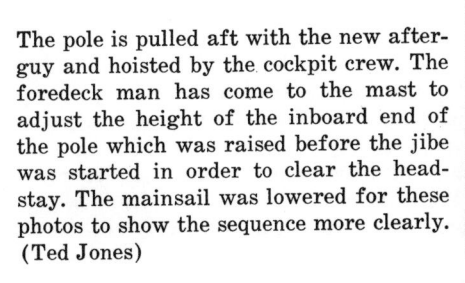

The pole is pulled aft with the new afterguy and hoisted by the cockpit crew. The foredeck man has come to the mast to adjust the height of the inboard end of the pole which was raised before the jibe was started in order to clear the headstay. The mainsail was lowered for these photos to show the sequence more clearly. (Ted Jones)

    5. Watch out for other boats that might interfere with jibing sequence and keep crew advised.

Mainsheet
    1. Cast off vang prior to jibing.
    2. Jibe mainsail.*
    3. Help Sheet (new guy) crew member with new foreguy.
    4. Set up vang on new jibe.

Larger boats ought to have two sets of sheets and two sets of guys, both rigged, to facilitate jibing. With this method, the "lazy sheet" (the one not in use on the leeward side) is taken forward to be clipped into the pole and become the new afterguy. Often this is a wire rope. When the jibe is complete, the lazy sheet on the new leeward side takes the strain, and the old guy (particularly if it is wire) is eased. With this system the single foreguy should be attached to the pole.

Another method, two-pole jibing, may also be used, particularly in heavy weather. The new pole is simply set up in position with the sheet clipped into its end—the boat is jibed—and the old pole is taken down. This takes longer, but assures complete control of the spinnaker at all times. Two poles, two pole-end fittings on the mast, and two sets of lifts and foreguys are needed for two-pole jibes.

The End-for-End Jibe

There is another jibing method which small-boat sailors will be familiar with—the end-for-end jibe. In this procedure the foredeck man takes the inboard end of the pole from the mast, clips this end around the spinnaker sheet (new guy), and, as the boat is swung and the mainsail jibed, moves the pole toward the new windward side. He then releases the old guy to become the new sheet and clips the end of the pole that held the old guy onto the mast.

This jibe works well in light air and on relatively smaller boats

---

* Sometimes it will be possible to flip the boom across the boat by grabbing all the standing parts of the mainsheet. This should not be attempted in heavy winds; it is preferable to jibe the mainsail by trimming the hauling part through the blocks and around the winch until the boom is amidships. When the new guy is secured to the pole and the helmsman lets you know that he has altered course, the sheet should be slacked until the boom is properly positioned.

The end-for-end jibing sequence is begun by unclipping the inboard end of the pole from the mast and clipping the pole to the old sheet (new guy). The pole foreguy must be attached in the center of the pole under the topping lift.

The foredeck man moves the pole across the boat as the mainsail is jibed (the mainsail is shown lowered to show the sequence more clearly and trips the starboard end of the pole to release the old afterguy, which now becomes the new sheet.

The pole is then clipped into the mast to complete the jibe. Perfect coordination with the cockpit crew is required to execute the end-for-end jibe properly. In more wind the foredeck man would have difficulty getting the pole pushed outboard, against the afterguy, far enough to get the inboard end hooked to the mast. Not recommended in heavy weather. (Ted Jones)

(under 25′ IOR rating). It does not require any special equipment or extra sheet and guys, but the topping lift and foreguy (if attached to the pole) must be in the center of the pole. The end-for-end jibe works best with double foreguys on the spinnaker clews.

A very fast jibe can be made using this method, but I recommend it only for small offshore racers in light winds. The end-for-end jibe used to be the primary jibing method for most boats, but it has been superseded by the dip-pole and two-pole methods described earlier as they are more positive in the way they are used to control the spinnaker.

Even in light air there is always great pressure on the spinnaker pole so that it is difficult for the foredeck man to push it outboard at the end of the jibe and clip the inboard end of the pole to the mast. The harder it blows and the farther aft the outboard end of the pole, the more difficult it is to push the pole outboard. For this reason it is very important for the person trimming the afterguy to understand the problems of the foredeck man. At the first sign that Foredeck is having difficulty with the pole, Afterguy should ease the pole forward. It may be necessary to ease it all the way forward even though the course is a dead run.

These difficulties with the end-for-end jibe tend to make the method unsatisfactory as standard procedure on offshore racers. However, in light air, the end-for-end jibe can be the fastest and the surest method of jibing.

The Lines-Through-the-End-of-the-Pole Method

The problem in giving credit for unpatented inventions is that two or more people in different parts of the world often think of the same idea at the same time. The clever rig I am about to describe has been credited to several people, both on the East and the West Coasts, but never to Fred and Lorna Hibberd, whom I first saw using it aboard their *Caprice* in 1964.

Here's how the "Hibberd method" works:

Two outhauls pass through a bell-shaped fairlead at the outboard end of the pole to either clew of the spinnaker. The other ends of these outhauls pass inside the spinnaker pole to the inboard end, where they come out through exit blocks and terminate in jam cleats. To jibe with this rig, the guy side outhaul is slacked, the pole lift is slacked, the pole is dipped (as in the dip-pole method), and the old sheet side (new guy) outhaul is taken up until the pole end fits up snugly against the clew of the spin-

SPINNAKER HANDLING

A variation of the "Hibberd" spinnaker pole described in the text is this one made by Products Engineering, Inc. Wires coming from bell fitting on outboard end are shackled to spinnaker sheets (shown without spinnaker attached). Pulling the tail of either wire pulls the pole out to the tack of the spinnaker. This model captures the ball on the wire in a lock which allows the inboard end of the pole to be moved without adjusting tail. A disadvantage is the probability of chafe with the wire riding on the aluminum bell.

naker on the new windward side. Pole lift and foreguy (a single one to the outboard end of the pole) are then adjusted, and the jibe is complete.

The advantages of this method are that no one needs to go forward of the mast, the sheet and guy do not have to be clipped in or out of the pole, and the spinnaker is under positive control at all times. Unfortunately, there are also a couple of disadvantages. The rig is complicated by many lines, there is danger of chafe of the outhauls on the outboard end of the pole, and the outhauls tend to pull the spinnaker in to the pole instead of pulling the pole out to the spinnaker.

This rig would be ideal if all the lines could be led aft to the cockpit since this would eliminate anyone having to go forward, even to the mast, to jibe. However, it is difficult to rig the outhauls out of the pole, down the mast, and back aft and still have the inboard end of the pole adjustable on the mast.

Leading the Topping Lift and Foreguy Aft

Rigs leading both the topping lift and foreguys to the cockpit ease the job of the foredeck man and give more control of the spinnaker to the cockpit crew. This rig is primarily used on smaller boats where there is a limited crew and where too many bodies on the foredeck would bury the bow and slow the boat significantly.

The only difference in procedure from having the topping lift on the mast is that someone aft handles both lift and foreguy(s), and the foredeck man has only to worry about getting the pole dipped and attached to the new guy.

Reaching Strut

The reaching strut is a short pole used to hold out the afterguy when close reaching and ease the strain and stretch on the guy by increasing the angle between the pole and the guy.

Use the reaching strut whenever the pole approaches the headstay. Hook the outboard end inside the afterguy, push outward, and hook the inboard end to the eyes on the side of the mast.

Spinnaker Takedown

Too many crews go all to pieces when taking in a spinnaker. Often the wind will increase while a spinnaker is set, and the sail must be doused quickly and in difficult wind and sea conditions. If the basic principles of spinnaker handling are adhered to, the sail should come down completely under control and with little fuss in any weather.

The helmsman must remember, above all else, that a spinnaker is easily controlled when the boat is headed off the wind. Too many novices, with the shouts of former instructors ("Head up, dammit, head up!") ringing in their ears, panic and head up at the onset of spinnaker trouble. Resist that impulse. Heading up only compounds spinnaker problems and makes it practically impossible

SPINNAKER HANDLING

The reaching strut is used as a spreader to improve the lead of the afterguy when reaching with the spinnaker pole well forward. The stretch of the line is reduced and the strain on the afterguy is much less with the strut rigged. (Dalgety Public Relations)

to take the sail down. Head off nearly dead downwind if necessary, and the spinnaker will become peaceful and tranquil.

Prepare to take down the spinnaker by first hoisting the genoa or other headsail that will replace the spinnaker. Do not remove the spinnaker without another sail in place—not only will the boat be slowed considerably with a bare foretriangle but the genoa helps blanket the spinnaker and keeps it from filling and becoming difficult to handle on takedown.

The spinnaker sheet (or lazy sheet, or lazy foreguy) should be taken forward under the boom and made fast taut if there is a strong wind. The spinnaker is tripped from the afterguy, whereupon it flies off to leeward. The former leech—with the sheet attached—is pulled down while the halyard is eased, and the foot and middle cloths of the sail are gathered in as it comes down.

He gathers the sail from close behind the mainsail to keep it from streaming out behind the yacht—possibly out of control. (Ted Jones)

In this spinnaker takedown, close hauled in light air, the crew member gathering the sail is well forward facing aft.

Two unconventional, but effective, spinnaker takedowns performed by these well-drilled Congressional Cup crews. "J" started taking the spinnaker down in the conventional manner, to leeward, but jibed in the process turning it into a windward takedown. "E" took their spinnaker down to windward and then jibed to round the leeward mark, which is out of the photograph to the right. (Chris Caswell)

SPINNAKER HANDLING

A typical crew assignment for takedown drill might be organized something like this:

Foredeck
1. Makes ready new sail for hoisting.
2. Calls for ease on foreguy when ready.
3. Removes lazy sheet.
4. Trips spinnaker from afterguy.
5. Lowers halyard.
6. Stows pole and cleans up lines on foredeck.

Sheet
1. Takes sheet (or lazy sheet or lazy guy) forward.
2. Gathers in sail.
3. Removes sheets and guy when sail is in boat.
4. Removes halyard and gives end to Foredeck.
5. Releads sheets and guys.

Guy
1. Eases guy to Foredeck.
2. Lowers pole to Foredeck (if lift is led aft).
3. Helps Sheet gather sail and clear lines.
4. Helps relead sheets and guys.

Helm
1. Bears off as necessary to keep spinnaker from getting out of control.
2. Heads up to proper course.

In tripping the afterguy shackle, the foredeck man must be careful that the spinnaker pole does not fall on him. He should avoid standing directly under the pole, for as soon as the sail is released, it is no longer exerting an upward force on the end of the pole. He should see that slack is kept out of the pole lift so that the lift catches the pole when the spinnaker is released. Even with all these precautions, the load on the foreguy will snap the pole down sharply when the spinnaker is released. It can give one a nasty bonk on the noggin!

Spinnaker Staysails

Staysails were "out" not many years ago. A good foredeck man would have nothing to do with them. He'd claim that all they did was louse up the spinnaker, and in spite of the extra sail area the boat would slow down. In many cases, these claims were valid. Today, sailmakers are making many different shapes and sizes of spinnaker staysails that can effectively and dramatically increase the speed of the yacht while carrying a spinnaker.

Another factor which helps in carrying another sail inside a spinnaker is the "penalty pole," a spinnaker pole made longer than the normal foretriangle base. Depending on rating adjustments, a penalty pole anywhere from 10 to 20 percent longer than the foretriangle base may be carried. A higher rating will result, but a larger spinnaker is permitted. The penalty pole has the additional advan-

Manitou shows a perfect double slot with the genoa set inside the spinnaker to provide more drive on a close reach. (One-Design & Offshore Yachtsman)

tage of holding the spinnaker tack well forward of the headstay when close or beam reaching, thereby allowing a genoa or larger staysail to be set and carried effectively.

With a penalty pole, it is possible to carry the number one genoa with the spinnaker under some conditions. This is called "double-slotting." The additional sail area is extremely effective in increasing speed. Care must be taken not to let the spinnaker collapse, since it is much more difficult to refill under the genoa than when it is flying alone. The best way to refill the spinnaker under these conditions is to let go of the genoa sheet completely. With practice in easing the genoa sheet quickly, double-slotting can sometimes be made to work even without a penalty pole.

A reaching spinnaker staysail is usually cut shorter in the hoist and is set so that the luff is parallel to the headstay with the tack about 30 percent of the foretriangle base aft of the headstay. A special halyard must be provided for this sail. The leech and foot of a reaching spinnaker staysail are usually cut to provide a substantial overlap aft of the mast.

The reaching spinnaker staysail is set with the luff taut and the sheet led outside the main shrouds to the rail. Reaching spinnaker staysails may also be set with a number one genoa or reacher when the spinnaker cannot yet be carried because the wind is too far forward of the beam. Some crews even find it possible to set a reaching spinnaker staysail inside a genoa which is inside a spinnaker—triple-slotting.

A spinnaker staysail cut especially for broad reaching and running conditions is cut much higher—filling or nearly filling the foretriangle—but also much shorter on the foot. This sail, sometimes called a "tall boy," is usually tacked to the rail or along an arc about 40 percent of the foretriangle base forward of the mast and tacked to the rail just aft of the mast on the leeward side. The purpose of this sail is to provide an additional slot ahead of the mainsail and to accelerate or promote the flow of air across the leeward side of the mainsail.

In light air, or whenever there is doubt as to the effectiveness of a spinnaker staysail, it should be taken down. Check the speedometer both before and after taking the staysail in and see if the boat slowed down or speeded up. Then either reset the sail or leave it down. There is always the possibility (probability) that conditions will change in a short time, so once the staysail is set up for quick hoisting, it may be left on deck even though it is not wanted at the moment. If the wind picks up, the sail can be reset in a flash simply by hauling on the halyard.

Changing Spinnakers

It is not enough that a crew be proficient at setting, jibing, and taking in a spinnaker like a precision drill team. A really good crew will also be able to set a new spinnaker while one is already set and take the old one down without either of them breaking. This is not as difficult as it may appear, but the maneuver, if accomplished quickly and properly, will raise the morale of the crew performing it at the expense of those watching.

To do it, the yacht must have a second spinnaker halyard as well as additional lines for sheet and guys. The new sail is temporarily tacked to the bow pulpit and set inside the sail already up. When it is properly trimmed inside the old sail, the latter is released from the tack in the conventional way and simply peeled off the outside of the new sail. One might need this procedure if a spinnaker has a small tear or if conditions change to require a different weight sail.

Sometimes it may be necessary to set a spinnaker on the genoa halyard. This happened in the St. Petersburg/Fort Lauderdale Race in 1969 aboard *outRAGEous;* the spinnaker halyard had chafed through, and there was no way, in the rough seas, to replace it. We shackled the head of the spinnaker to the headstay so that it rode up and down on the stay like a jib hank. This kept the jib halyard from jumping out of its sheave and jamming in the sheave box. It also made the spinnaker very easy to lower—we just let it fall on the foredeck like a jib—but we were without another headsail when changing from genoa to spinnaker or vice versa.

Mizzen Spinnaker and Staysails

One of the great advantages of the yawl or ketch rig is that it allows a staysail to be set from the mizzenmast when reaching. A mizzen staysail is set from the mizzen masthead from a special halyard. It is tacked to the deck aft of the mainmast and normally sheeted to the end of the mizzen boom. The mizzen itself may be either up or down when a mizzen staysail is set. A normal triangular mizzen staysail should be set as soon as it can be trimmed, as long as it does not increase weather helm so much that it threatens to overpower the yacht. Under some conditions it may pay to set the mizzen staysail and take down the mizzen to keep from producing too much weather helm.

When broad reaching and running, it is possible to set a mizzen

(Right) Replacing one spinnaker with another without first taking down the one that is set can only be done aboard yachts equipped with two spinnaker halyards and then only three times without fouling halyards unless alternate takedowns are to windward.

(Below left) The new spinnaker is hoisted inside and tacked to a sailstop or short wire pennant attached to the genoa tack fitting. Alternately, as here, a second afterguy can be led through the pole. This can usually only be rigged on small yachts.

(Below right) When the new spinnaker is set and drawing, the afterguy on the old sail is released and the sail is peeled off the outside of the new spinnaker. Alternately, the afterguy shackle can be released if the yacht is small enough that a crew member can reach it.

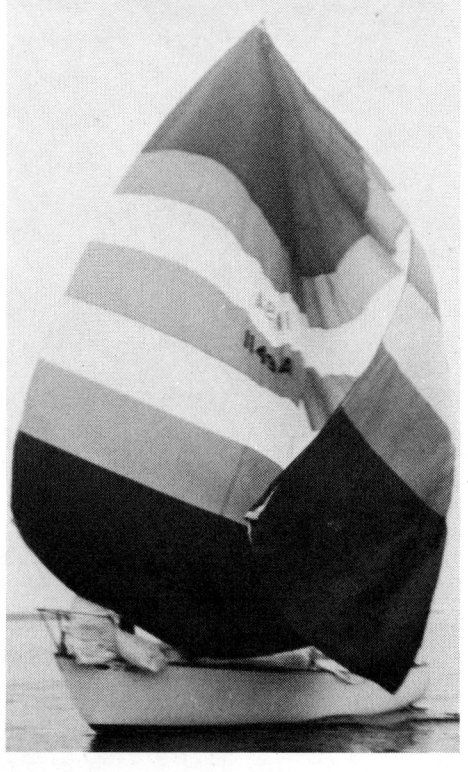

The mizzen spinnaker is shaped like a fore triangle spinnaker. It cannot be set from a pole but is tacked on deck with a long pennant to allow it to lift. (One-Design & Offshore Yachtsman)

The mizzen staysail is shaped more like a genoa or reacher and is used on a close or beam reach when the mizzen spinnaker cannot be carried. (Charles Mottl & Company)

spinnaker—a sail cut just like a spinnaker but set as a mizzen staysail. A mizzen spinnaker can be flown with great effectiveness downwind, although sometimes it will be necessary to take down the mizzen to keep it drawing. This sail is not set on a pole, but must be tacked to the deck.

When setting either a mizzen staysail or mizzen spinnaker, the halyard must be to leeward of the mainmast permanent backstay, and the mizzen windward backstay must be set up before the staysail is set and drawing.

Chuck Blair's *Hotfoot* reaching in heavy weather. (Norman Fortier)

Chapter 13 **Heavy Weather Racing**

When boats fail to finish a tough ocean race or finish poorly, it is most often the crew rather than the boat that has come apart. The crew that wins in heavy weather is most likely the crew that knew just how hard to push to keep going in order to get there first.

Keep in mind that we are still considering *racing*. Often, even when the weather has not yet reached "survival" conditions, some of the less experienced crews will conclude that survival *is* the issue and will pack it in. Don't let yourself be rationalized into thinking that everyone will quit, so you might as well, too. Of course, you and your crew must still *want* to keep racing. Remember: No matter how severe the storm, *someone* will finish the race.

Not long ago, there was a feeling among a few sponsoring organizations that anyone who dropped out of an ocean race was a bad guy who should be punished. Apparently a few solons got upset with the large number of nonfinishers and decided to penalize those who didn't have a reasonable excuse. The penalty was 10 percent of their elapsed time the next time they entered that race. Fortunately, this rule did not prevail. Had it continued in force, it might have pressured crews to continue in a race when their best judgment told them they ought to quit. The increasing hazards of crew fatigue or gear failure might have caused serious accidents if the yacht carried on. My personal feeling is that regardless of the circumstances, when it is no longer fun, interesting, or challenging to continue racing, you may drop out. If it's unsafe to continue, you must drop out, notifying the race committee of your action. To continue in a race when you really don't want to is foolish.

An example of a situation that might have been more serious if a failure-to-finish penalty had been in force occurred aboard

CCA Commodore Fred Adams' *Katama* in the 1966 Transatlantic Race. *Katama* was running under spinnaker when a particularly severe combination of wind and sea action caused her to jibe-broach. Her spinnaker pole buried deep in the water as she rolled to windward, and the force of the pole against the mast bent the mast just above the deck. The spar was in no immediate danger of failing, but Fred and his crew thought it prudent to discontinue the race. They still sailed Transatlantic to England (the race finished in Denmark) over 1,000 miles from the point of the accident without further incident. They did so in safety with reduced sail.

Had the 10 percent penalty for failure to finish been in effect, *Katama*'s crew might have tried to continue the race. They might have continued by flying a spinnaker and pushing just a little harder than their good judgment told them they should.

There are times, though, when a simple solution to what seems an insurmountable problem can keep you in the race when you're on the verge of giving up. As long as winning is important to the crew, you've got to keep fighting.

One of the roughest races I was ever in took place in the relatively sheltered waters of Long Island Sound. I was sailing with Nick Baker aboard his new 38' sloop *Soufflé*. We were doing extremely well, judging by the large boats around us—much larger than *Soufflé* and with reputations for being well sailed. The wind had been increasing all day until it was blowing close to 40 knots off the Connecticut shore. The temperature was below freezing. Although we were only a few miles to leeward of the shore, it was quite rough. When it came time to change from the number two genoa to a smaller jib, we could not get the job done. Three men on the foredeck had all they could do to hang on, and after they had reached the point of near-exhaustion and stiffness from the cold, they came aft and gave up.

We hung on, trying to get to windward with only a reefed mainsail, but we made practically no headway. After a few hours we realized that the race was lost, so we gave up and reached in to Saybrook.

Later, I was telling our tale to boatbuilder Bob Derecktor who suggested, "Why didn't you run off before it, take the genoa down, and hoist the jib?"

"But we were trying to get to windward," I said.

"Yeah," he said, "but you didn't get there. So you lose a few miles; it would have been easy to change headsails while you were running away from the wind, the boat would have been level, and there'd have been no spray. When you got done, all you had to do was sheet the jib and head up on course. At most, you would have lost a couple of miles and you might still have won the race."

Among our crew was a famous yacht designer, a Star Class World Champion, and five other very experienced sailors. Yet the obvious and simple solution to our problem had never occurred to any of us.

The lesson: if you want to win in heavy weather, you've go to keep thinking. No matter if you're tired, wet, or even seasick, if you want to keep going, you've got to pull yourself together and use all your resources.

One of the toughest things to do in heavy weather is to keep working. You get tired much more quickly when you must work just as hard (or harder) hanging on as to get things done.

In the 1960 Bermuda Race, after *Astral* had been hove to most of the night (see Chapter 17), I was on deck the following morning and went forward to reset the working jib. The wind was down and we should definitely have been sailing again, but the seas were still large, steep, and angry. It took me quite a while to get the sailstops untied, the halyard attached to the head, and the sail hoisted. In fact, it seemed to take an incredibly long time, because I spent most of it on the foredeck just hanging on. In addition, I was very hungry, since I had not eaten in nearly twelve hours. By the time I was finished and *Astral* was sailing again, I was exhausted and nearly ill. Barney Compton came to my rescue and thrust his arm out of the hatch with an ice-cold orange, which I devoured. The effect was almost immediate. I felt alive again.

A short time later, I took the wheel as we were making four or five knots close reaching under working jib and mizzen. The wind had swung during the night so that there were two components to the waves—with the present wind, abeam—and from the old wind direction, about 45 degrees off the bow. Approximately every tenth wave the two wave systems would meet and lift up a particularly large wave that looked like a mountain peak. I had no trouble avoiding these extra-large waves, but because I was tired I let *Astral* have her head for a moment. Suddenly her bow went straight up the face of one of these double-wave mountains. I knew that I had made a mistake, but there was nothing to do at that point but hang on. It seemed like a bottomless pit on the other side of the wave. *Astral* leaped off the peak, her bow fell—it seemed like 30 feet, but was probably no more than 15—and

The author at the helm of Humphrey B. Simson's *Kittiwake* doing 10 knots in n ocean during the 1966 Transatlantic Race. (Steve Lang)

crashed into the trough below. I watched horrified as the mast popped forward as we hit. I expected it to double over and collapse, but fortunately it did not.

Walter Fink, who had been trying to sleep in the forward cabin, appeared in the companionway, bleary-eyed and shaken. "What was *that?*" he asked, rather shaken.

Walter had been lifted out of his bunk, hit the overhead quite hard, and smashed back into his bunk again. It is a wonder he wasn't more seriously hurt.

I never did tell him that I could have avoided that wave. However, you can well believe that I was more alert thereafter and had a new respect for the power of waves and for the strength of

Astral's hull and rig. Many boats I have sailed since certainly would have lost their masts in those same conditions.

In just a little over an hour I had learned how difficult it is to work in rough seas, how important it is to keep one's strength up through proper eating, and how costly it can be if the helmsman doesn't stay alert.

"... battered and torn in a kind of mob violence ..." (Seth Hiller)

Chapter 14 **Survival Storms**

As pointed out in the previous chapter, what are survival conditions for one crew and yacht may be only very heavy weather for another. You must know your own boat and your crew's capabilities. When crew safety or vessel integrity is in doubt, you should stop racing and start surviving. Yet there may be a very fuzzy line between continuing to race—or thinking you are still racing—and realizing that you'd better give up and do whatever you can to keep the boat in one piece. Storms are often unexpected. You may not know where they came from, you may not know how hard they are going to blow, and you may not know how long they will last.

The action you take at the beginning of a storm may have an effect on your ultimate survival. In fact, you may be prevented from taking a particular action later because of some action you took earlier when you were still focusing upon racing and not yet worried about survival. Therefore, it is important to assess the seriousness of the storm and your relation to it at the very beginning and to do nothing that might jeopardize your yacht's safety should the storm get worse.

For instance, your racing course may be rushing you hell-bent toward a lee shore. The wind is picking up all the time. Assuming that you believe that you can get into harbor in the conditions that prevail at the moment, will you still be able to make it if they get any worse? Will you be able to beat away from the shore if you can't make it to shelter? Have you sufficient confidence in the weather report to be sure that it won't get worse or that it will blow itself out before you get there? If you can't answer these questions with a confident affirmative, it would be prudent to heave to now rather than stand further into danger.

Even once you have abandoned the race, it may be that the

action you take early may keep you from changing your mind and taking an even more conservative position if the storm gets further out of hand. Suppose the decision is to run before the wind and sea. You put out a warp to help control the boat as it plunges down the face of the ever larger waves. The storm might continue so long that you wear out the crew on the helm trying to keep her stern-to. The seas might become so terrifyingly large that you can no longer control the boat in this way. How would you then stop running before it and heave to without risking a disastrous broach? You might have worked yourself into a hopeless position from which there is no escape.

Good judgment and good seamanship demand that all possibilities be considered carefully before one takes any action that may be irredeemable.

I have been fortunate that, with the possible exception of my first race to Bermuda aboard *Astral* (see Chapters 13 and 17), I have never had to cope with a survival storm. In fact, I have never been in a position where survival was even in doubt. I hope to keep it that way! There are, however, well-documented adventures that may serve as valuable lessons to teach us to be prepared for such unfortunate situations.

Without a doubt, the best compilation of sea stories dealing with survival in modern yachts is K. Adlard Coles's *Heavy Weather Sailing*, which is an exhaustive study of storms encountered by the author and many others while racing and cruising offshore. I recommend this book to anyone intending to sail offshore, although not for bedtime reading.

Of survival storms, Coles writes:

> The difference between a gale and what has become known as a "survival" storm is that in the former, with winds of Force 8, or perhaps 9 (say 30 to 45 knots mean velocity), the skipper and crew retain control and can take the measures which they think best, whereas in a survival gale of Force 10 or over, perhaps gusting at hurricane strength, wind and sea become the masters. For skipper and crew it is then a battle to keep the yacht afloat. There is no navigation, except rough DR because the course is dictated by the need to take the breaking crests of the seas at the best angle.[1]

---

[1] K. Adlard Coles, *Heavy Weather Sailing* (Tuckahoe, N.Y.: John de Graff, 1968), p. 213.

SURVIVAL STORMS

The most experienced person to have written about survival at sea is Miles Smeeton. Following the 1956 Olympic Games in Melbourne, Australia, Smeeton, his wife Beryl, and John Guzzwell set off for England in the Smeetons' 46' ketch *Tzu Hang*. It was a bold undertaking, following a route rarely traveled by yachts (no more than a dozen before or since), from Melbourne south of New Zealand, around Cape Horn (the infamous southernmost tip of South America), and north in the Atlantic to England. Nevertheless, this was far from a foolhardy adventure, for the Smeetons were experienced ocean cruisers, and their yacht was well found and well suited for such a voyage. They also had, in John Guzzwell, the most capable shipmate that anyone could ask for. Guzzwell was taking time out from a solo circumnavigation (which he subsequently completed) in a 20' boat he had built himself.

All went well for *Tzu Hang* until they were 1,000 miles due west of the Straits of Magellan. They encountered a storm and were running before it, towing sixty fathoms of three-inch hawser to help slow *Tzu Hang* as she raced down the face of each giant sea. Miles Smeeton described it as follows.

When John went below, Beryl continued to steer as before, continually checking her course by the compass, but steering more by the wind and the waves. She was getting used to them now, but the wind still blew as hard as ever. In places the sun broke through the cloud, and from time to time she was in sunshine. A wave passed under *Tzu Hang*, and she slewed slightly. Beryl corrected her easily, and when she was down in the hollow she looked aft to check her alignment. Close behind her a great wall of water was towering above her, so wide that she couldn't see its flanks, so high and so steep that she knew *Tzu Hang* could not ride over it. It didn't seem to be breaking as the other waves had broken, but water was cascading down its front, like a waterfall. She thought, I can't do anything, I'm absolutely straight. This was her last visual picture, so nearly truly her last, and it has remained with her. The next moment she seemed to be falling out of the cockpit, but she remembers nothing but this sensation. . . .

. . . I felt a great lurch and heel, and a thunder of sound filled my ears. I was conscious, in a terrified moment, of being driven into the front and side of my bunk with tremendous force. At the same time there was a tearing, cracking sound, as if *Tzu Hang* was being ripped apart, and water burst solidly, raging into the cabin. There was darkness, black

"... a great wall of water was towering above her, so wide that she couldn't see its flanks, so high and so steep that she knew *Tzu Hang* could not ride over it."

darkness, and pressure, and a feeling of being buried in a debris of boards, and I fought wildly to get out, thinking *Tzu Hang* had already gone. Then suddenly I was standing again, waist deep in water, and floorboards and cushions, mattresses and books, were sloshing in wild confusion around me.

I knew that some tremendous force had taken us and thrown us like a toy, and had engulfed us in its black maw. I knew that no one on deck could have survived the fury of its strength, and I knew that Beryl was fastened to the shrouds by her lifeline, and could not have been thrown clear. I struggled aft, fearing what I expected to see, fearing that I would not see her alive again. . . .

As I reached the deck, I saw Beryl. She was thirty yards away on the port quarter on the back of a wave, and for the moment above us, and she was swimming with her head well out of the water. She looked unafraid, and I believe that she was smiling.[2]

John Guzzwell's account of this accident is of interest as well. He writes his impressions in *Trekka Round the World*.

> B. raised her hand and shouted, "I'm all right, I'm all right." While she started to swim towards us I looked about me and saw that both masts were in the water and all smashed into short lengths as though they had exploded apart. The doghouse had been wiped off at deck level and I noticed that both dinghies had gone. The side skylights were both smashed and the lids had gone too. I looked up and saw another monster of a sea approaching and I thought, "What a bloody shame! No one will ever know what happened to us."
>
> "Hang on," I shouted, and *Tzu Hang* lifted sluggishly to meet the crest; she had a slow hopeless feel about her and I watched more water pour down the great hole in the deck.
>
> "Well, this is it, Miles," I said, knowing that we had come to the end of the trail.
>
> He nodded. "Yes, it looks like it, John."
>
> "Hang on!" I cried, as another big sea came along. *Tzu Hang* again made a tremendous effort, but she lifted, and I felt a

---

[2] Miles Smeeton, *Once Is Enough* (New York: W. W. Norton, 1959), p. 79.

spark of hope. "We've got a chance," I cried. And just then B. said, "I know where the buckets are." [3]

The story of *Tzu Hang*'s recovery from disaster is one of the most outstanding in all of seafaring lore. She had been rolled over, pitchpoled stern over bow by the giant wave. That the Smeetons and Guzzwell were able to rescue themselves, bail *Tzu Hang*, seal the holes in her deck where her hatches and doghouse had been, jury rig and sail her, without a rudder, nearly 1,000 miles to Chile ranks as one of the most outstanding feats of seamanship of all time.

As if that weren't enough, after *Tzu Hang* was rebuilt, the Smeetons (this time without Guzzwell aboard) set out from Chile and were rolled beam over beam by a giant wave 300 miles off the coast. This time they were hove to with *Tzu Hang* lying "ahull," beam to the seas.

At four o'clock I thought that I'd make some tea. It was summer and for ten hours now it had been blowing a full gale, so I thought that the change must come soon, now that the glass had steadied. When the glass began to rise, the wind would still blow for a few hours, but this must be the worst of it now. Almost as I thought this, *Tzu Hang* heeled steeply over, heeled over desperately into a raging blackness, and everything within me seemed to rebel against this fate. All my mind was saying, "Oh no, not again! Not again!"

Again the water burst violently into the ship, and again I found myself struggling under water in total darkness, and hit on the head, battered and torn in a kind of mob violence, and wondering when *Tzu Hang* would struggle up.... [4]

This time, without Guzzwell to help, the Smeetons saved *Tzu Hang*, jury rigged her, and sailed her once again to Chile from where they shipped her home to England to be rebuilt. They continued cruising her all over the world until 1970, when they sold her to a former crew member. They eventually sailed around Cape Horn on their final voyage.

The Smeetons, having tried two different methods of dealing with storms and having failed twice to keep their yacht from being

---

[3] John Guzzwell, *Trekka Round the World* (London: Adlard Coles, Ltd. in assoc. with Rupert Hart-Davis; New York: John de Graff, 1963), p. 77.

[4] Smeeton, *op. cit.*, p. 177.

overwhelmed, are unquestionably the greatest living authorities on coping with severe storms.

Survival Methods

There are three basic methods of dealing with severe storms: lying ahull, running before it, and heaving to. Lying ahull simply means that the crew lets the boat fend for herself with the helm lashed. Most boats will lie broadside to wind and sea when left to their own devices in this way. Running before it, probably under bare poles, means that someone must be on deck to steer the whole time. Warps or some sort of drogue may be towed to slow the boat and to help keep her stern-to. Some have found that having a small headsail set and sheeted flat helps maintain control. Heaving to requires a small bit of sail—perhaps a reefed mizzen and storm jib or a storm trysail—to keep the boat's bow more or less into the sea. Some boats may require a drogue from the bow, and others may not heave to successfully at all. This latter method is the most difficult position to attain. You should try various combinations with your own boat in order to know how she will heave to. This means that you must venture forth in rough weather (rather than waiting until the crucial moment) to try things out.

The Smeetons tried the first two methods of dealing with severe storms and failed. Their exhaustive studies of survival methods convinced them that heaving to was the best method.

"In the end," writes Miles Smeeton of survival storms, "in a battle for survival, there is no final answer, and no one can be assured that a small yacht will see it through. It depends whether or not she is hit by some particular wave, towering and breaking at just the wrong time. As far as *Tzu Hang* is concerned, if caught out in a severe gale, I should follow the old and tried practices of the sea. If possible, I would ride out the gale by heaving to. If it was impossible to set or carry sail, I would turn and run. If my ship threatened to get out of control by surfing or broaching, I would tow warps astern to which were attached some form of sea anchor. I would avoid, at all costs, lying broadside to the sea." [5]

This chapter and the retelling of *Tzu Hang*'s two rollovers are not intended to frighten but to forewarn. One may sail many thousands of miles at sea, as I have, without ever encountering

---

[5] Miles Smeeton, *Because the Horn Is There* (London: Grey's Publishing, 1970), p. 169.

conditions that even come close to what Miles Smeeton describes. And certainly, Smeeton's story should not make anyone so fearful that he decides to give up the many years of pleasant offshore sailing and racing that are there to be enjoyed. Rather, we should take advantage of the experiences of others to prepare for what they tell us may occur.

Before we dismiss the *Tzu Hang*'s experiences as freaks which could not occur with "our" kind of boats in the waters where "we" sail, there is another story of a double rollover that occurred to Joe Byars' 39′ yawl *Doubloon* on her way from Florida north for the start of the Bermuda Race. *Doubloon* was lying ahull in a gale off Charleston, South Carolina. She was turned over and lost her rig as well as a man overboard, who managed to swim to the boat and climb aboard unassisted. Later, *Doubloon* was rolled over again in the same storm. It could happen to you!

Most of the boating periodicals carried stories of *Doubloon*'s adventure in 1964. A concise account, with many factual details, may be found in Adlard Coles's *Heavy Weather Sailing* (Chapter 18).

Many people will assume that most boats built and equipped for offshore racing will be reasonably ready to meet whatever the sea may have in store. Sadly enough, this is not always the case. Most custom boats, designed by competent designers and built by competent yards for offshore racing, will be suitable, but many of the thousands of stock fiberglass boats built recently will not. There are, of course, responsible and competent builders of fiberglass boats who build sound yachts that have true offshore capabilities when properly equipped by their owners. As a matter of fact, most of the potential buyers of these boats have no interest in taking them offshore. The stock boat companies realize this, and many insist that to build boats tough enough to go offshore is to overbuild them, making them more expensive than they should be, for customers who simply want weekend cruises in sheltered waters. Whether one agrees with this philosophy or not is immaterial. The fact is that many boats are being built that one might expect to be suitable offshore racers when in fact they are quite unsuitable.

The best safeguard against getting an unsuitable boat is to seek expert opinion. When buying a boat, either new or used, purchase it from a reputable dealer or broker, one with experienced offshore racers on its staff. Tell them that you intend to race offshore—to Bermuda, to La Paz, or the Transpac—and that you don't want the boat to come apart on the way. Beware of bargains, either new or used. Survival does not come cheaply.

Chapter 15 **Safety**

T. Vincent Learson's *Nepenthe* safely taken in tow after being dismasted near the reefs north of Bermuda in 1972. (Yacht Racing)

The safety of the yacht and the people aboard it is ultimately the responsibility of the skipper. The safe conduct of the yacht, the conscious consideration of safety in every evolution of a race or passage, the awareness that safety is a paramount part of each decision must be so much a part of the skipper's mental attitude that safety is second nature to him. When he is presented with any situation demanding immediate action, his automatic response must be based on considerations of safety.

There is no one at sea to look after the foolish and ignorant. There are no "consumer protection" agencies to make certain that we aren't taken in by an innocent-looking little cloud that turns out to pack hurricane-force winds. There are no "service departments" to inspect our hull and rigging and pronounce them fit for another 2,000 miles. There is no police department directing traffic or erecting stop signs at the intersections of busy shipping lanes. There is no fire department to come and put out our galley fire nor an emergency unit to resuscitate an unconscious crew member. There is no ambulance, and if there were, there is no hospital to which it could go with the sick or wounded. Safe sailing is the original do-it-yourself job, and the captain is responsible for a botch-proof product.

It should be obvious that one person alone cannot reasonably effect total safety. Safety is the job of every person aboard. It must be in everyone's mind all the time. Each crew member, depending upon his experience, must be responsible for the myriad of small considerations that add up to a safe or an unsafe yacht.

Safety covers virtually every activity aboard, from the shoes on the crew's feet to the attitude of the navigator. And, if you check back in previous chapters, you will find discussions of safety in all aspects of sailing.

SAFETY

Safety begins with one's first lesson in boating—"Step into the middle of the dinghy, not onto the gunwale"—and continues throughout the learning phase from beginner to offshore expert. Then, too, even the experienced small-boat sailor has to be shown how to handle safely the heavy equipment aboard a large offshore racer. One must learn, for example, that it is dangerous to stand in the bight of a taut line or to stand under the spinnaker pole when releasing the spinnaker. Hopefully one doesn't learn this by getting hit in the head. Only through experience can one acquire a thorough knowledge of sailing so that safety is something that one practices naturally and unconsciously.

The experienced seaman will think automatically about things like chafe. He will make it routine to look at all the lines periodically and to check them for excessive wear across one another, over sheaves, on the cheeks of blocks, and under the boom. And even though he can't see the spinnaker halyard aloft, he will occasionally adjust the halyard so that the wear is spread rather than concentrated.

Expert eyes will search out cracks in swaged rigging terminals or on a welded bail rather than just blankly looking at the fittings. The ears will be attuned to the thumps and bumps, grunts and groans that are normal to the working of a hull at sea and know instantly when an abnormal sound mingles with the usual ones.

The wary foredeck hand does not step on a sail spread over the hatch to dry. Someone may have left the hatch cover open.

You don't consciously think about these things; they happen or you feel them because through experience you have developed a sixth sense about them.

"I used to worry all the time," says Patrick Ellam, "about what we should do if the wind went 'round to the northeast or something, but for the last fifteen years or so I've stopped worrying about things like that." Ellam, who operated a very successful yacht delivery service, is one of the most safety-conscious people I know. His statement surprised me until he added, after a few seconds pause for thought: "I suppose all those things are recorded in your subconscious so you don't worry about them after a while. You'll know what to do when the time comes."

Some of the little things that Patrick does are matters of convenience or expediency which can ultimately have an effect on safety. When he owned a large schooner that had no auxiliary power, Patrick would drill his crew on the procedures and duties of each before entering port. Then, as he'd shoot into a tiny harbor under sail, a series of hand signals would be all that was required to have sails lowered smoothly and at the proper time. The schooner would glide gently into her berth with neither shouted orders, cursed recriminations, nor splintering crashes—sounds that often mark the undrilled, *unsafe* crew.

Drill may, perhaps, epitomize safety, because if each crew member has a specific duty in a specific situation and each crew member can rely upon the other to do his job, each evolution will be done properly and on time to the ultimate safety of yacht and crew. And if this is true of routine situations, it is doubly true in emergencies. Emergency procedures must be worked out for such unhappy eventualities as man overboard, dismasting, fire, and sinking. To be sure everyone knows his job, it is best to have drills. It is perfectly well to work out emergency procedures by the fireplace on cold winter nights and say, "In the event of a such-and-such, we'll do so-and-so," but all too often these procedures, no matter how carefully thought out, don't work in the heat of the emergency.

Why, when there are at least these two important reasons for having emergency procedure drills, don't more people have them? There is always something more pressing to do, I suppose, and while safety is usually on everyone's mind, it still isn't popular to interrupt a practice sail to go through them. Whenever, as skipper or boat owner, I have to grapple with a safety problem, I visualize myself being in jeopardy. I am quick to see how much I'd like everyone else to know exactly what to do and have them do it right—*the first time.* The only way to assure that is to practice.

It will not be possible to outline detailed procedures for every conceivable emergency situation. These must be worked out for each yacht and for each size of crew. What follows should be used as rough outlines from which each crew can develop its own detailed emergency procedures.

Man Overboard

The most fearful and urgent emergency requiring instantaneous reaction on the part of the crew is "Man overboard!" With that dreaded call everyone must spring to action immediately and do just the right things, otherwise those two words may be the last the man in the water hears. It is vital that everyone know exactly what to do and when to do it if the person in the water is to be recovered.

Initially, there are several things that must happen at once.

The helmsman must get the horseshoe life ring, water light, tall buoy, and drogue into the water. The helmsman must designate someone to watch the man in the water. The helmsman must immediately come to a reaching course, note the course he is steering, and carefully maintain that course until sails can be lowered or cleared away to allow a tack or jibe to reverse course. If any one of these things isn't done or is delayed, the chances of recovering the man are greatly diminished. If the man in the water doesn't get to the life ring, he probably won't stay afloat long enough for the boat to get back to him—particularly in water below 60 degrees Fahrenheit. If someone doesn't keep a constant watch on the man in the water, he may be lost from sight forever. It will no doubt be difficult to keep him in sight as he alternately bobs up and disappears beneath the waves, but a second's inattention could lose him, particularly if the boat has been running or reaching with the spinnaker set. Thus, the person watching the man in the water *must do nothing else.* It is also imperative that the helmsman know his course so the reciprocal can be sailed.

The rest of the crew should concentrate on getting the boat ready to tack or jibe. Since the helmsman will most likely be the one best tuned to the situation, it may be a good idea for him to direct the others. The skipper will have to assess the situation to decide whether he, the helmsman, or one of the watch captains should give the orders. Certainly only one of them should, and if the skipper has been on deck or is thoroughly aware of all the circumstances, he should probably assume command, although he should not take over the helm unless or until everything is under control.

The navigator should immediately make note of the heading, the log reading, the time, and the exact position (as near as possible) of the yacht when the man went over. The heading is particularly important in case the helmsman forgets in the heat of the emergency. If he is not needed on deck, the navigator should maintain a plot of the position of the yacht and the man in the water so he can give a course and distance to the man at any time that the boat is ready to tack or jibe.

Remember, the skipper, navigator, or one of the watch captains may be the man overboard. Whoever it is, his duties, if they are critical to the rescue operation, must be assumed by someone else. Remember, too, that there may be more than one person overboard. The more crew members in the water, the less crew to handle the yacht.

It is a lot more difficult than you might imagine to maneuver a yacht alongside a person in the water. Most likely the sea will be rough. You must avoid letting the yacht overrun or smash down on top of the man in the water. In moderate weather I would approach from the windward side of the man in the water, stop the yacht, and let her drift down to him—creating a lee which will make it easier to get hold of him and haul him aboard. If it is extremely rough, the yacht may make too much leeway or be in danger of falling down on the man in the water. In this case, it will be necessary to get a line to him and pull him to the lee quarter or over the stern.

Once he is alongside, the man in the water may be very hard to pull aboard due to the weight of his clothes and the bulk of his life vest or horseshoe. (Try pulling someone or something aboard at anchor in smooth water to see how difficult this can be.) San Francisco sailmaker Don Goring has suggested that every yacht have built-in steps on the transom, or in the rudder, or elsewhere, convenient for a person in the water to climb out onto. This is a good idea that is seldom followed through.

Then, too, the man in the water may be unconscious or unable to help get himself aboard because of injury or exhaustion. In this case, if no other means succeeds in getting him aboard, someone may have to go over the side (secured with a line to the yacht) to get him into a sling. This is an extreme situation, however, and is the only time another person should enter the water. Never jump overboard to assist someone who has fallen overboard. Robert Ames went overboard from his yacht *Hamrah* in the 1935 Transatlantic Race to Norway. His son Richard went overboard with a line, but couldn't reach his father. Finally, Richard let go of the line and swam to his father. When they were missed in a first attempt to reach them, the younger son Henry launched the dinghy and rowed to his father and brother. Now severely shorthanded, those remaining aboard *Hamrah* could not bring her about. The dinghy swamped, they lost sight of it in the waves and all three men were lost.[1]

There will be times when it is a good idea to wear a life jacket. Whenever there is a danger that someone might go over the side—whether because he is on an especially dangerous assignment or because the sea conditions are very rough—those in jeopardy should wear life jackets. If there is a general emergency and the

---

[1] Alfred F. Loomis, *Ocean Racing*, rev. ed. (New York: Yachting Publishing, 1946), pp. 213, 214.

yacht is in danger or sinking, everyone should wear a life jacket.

In these cases the skipper should give a definite order. Let there be no mistake that it is an order, and let there be no quibbling. There can hardly be any valid reason for not wearing a life jacket in rough weather conditions, especially if the jackets provided by the owner are of the most recent type that can be worn comfortably by active crew members without interfering with their movements.

It shouldn't be necessary, however, to wait for an order if you think it would be wise to wear a life jacket. At night, in rough conditions when working forward, or any time you feel there is a chance you could go over the side, it makes good sense to wear a life jacket or one of the floater coats mentioned in Chapter 3.

Never is it truer that an ounce of prevention is more valuable than a pound of cure than in a man-overboard situation. Safety harnesses are the answer. They may not prevent you from going overboard, but they will keep you with the yacht, even though you may be over the side. I have never been snapped up short by a safety harness, but I'm sure it is not a pleasant experience—painful at least, and possibly causing injury. Nevertheless, it is preferable to losing contact with the yacht. I find that a safety harness gives me peace of mind and allows me to work more quickly and often with both hands (instead of one for me and one for the yacht), although there still is no substitute for a firm grip on something solid.

Falling overboard is likely to occur when the safety harness is not attached—when changing helmsmen, changing the watch, or, as Adlard Coles points out, when rushing on deck to avoid being sick in the cabin. [2]

The rules (ORC Special Regulations) require that there be a safety harness for every crew member. It should be worn all the time at night and any time the sea conditions are rough or the sailing is fast and strenuous. The harness will do no good if it is not hooked onto something. Make sure that it is always hooked to something *secure*. In moderate conditions the harness may be hooked to a piece of rigging or a lifeline, but when it comes on to blow a gale, hook to something more substantial, such as a stanchion base, cleat, or deck plate. If the rig goes over the side, you don't want to go with it. Of course, if Beryl Smeeton had been hooked to "something solid" instead of the rigging when *Tzu Hang* pitchpoled (Chapter 14), she would very like not have survived, but

---

[2] K. Adlard Coles, *Heavy Weather Sailing*, p. 297.

that was an extreme case. The rules must be tempered by good judgment and a proper assessment of the situation at hand. If the yacht is in danger of being overwhelmed, you are better off below.

Most acceptable types of safety harness have two hooks: one on the end of a long line and one in the middle of the line. When both hooks are attached to the harness, the loops should be short enough so that you don't trip over them. Hooking on with the end hook and releasing the middle hook will give you a wider working radius. When going forward in rough conditions, clip the second hook onto the lifelines around stanchions or the shrouds before you unclip the first one. That way you will be sure that you are always hooked on.

Fire

The only fatality in the history of the Bermuda Race was the result of fire. Had it not been for fast work and excellent seamanship on the part of the late Robert Sommerset, skipper of *Jolie Brise*, who reversed course and put his yacht alongside the burning *Adriana*, the toll of lives would surely have been greater. A galley fire had broken out aboard *Adriana* and quickly got out of hand. The timely arrival of *Jolie Brise* allowed all hands to jump clear of the burning yacht. Unfortunately, the helmsman, Clarence Kozlay, fell between the yachts as he jumped and was lost.[3]

What can be done about fire at sea? Prevent it. Gasoline engines are probably the most probable cause of fire, with galley stoves a close second. Cabin heaters are probably more dangerous than either, but they are seldom used. Fuel tanks, lines, vents, and the carburetor are all sources of potential fire. Check them frequently, keep the fuel tank shut off when not in use, sniff the bilge before starting the engine, *and* run the blower. If there are fumes present, don't start the engine, don't throw electrical switches (battery/blower switches should be vaporproof), and don't let anyone smoke.

Galley fires get out of hand because of improper handling. Make sure no one operates the stove who isn't familiar with it. Care must be used not to overprime an alcohol or kerosene stove or it might flare up and start something else burning. Keep towels away from

---

[3] Loomis, *op. cit.*, p. 83.

the stove; resist the temptation to hang them on a handrail above the stove to dry. Shut off the stove fuel after each use, particularly the main valve if using bottled gas. Follow the same precautions with the cabin heater, and put it out or don't light it in rough conditions when there is a danger of spilling the fire out of the stove. Most cabin heaters are properly designed so that they can take considerable jostling without dumping the fire on the cabin sole, but if in doubt . . . well, would you rather be cold or too hot?

If it is too late for prevention, the fire must be put out. Federal requirements specify the type, size, and number of fire extinguishers that must be aboard, but they cannot tell you where to place them. A lot of thought should be given to the placement of fire extinguishers, and everyone aboard should know where they are. If you think you could use more than the law requires, don't hesitate to provide them. There are several tales of crews emptying all the available fire extinguishers into a fire with little or no effect. This often happens because the discharge from the fire extinguisher has not been directed at the source of the fire. Make sure you know where the fire is coming from before emptying all the extinguishers blindly into the cabin or down a hatch.

Alcohol stoves have an advantage over other types in that their fire can be put out with water, which is available in abundance. Kerosene, and gasoline stove fires cannot be extinguished with water, nor should you attempt to put out a grease fire with water.

If a fire gets out of control, there is no recourse but to abandon ship—and the sooner the better. Get everyone off the yacht but don't cast off until it is certain that the yacht will sink. The fire may burn itself out. A steel or aluminum hull may remain seaworthy even though burned out and should afford more protection than a life raft until help arrives, though you might be hard pressed to sail it anywhere.

Sinking

When, because of uncontrollable leaks, holing, or fire, your yacht is irrevocably sinking, there is nothing to do but to abandon it. Again, thanks to the ORC Special Regulations, you will have aboard the items necessary for your crew to abandon ship with the reasonable expectation that they can survive the ordeal. If, however, panic sets in, the crew members don't know what to do, and the proper orderly procedures are not followed, you may all drown, starve to death, or die of thirst. Once again, a thorough drill with exact duties for each crew member can spell the difference between survival and death for the whole crew. When your once comfortable and secure yacht has slipped beneath the waves, it is gone forever with everything in it.

The key to surviving a sinking is to get everything you will need into the life raft. To assure that this happens, it must be planned in advance, along with the particular duties and responsibilities of each crew member. To leave to chance getting food, water, flashlights, radio transmitter, etc., into the raft with the survivors is to risk not having them. Modern rafts are packed with emergency supplies, but extras, when they are available and there is time to get them, could be (literally) lifesavers.

Although we were not as well equipped in *Astral* in the 1960 Bermuda Race as are offshore racers today, we had an excellent abandon-ship routine which was sufficiently detailed to get the job done safely, yet not so cumbersome that you couldn't remember everything you were to do. The *Astral*'s abandon-ship procedure was prepared by the skipper, Howard Johnson, and is reproduced here as an example of good planning. *Astral* carried an eight-man raft, which could take off her entire crew. In addition, she had a smaller raft as a standby, to which several crew members could transfer so as to ease crowding in the main raft. There was also a dinghy aboard.

Astral Abandon-Ship Procedure

Objectives
 1. Get large raft safely launched and inflated.
 2. Get everyone into it.
 3. Get other equipment into and secured to dink and dink secured to raft.

Preliminaries
 1. Harnesses to remain on—whistle attached.
 2. Rubber vest [4] inflated—lights attached.
 3. Check to see that two rafts and dink are tied to ship.
 4. Each person to take flashlight.

---

[4] In addition to approved life jackets, *Astral* carried inflatable vests. This was before unicellular foam jackets were available, which would have been preferred.

SAFETY

Howard
1. Direct operation with searchlight.
2. Make sure all others are in raft.
3. Cut loose main dink painter.
4. Hook searchlight to harness.
5. Unhook raft painter from ship and hook to harness.
6. Tally ho!

Barney
1. Launch dink—with Bob's help.
   a. Turn over and prepare for launching, leaving main painter secure to ship.
   b. See that following are in dink and secured to it: emergency radio, fresh water, small raft, water light (if time).
   c. Wait for large raft to be launched and inflated.
   d. Launch dink to leeward aft of mast, leaving main painter fast to ship.

Bob
1. Assist Barney to launch dink.
2. Go over bow and follow line to raft.

Buzz
1. Launch and inflate large raft—with Ted's help—over lee bow.
2. Leave painter fast to ship.
3. Go over bow and follow line to raft.

Ted
1. Assist Buzz to launch raft.
2. Go over bow and follow line to raft.

George
1. Put fresh water into dink.
2. Secure it.
3. Go over bow and follow line to raft.

Walt
1. Put emergency radio in dink.
2. Secure it.
3. If time, put water light in dink and secure it.
4. Go over bow and follow line to raft.

Al
1. Prepare small raft for launching and wait.
2. When large raft is inflated, put small raft in dink and secure it.
3. Go over bow and follow line to raft.

Fortunately, we never had to test this procedure, but it seems a reasonable one to follow. Different particulars would have to be developed for different yachts and crews.

We never practiced this drill other than to check to see that we each knew our duties. It is difficult to go through an abandon-ship drill with life rafts, although it could be done at the end of the season or before rafts are sent to their manufacturer for checking and repacking. Why not try it out one day and see if it works or if improvements can be incorporated? You also get to see if the raft really will inflate and find out how difficult it is to inflate it with the emergency pump if it doesn't.

Dismasting

Rigging failure and dismasting are less serious emergencies than those just detailed, but they must be dealt with promptly and with a well-thought-out procedure. There are two contradictory things you want to accomplish in the event of dismasting: you want to save as much of the spars, rigging, and sails as possible, and you want to get the wreckage away from the boat as soon as possible to prevent the spars from holing or otherwise causing damage to the hull.

It is very unlikely, assuming a mainmast collapsed because of the stress of the weather, that conditions will permit the salvage of the mast. It may be possible on a small boat, but certainly it isn't on large ones. When *American Eagle* lost her mast in the Miami/Nassau Race in 1969, her crew tried for several hours in darkness, waited for dawn, and failed after several more hours' effort to get the spar under control. It finally was necessary to cut it away, losing mast, mainsail, genoa, and most of the rigging. They took a chance hanging onto the rig that long, but as soon as it looked as if it could do damage to the hull, it was cut away. Had *American Eagle* been far at sea with no chance of rescue, she would have been hard pressed to have enough material to make a jury rig.

When dismasted in a severe gale, some have tried to hang onto the wreckage in the hopes that it would act as a drogue and keep the bow into the seas. In *Doubloon*'s case it seemed to work, with help.

> It seemed that *Doubloon* could stand anything more that would come her way, and the spirits of her crew rose a little. The next thing to do (it was now daylight) was to clear the

rigging. The wire cutters had been in the cockpit and had gone to the bottom when the yacht rolled over. Nevertheless, Gene managed to cut the halyards and remove all clevis pins to rigging except the forestay, which was attached to a good piece of the mast which acted as a sea anchor. He then rigged another sea anchor out of a number two genoa, a sail bag, and an anchor. *Doubloon* was riding 60 degrees from the wind.... [5]

Rigging cutters, long thought a necessary piece of emergency gear, have proven incapable of cutting wire larger than one-quarter inch under the severe conditions one would expect in a dismasting. Instead, a hacksaw is required by the ORC Special Regulations with the hope that clevis pins could be loosened (as Gene Hinkle did aboard *Doubloon*), the hacksaw being the court of last resort.

Getting the spars aboard seems to be a near impossibility, judging by the experience of those who have been dismasted at sea. Nevertheless, the recovery of at least some spars—the main boom or part of the mainmast—would seem worthwhile if it is possible. With only a spinnaker pole, *Tzu Hang*'s crew was hard pressed to be able to set enough sail to make headway. As long as the spars are not damaging the hull, they may be left attached to the yacht and recovered later if conditions permit. However, conditions could get worse, too, and it would be a serious error to leave broken spars and rigging attached that cannot be gotten rid of quickly should they start pounding against the hull.

Steering Failure

I have twice been aboard a yacht offshore when loss of steering occurred. The first time was aboard the prototype C&C 35 *Redhead* in the St. Petersburg/Fort Lauderdale Race when the entire rudder assembly sheared off and was lost. The second time occurred off Cape Kennedy. I was helping Peter and Lucia Church take their 40′ yawl *Domino* to Fort Lauderdale when the steering quadrant broke. Fortunately, in neither case was the yacht in immediate danger, although in both cases assistance was available (and accepted) from the U.S. Coast Guard. I believe that both yachts could have reached port safely on their own.

[5] Coles, *op. cit.*, p. 198.

When *Redhead*'s emergency tiller had no effect, we realized that the rudder had gone. The first thing was to get sail off and rig some way to steer her. Using the spinnaker pole and a locker top, I made a jury rudder which I put over the stern, only to discover that the leverage was such that the rudder tended to throw me about on deck rather than steer the boat. After a few tries, this device was temporarily abandoned. It was possible to affect the boat's heading with this oar, but it was too difficult to try to use it to maintain course.

Next we tried a drogue astern, consisting of the bosun's chair, to which was shackled a medium-size Danforth anchor. The weight of the anchor held the wooden chair under water, and this drogue proved very effective in holding *Redhead* on course, broad reaching, under number four genoa, and no mainsail. This drogue was later bridled to the winches on either side of the cockpit. By adjusting the length of the bridle on either side, we could alter *Redhead*'s heading about 20 degrees either side of dead downwind. In a 20-knot-plus wind, we could make two or three knots under this rig.

Later, when we rounded Rebecca Shoal, we were able to beam reach under genoa and reefed mainsail, making four or five knots. I am confident that we could have gone to windward with this rig or perhaps with the drogue reduced to just the Danforth anchor.

When *Domino*'s quadrant broke and it became apparent that we could not control the rudder (a former owner had removed the fittings for attaching an emergency tiller), I rigged the same bosun's chair/anchor drogue that had worked so well on *Redhead*. It did not seem to work as well as it did for *Redhead*, but perhaps this was because *Domino* was quite a bit heavier (although not much larger) and because she was sailing in a much steeper and larger sea than we encountered in *Redhead*. Nevertheless, with *Domino*'s yawl rig and centerboard, it would have been very easy to sail her on any point of sail in almost any condition. Had we not been towed into Port Canaveral, the next step would have been to rig a line through the rudder when the sea calmed down. In her case, we would have had to drill a hole through the rudder, which would have been quite difficult in the water. In fact, some boats have a hole already drilled for this purpose. With a line rigged to the winches on either side of the cockpit, we could have easily controlled *Domino* even entering the narrow inlets along Florida's east coast.

Safety is a tiresome subject, but a necessary one, nevertheless. We would all rather be enjoying ourselves instead of thinking about how to stay out of trouble, but if we stay out of trouble, our sailing will be that much more enjoyable. As Patrick Ellam points out, after a while you don't have to think about safety, it becomes second nature—and that's as it should be. The essential ingredients for safety are well-thought-out and rehearsed plans and common sense. Emergencies still will occur in spite of the most careful preparation, but they need not spell disaster if you plan ahead and think.

Try to think of everything that could go wrong with the yacht. Then work out how you would cope with each situation. What would you do if a floating object or a whale should stove a hole in the hull? What about a wave breaking in a hatch or into the deckhouse windows? Can your crew cope with rudder loss, quadrant breakage, or a broken tiller? What will you do if you break a boom? Can you fix a broken chainplate? Are there spares for broken turnbuckles and toggles? Ask yourself all these questions and then work out the answers in advance. If the necessary equipment to cope with these emergencies is not aboard, it must be obtained and stowed in appropriate places.

Plan for disaster and the chances are good that you won't have one.

Healthy, fit crew members in the rigging of Charlie Morgan's 12-meter *Heritage* on her nonstop offshore passage from Fort Lauderdale, Florida to Stamford, Connecticut. (Ted Jones)

Chapter 16 **Health**

I am not a doctor. I cannot give you specific advice about matters relating to one's health on an offshore race or a long ocean voyage. Furthermore, in the event that medical problems do arise on board, they should be handled with the utmost care and circumspection.

Although, as pointed out before, there are no ambulances or hospitals at sea, it is possible, and in most races entirely probable, that medical help can be summoned by radio transmission. There will be long races, however, where the yacht may be out of touch for a week or more, and in these cases, familiarity with proper first-aid techniques is essential. Even with a physician in the crew, he will be very limited in the things he can do at sea in a confined and bouncing cabin.

Each crew member should give considerable thought to the kind of medical problems that might develop. Toothache, for instance, is very difficult to deal with at sea. A dental checkup is a must for each crew member, and he should tell his dentist that he is leaving for a race in case there is only preventive maintenance that should be performed beforehand.

Toby Baker was taken off the yacht *Magic* by helicopter in the 1964 Bermuda Race. He had been so thoroughly briefed by his skipper, William Apthorp, that he recognized his symptoms immediately. Before *Magic* had reached Bermuda, Toby's appendix had been removed. Every crew member should know the danger signals of appendicitis and what to do if help is not available.

People with heart trouble, trick knees, bad backs, shoulders that dislocate, and those subject to epileptic fits or other seizures should not go offshore racing. If they do, they present a hazard not only to themselves but to their shipmates as well. However, many people with physical disabilities do race offshore, making certain that their shipmates are well aware of the situation and are prepared to help if trouble develops.

When preparing for a Transatlantic Race, one aspiring crew member tried out with us in the Southern Circuit. Unknown to any of the rest of the crew, he had a history of shoulder dislocations. At a very tense moment in the Gulf of Mexico his shoulder went out. He was in pain, and immobile. It took considerable effort on the part of two other crew members to get the shoulder back in its socket. Meanwhile, the three of them could have been useful on deck and, of course, the disabled crew member was no help for the rest of the race. The skipper decided that this fellow, although he was knowledgeable and a companionable shipmate, should not go Transatlantic. A severe disappointment, I'm sure, but a wise decision nevertheless.

Few of us are without some potential medical problems, and before we go offshore, where we must be self-sufficient, we should see to anything that might give trouble. A medical as well as a dental checkup is a must.

If there is no physician among the crew, someone should be appointed by the skipper to be medical officer. This person should be a volunteer (hence he will have some interest in the job) and should be thoroughly familiar with first aid. It is a good idea to have at least one other person among the crew with first-aid training, in case the medical officer needs attention.

The medical officer should make an appointment with his family physician and explain to him the nature of the voyage and the dangers involved. While the physician cannot prescribe treatments for potential medical problems, he may provide the medical officer with prescriptions for certain drugs that may be required should someone aboard be injured or become ill. It is important that the medical officer be well known to the physician; otherwise there may be considerable reluctance to provide prescription drugs. It is for this reason that the "family physician" is recommended. Along with the prescriptions, the physician may give general instructions regarding their use and dangers. This information should be written down. Only the medical officer should have access to medical supplies and only he should have the authority to dispense them.

Obviously, if one of the crew members is a physician, he should be the yacht's medical officer. The skipper should make the appointment and ask that the physician stock whatever medical supplies he would like to have aboard. Be sure this point is understood—

physicians like vacations, too, but they'll certainly accept the responsibility if asked.

If any crew member has a known physical problem or requires special medication, he should tell the medical officer. Even though he may have everything well under control, the health of the yacht is the medical officer's responsibility, and he should be informed of any special requirements of the crew members. If someone is allergic to penicillin or to other drugs, the medical officer should be told about it before the voyage begins. Obviously, if that person were injured and unconscious, the medical officer could make a serious mistake if he gave him the offending drug.

Drugs can be dangerous even when properly dispensed. I had a bad experience with one of the "mycin" family of drugs. Apparently they increase the skin's tendency to absorb ultraviolet radiation, and I was severely burned on the face and hands after only a couple of hours of exposure to the sun. I am told that there is a danger that permanent damage may be caused by this combination of drugs and sunlight.

Seasickness is a common malady, causing difficulties ranging from minor inconvenience to total disability. It is not something to be ashamed of—something you hide in your personal "closet" of secrets—but should be acknowledged and dealt with. Seasickness can be prevented and it is more easily prevented than cured.

In regard to seasickness propensities, I have been shipmates with four types of people: those who never get seasick or feel squeamish, no matter how rough it gets; those who sometimes feel squeamish or listless for a while but who don't get actively ill; those who are actively sick for a time and eventually get over it; and those who are sick for as long as they are at sea. There are two types of reaction to seasickness: a person can throw up and go back to doing whatever he was doing, or he can throw up and collapse, unable to continue. Those who can continue working are preferred shipmates. The other kind should stay ashore.

Seasickness remedies can be helpful to some people and useless to others. I find that I'm a "number two" type, who gets squeamish and doesn't feel like working for the first day or so at sea. However, if I take Bonamine—one tablet the night before the start and one in the morning—seasickness symptoms do not develop. I sometimes feel nauseous when below in rough weather, but I find I can overcome this feeling by lying down in a bunk. Preparation of food—even making sandwiches—gets to me, but I can work cleaning up the galley for a short time without feeling ill. I find that a full stomach is less likely to complain than an empty one, so I eat frequently in rough weather. What works for me may not work for you, however, and it is helpful to know how you react to heavy and not-so-heavy weather—and what you can do to prevent seasickness.

Often it is a good idea for the yacht's medical officer to dispense seasick pills to all the crew with instructions to take them before the race and to report to him if they need more. Taken properly, seasick pills are not harmful (pregnant women crew members should not take them, however), and even persons who are borderline cases will benefit considerably from them.

Rest is universally beneficial, of course. Then, too, someone who is very tired will be more prone to seasickness than a well-rested crew member.

There is another type of problem which might well come under the heading of "seasickness," and that is caused by a combination of motion and interruption of shore-based routine—constipation. This frequently occurs among offshore racing crews and usually takes care of itself within a couple of days. If it does not, it might be well to take a mild laxative to get things rolling again. The medical officer should be cognizant of this problem, should have discussed it with his doctor ashore and with the crew members before the start, and should inquire casually of each crew member during the first two days at sea if he is having any problems and dispense laxatives and dosage instructions to those in need.

Urination can be affected also. I frequently have difficulty urinating during the first day of a race. This is due, I think, to tenseness caused by the motion of the boat. It does not help to be trussed up in foul-weather gear while on deck and to have the world at an odd, constantly varying angle when below. Whether there is any direct causal relationship or not I don't know, but I seem to be bothered less by this problem when I have followed a routine of taking Bonamine before the race.

One's state of mind must play an important part in any form of seasickness. At least I know it surely does for me. The start of the 1966 Transatlantic Race was about as miserable as one could imagine. With 3,600 miles to go, we started in the teeth of a gale beating to windward. We knew before we left the dock at St. George's what we would be facing, and any other time I would have been at least apprehensive if not absolutely discouraged. This time I was psychologically ready. In any other sport it would have been said that I was "up for the game." I knew *Kittiwake* would sail well to windward in the heavy weather—which must have been a factor in my attitude—and I just didn't give a damn. Frankly, this was not the normal "me," but I thoroughly enjoyed being so completely confident.

The attitude continued through the critical first day. I never felt seasick or squeamish. I had no trouble with my bowels or with urination. In fact, a few hours after the start, I discovered that our entire supply of twelve dozen eggs, which had been stowed in a locker in the head, had been flooded from the head basin. The locker was a mass of eggshells, cardboard carton bits, mixed raw egg yolks and whites, and seawater. It was enough to turn the strongest stomach, watching that mess churn as the boat leaped and crashed to windward. The sight didn't bother me at all, and I spent a positively cheerful forty-five minutes cleaning up the mess —cheerful because I knew I was overcoming what would normally be a serious handicap. Had I not been in such a psychologically euphoric state, the sight of the inside of that locker would have sent me bolting for the rail.

Psychology can often play an important part in how you feel. If you think you are going to be sick, you very likely will be. I sometimes wonder if psychology isn't at work with seasick pills—you have taken something so you don't worry about it; hence, you aren't seasick. If you can mentally talk yourself into being seasick, there is no reason why, with a lot of concentration and self-discipline, you can't talk yourself out of it as well. Try it; it's much more fun not to be seasick.

To paraphrase an old saw, seasickness can ruin your whole day— and spoil an otherwise pleasant voyage.

Smashing through Gulf Stream seas on the way to Bermuda. (Seth Hiller)

Chapter 17 **What It's Like**

There are many fascinating offshore races sailed throughout the world both regularly—annually or semiannually—and irregularly—such as the Transatlantic Races or Tahiti Races, which take place every three or four years. There is ample opportunity for the enthusiast to get his belly full, if he has the time and the energy, whether it be winter or summer or whether he is in North America, Australia, Europe, or South Africa. There are owners, such as Sumner A. (Huey) Long, whose globe-circling *Ondines* have participated in practically every ocean race in the world, who go all out, all the time. There are the sailors who crew for them and who spend all their time sailing and racing. There are also those, less fortunate perhaps, who must work for a living, who have business and family commitments that take precedence over sailing, but who nevertheless get as much sailing in as possible, either on their own boats or with others as crew in a Bermuda Race, Southern Ocean Racing Circuit, or Transpac. Regardless of time, geography, or season, however, it is possible in the "jet age" to find an offshore race somewhere, a willing crew to sail your boat, or a boat looking for a willing crew. With only a week or two to spend, you can sail in an offshore race somewhere and return to the office with salt in your socks and that satisfying feeling that comes from having tackled the sea and won.

Since I belong to the category of slaves committed to family and employer, I have not had the opportunity to sail in all the world's offshore races. I am more fortunate than most, however, in that I have a family whose members all sail and an employer who requires that I participate in as many offshore races as possible. These things notwithstanding, it is still necessary for the family to pursue the chores of keeping house and attending to education and for me to help assemble a magazine every month, all of which tends to keep one ashore.

Not having been on several of the world's more important offshore races, I must therefore turn to others for descriptions of some of those races that are important if one is to achieve a broad understanding of offshore racing. Several of the following accounts come from stories published in boating periodicals whose publishers have kindly given permission to include them in this chapter.

While specific offshore races have general reputations as being easy, either light-wind affairs or long reaches and runs (Bermuda, Miami/Nassau, and Mexican Coastal races); or tough, with frequent gales or long, arduous beats (Fastnet and Sydney/Hobart), each offshore race will be different from the last. Whether it be the North Atlantic, the Irish Sea, or Tasman Sea, the ocean is always different, always changing, always presenting a new challenge. To this, add the challenge of competition from yachts and crews similar to yours, and you begin to understand the infinite variety that is part of offshore racing. It is this variety that contributes to its popularity.

The Bermuda Race

The oldest regularly scheduled *ocean* race is the even-year biennial Bermuda Race. (The Chicago–Mackinac Race was started earlier and therefore qualifies as the oldest *offshore* race.) Ed Cotter, writing on navigating to Bermuda, introduced his story with a colorful background of the Race.

> Air travelers to the Bermuda Islands endure only a minimum of hardship while jetting in 90 minutes from east coast airports to that sun-kissed archipelago 580 miles east of the North Carolina coast. The flight is a means to an end, to a pleasant vacation. Other vacationers make the passage aboard luxurious cruise ships, enjoying a pampered and relaxing 36 hours en route.
>
> But to the blue water racing yachtsman, the voyage is the whole interest, and arrival is but the climax of four to seven days of testing, in a relatively fragile wind-driven craft at the mercy of sea and weather.
>
> To quote from this year's Bermuda Race announcement, "The long range objectives of the Bermuda Race are to encourage the designing, building, and sailing of seaworthy yachts,

and the development in the amateur sailor of the art of seamanship and proficiency in the science of navigation."

Since the inaugural race by three boats in 1906 (then sailed from New York to Bermuda), these objectives have been well served. In 1968 the race entries had grown to 152 sleek, expensive yachts divided into six classes and manned by an estimated 1,500 part-time mariners. All but 10 finished.

Only the master and the navigator in a Bermuda Race must be amateurs—that is, not paid for their services. The master of a Bermuda entry is a special breed. To play this ultimate of games, offshore racing, he needs interest, capability, money, and free time in large quantities. He may spend years trying to win this race; designing, building, outfitting, re-designing, tuning, returning, campaigning in lesser events to prove or disprove ideas for faster sailing; selecting, organizing, and training his crew. Beginning early in the Bermuda year (the race is biennial, in the even years), he must finalize his plans. His goal is to have yacht, crew, and gear at the starting line at the peak of perfection. [1]

If only I could relive my first Bermuda Race in 1960! *There* was one to occupy my mind, and I'm sure the minds of the rest of the crew, for many a winter evening. It wasn't as dramatic as Bob Johnson's record passage in *Ticonderoga* (Chapter 1), but it contained the usual ingredients and provided good lessons. Most of us were green to offshore racing, although we had a wide variety of big-boat racing experience in alongshore events. It turned out to be the slowest race on record; by a combination of good luck, skillful navigating by Buz Knowlton, and hard work by the rest of us, the fourth day found our little Block Island 40' yawl up with the 50- and 60-footers.

Walter Fink, later to become famous in Midget Ocean Racing Club events, was on the helm that morning. The wind was nearly nonexistent, but Walter managed to take full advantage of what little there was. We had over 80 boats in sight out of a fleet of 135, and Al Kappel and I watched incredulously as Walter moved *Astral* past boat after boat. We abandoned our usual half-hourly

---

[1] Ed Cotter, "Looking for Bermuda," *One-Design & Offshore Yachtsman*, vol. 9, no. 6 (June 1970), p. 35.

rotation of helmsmen and let Walter sail as long as he could keep her moving so beautifully.

It was impossible to tell how many boats we actually passed, but we appeared to move from the back of that 80-odd boat fleet to near the front of it. We were ecstatic. We saw only one boat near us that was our size. We knew we must be doing fantastically well, and with just 100 miles to go, we began to have visions of a whopping victory celebration.

The reports of the leading big boats began to come through on the radio from Bermuda. We were easily close enough to them to be within our handicap if we could just get some wind to finish on.

Later that afternoon, the breeze began to fill in from the south, and we began beating our way to Bermuda. As the afternoon went on, the wind got stronger. All hands were called to change headsails—number one genoa to number two, then number two to number three. We reefed; we reefed some more. We gradually wore ourselves out, but it didn't matter. We were within a few hours sail of Bermuda with this wind; we could sleep when we got there.

Supper wasn't as planned. It was too rough to cook. Walter, Al, and I formally relieved the other watch, who collapsed into their bunks without having had much to eat. We were pretty tired ourselves as we had been up and down most of the afternoon along with the headsails. Buz and skipper Howard Johnson had been up all day, too, but Buz helped me change the number three for the working jib as the wind continued to pipe up.

By now the mainsail had been furled completely and Barney Compton's watch had set the storm trysail—a small, heavy, shred of a sail, meant for use in the worst possible conditions. Al was at the helm, and as I hoisted the jib it created an infernal racket as it flailed in the wind. We sheeted the sail in and . . . *wham!* We were aback and laid over on the other tack.

The wind and sea—as much of it as we could see in the dark—were raging beyond anything we had ever seen before. The jib sounded ready to explode off the stay as Al tried to keep her on course. We knew we should have set the storm jib, but that was worthless hindsight.

The hatch opened a crack and a bleary-eyed, ashen-faced Howard told us to heave her to. He and Barney and Buz had held a council of war; it was a divided opinion but the responsibility was Howard's. He feared for our safety—which was his ultimate responsibility—and for the safety of our vessel. We were exhausted. For us, the race was over.

Buz came on deck to help me take in the jib while Walter furled the mizzen. Buz cast off the halyard, and was coming forward to help me get the jib down when we were hit by a wave that sent *Astral*'s bow high into the air and us with it. I came down between the bow and the pulpit and fetched up with only my arms over the pulpit rail, the rest of my body dangling in the water. I got back aboard in time to see Buz dragging himself over the rail under the lifelines. He had somehow somersaulted around the lifelines and ended up clinging to the toe rail with his fingers and heels; the rest of him was overboard through the lifelines. We were both secured to the boat by safety harnesses but, just the same, I shiver at the thought of either of us having lost our grip.

Our race was over, but we still had to get to Bermuda. We set two-man, two-hour lookout watches as *Astral* rode safely but uncomfortably beam to the seas with the helm lashed (so as to head her up) and the storm trysail sheeted to windward. We were one of the last to get going again in the morning when the wind slackened. (The seas remained high, steep, and confused for many hours.) We finally made Bermuda on a sparkling, clear, beautiful, tropical morning. We were all in one piece. We had broken nothing. No one was hurt. But we were next to last in our class and sixty-sixth in the fleet on corrected time.

Our big mistake, of course, was in assuming that we could put on a successful sprint effort when within 100 miles of Bermuda. We had no warning of the storm—few did—but a prudent crew will always leave something in reserve for the unexpected. When the high winds hit, we did not know enough to reach or run before it. Our course was to windward to Bermuda, and we clung doggedly to it until we could sail no further. The experienced crews reached through the worst of the gale, kept moving in the *general direction* of Bermuda, and the wind let them up to course—as they expected it might—as the storm passed. By contrast, the race winner, *Finnisterre,* made 120 miles on her last day while we made 42, and our noon positions for the two days previous to that put us nearer Bermuda than *Finnisterre.*

Windward Passage's Record Jamaica and Transpac Races

The Transpac Race is the longest (2,225 miles) regularly scheduled offshore race in the world. It is sailed every odd-numbered year, alternating with the Bermuda Race, which is sailed in even-number years. In Chapter 1, we read Bob Johnson's account of

Windward Passage moves out from the fleet at 10-knots-plus on her way to record-smashing 811-mile run to Jamaica in 1971. (Miami-Metro)

the 1965 Transpac in which his *Ticonderoga* broke the ten-year elapsed-time record. In 1968 Johnson built a new boat, *Windward Passage*, which was designed by Alan Gurney to be the ultimate ocean racing speedster, the largest (73' overall) then allowed under the rules, and was figured to break existing ocean racing elapsed-time records. And that's just what she did.

But when it come to the 1969 Transpac, *Passage* had a disaster. A minor starting line foul cost her two hours of her elapsed time in penalty. While she had broken *Ticonderoga*'s 1965 record, the penalty took it away, and Ken Demuse's *Blackfin*, another 73' "maxi," was awarded first-to-finish honors and the official Transpac record. Saddest of all, Bob Johnson died of a heart attack later that summer.

Fortunately, Bob Johnson's death did not put an end to the saga of *Windward Passage*. Her campaign to break offshore race records was continued by Johnson's son Mark and *Passage*'s crew, who maintained a loyal respect for their dead skipper and an almost fanatic will to continue what he had started. Following the 1969 Transpac, *Windward Passage* went on winning offshore races and smashing records. Each time she'd have a particularly spectacular sail, her crew would wave to the heavens with a "How'd you like that, Bob?" or simply, "Thanks, Bob!," and it was obvious that Bob Johnson's spirit was continuing to guide *Windward Passage*.

I had the good fortune to be aboard *Windward Passage* during what may prove to have been her most spectacular race, the 1971 Miami/Jamaica Race. We not only beat *Passage*'s record for the race set in 1969, but we beat it by over thirty hours to establish a race record that may never be beaten.

At the start, we were fearful that there would be no chance to approach the 1969 record. The forecast was for head winds all the way to Eleuthera, about a third of the course, and with that much beating, we'd be lucky to stay out in front of the very weatherly converted 12-meter *American Eagle*—to say nothing of trying to break the record. We were lucky, though, and as we crossed the starting line, we could just hold our course for Great Isaac Light, the first mark of the course on the other side of the Gulf Stream. *Passage* surged ahead, the best start she had made in her career, taking the lead within seconds and leaving the fleet astern at a speed of ten knots.

As we passed Isaac, where the course required that we come almost 20 degrees closer to the wind, we were lifted. With only Huey Long's 73' *Ondine* in sight astern, we headed for Eleuthera with the wind freeing all the time and the speed climbing from 10 to 12 knots. Soon *Ondine* was a speck of white, hull down on the horizon, and as we passed Cat Island *Ondine* took an inside course, hoping for a better wind. The strategy did not work, and we were not to see *Ondine* again until she tied alongside at the dock in Montego Bay.

Not far from Cat Island, our navigator, Peter Bowker, told Mark Johnson that he had been checking Bob's log from the previous race, and that we were four hours ahead of *Passage*'s 1969 position at noon the first day. In addition, we had covered 262 miles from noon to noon for an average speed of almost 11 knots—startlingly fast even for a boat of *Passage*'s size.

By this time the wind was out of the northwest, and *Passage* was surging to 12 and 13 knots under spinnaker headed for the Windward Passage between Cuba and Haiti (Hispaniola), a notoriously rough stretch of water after which the Johnson yacht is named. A general lightening of the wind during the hours of darkness the second night slowed us to eight and nine knots, but with the dawn the wind returned. We thundered away from the Bahamas, past Inagua Island, and toward Cuba at speeds approaching 15 knots. At noon the second day we were sixteen hours ahead of *Passage*'s old record, and as we passed Cuba's Point Maisí we were twenty-four hours ahead.

Racing for Jamaica and a record we knew was ours if the wind held, *Passage* surfed to two bursts of over 20 knots in the early evening hours of our third day. It was the most spectacular sailing I have ever done. *Passage* flew along, throwing a tremendous bow wave that curved out thirty feet on either side and kicked up a "roostertail" astern like a racing hydroplane.

We picked up the easterly trade winds during the early morning and surged across the finish line at a comparatively leisurely 10 knots. Our elapsed time for the 811-mile course was three days, three hours, and eleven minutes.

We did not win on corrected time. That honor went to a San Francisco flyer, *Improbable*, designed by Gary Mull for Dave Allen. *Windward Passage* was third in class and fourth in fleet on corrected time.

From Jamaica, *Passage* completed the trip west through the Panama Canal and up the Mexican Coast to Los Angeles, where she was extensively refitted for the Transpac Race. She was being readied to avenge the disastrous race of 1969, and the crew was anxious for record-setting weather. They looked to the heavens and to Bob Johnson for guidance. They got it!

Chris Caswell's eyewitness account of the 1971 Transpac Race tells the story:

Mark Johnson's 73-foot ketch *Windward Passage* drove across the Pacific with a vengeance in the 26th race from Los Angeles to Honolulu, wiping away the stigma of the foul and penalty that erased her 1969 elapsed time mark and further burnishing the record that makes her unique among ocean racers. *Passage* walked off with all the hardware, being first to finish, winning on corrected time over the 69-boat fleet, and setting a new elapsed time record for the 2,225-mile course.

This year was both the fastest race, and also one of the slowest races, depending upon where you viewed it from. *Passage* sailed the course in nine days, five hours, 34 minutes, and 22 seconds—breaking *Blackfin*'s 1969 elapsed time record by one hour and 14 minutes, and her own unofficial (pre-protest) 1969 finish by 18 minutes. But for everyone except the Class A boats, it was a long, slow grind. Class A walked off with the top nine overall trophies, as the wind steadily shut off while the smaller boats were still at sea. For the Cal-40 sloops, winners of the last three Transpacs, the race took more than 14 days, and the last finisher straggled across the line after 16-and-a-half days at sea.

Early weather predictions of light airs were negated by the last-minute weather packet from the race committee that predicted a record-breaking year. As it turned out, it was a record breaker only for the leaders, and a drifter for the rest.

Lol Killam's 73-foot ketch *Graybeard* jumped out to an early lead in the light airs, reinforcing the results of the California Cup when she showed excellent speed in moderate air. Taking a long port tack up the coastline before heading across the Catalina channel, *Graybeard* had a solid lead at the west end of Catalina, the only mark of the course. Second was *Passage*, followed by *Blackfin* and Jim Kilroy's 73-foot yawl *Kialoa II*. Most of the fleet slanted off to the south after rounding Catalina, with fresh northwest breezes of 20 knots, but the few boats choosing to head north found themselves slatting in light airs.

Windward Passage took over the boat-for-boat lead on the next day, after moving 419 miles from the start. *Graybeard* and *Ondine* did not report in at roll call, so the second-place yacht was *Buccaneer* at 417 miles, still with northwest winds of 15 knots and no spinnakers yet set.

Windward Passage moments before crossing the finish line of the Transpac Race in 1971, in which she set the course record. (A. G. Thoma)

Passage turned in a 255-mile run in moderate northerly winds on the next day, moving up to second on handicap behind *Dakar*. The 42-foot sloop *Nimble* became the first casualty with a broken mast step, but continued under jury rig.

Windward Passage had moved ahead of her position in the 1969 race by the fourth day despite the generally light airs of 11 knots, and was in a good spot to break the record. *Blackfin* reported in for the first time in two days with a position that put her second in fleet and 34 miles behind *Passage*, which had 1,328 miles to the finish.

The wind gods began their private joke on the following day as the breeze steadily increased for the rest of the fleet. *Passage* had a 227-mile day and *Blackfin* logged 224, with *Passage* now a full day's run ahead of her 1969 position. *Graybeard* slid into third place and *Buccaneer* was fourth, all with 20+ knot winds.

Passage logged 227 miles for the sixth day, moving her to within 874 miles of the finish and 60 miles ahead of *Blackfin*. At this point, the National Weather Service put out a warning on Hurricane Denise, previously a mild tropical storm, but now boasting 100 mph winds on a collision course with the lead yacht.

Passage started slanting south on the next day to pick up some of Denise's outer winds and was 633 miles from Diamond Head, with *Blackfin* 34 miles astern and 34 miles to weather, but handicap honors at the time were held by Al Cassel's 50-foot cutter *Warrior*, 240 miles behind *Passage*.

The hurricane dissipated suddenly, along with most of the Pacific high, leaving the leaders sliding toward Hawaii with full chutes and the rest of the fleet listening to the slatting of mainsails. *Passage* had only 388 miles to the finish, with *Blackfin* behind by 70 miles.

Passage slid past Diamond Head late the next afternoon surrounded by hundreds of cheering spectator boats, with *Blackfin* crossing nine hours later and Huey Long's *Ondine* 40 minutes behind. Fourth boat to finish was *Buccaneer*, six hours later.

Graybeard, the early leader which had dropped to third in the lighter air, made a strong bid to regain the lead before being forced out of the race and almost sinking when her rudder and skeg broke off. Three days before she broke down, the big Vancouver ketch was 77 miles behind *Windward Pas-*

sage; the day she broke down she was estimated to be about 50 miles behind *Passage* and several miles ahead of *Blackfin.*

The wind gods resumed their big laugh after *Buccaneer* finished and shut off all winds across the Pacific. Roll call the next morning brought consistent reports of calms and oily swells. Even the Molokai channel, usually a wild spinnaker surf in 30-knot winds and 10-foot seas, was a millpond. The handicap leaders now were the six early finishers as the Class A rout began.

By the next morning, the Class B, C, and D yachts were still slatting with 300 to 500 miles to go. The clock became the biggest competitor, as each yacht still offshore counted the seconds as their time allowance steadily ran out and the race became a battle for class honors only. By the 14th day, only 35 yachts had finished, but the majority of the fleet crossed in the next 24 hours, and the last four boats crossed on the 16th day.

But for everyone involved there was satisfaction in *Passage*'s sweep. Most skippers commented that if they couldn't have won themselves, then they wanted the victor to be *Windward Passage.* And all the crews, running low on food and water, were glad to be back on land after the fastest, and the slowest, Transpac in history. [2]

Racing to Mexico

The California Coast is not blessed with a great many harbors. As a consequence, there are not as many port-to-port races here as elsewhere in the world. Races either to or from San Francisco and Los Angeles or San Diego, which would seem to the casual observer to be natural, have not developed. The absence of ports in between, and a hostile coastline, make the prospect a dangerous and not very attractive endeavor. The Midget Ocean Racing Association of Northern California has run several races from San Francisco down the coast to Los Angeles and San Diego, but while these have been successful and popular with crews in boats under thirty-one feet overall length, they have not been run on a regular basis or been attempted by larger offshore racers.

---

[2] Chris Caswell, "Transpac 71," *One-Design & Offshore Yachtsman,* vol. 10, no. 9 (September 1971), pp. 34–36.

By far the more popular courses are several run from Southern California down the coast to Mexico's Baja Peninsula to Acapulco, a distance of 1,430 miles; to LaPaz, 900 miles; and Mazatlán, a little further. These are long races, often sailed in light air and off the wind, with winning strategy dictating playing inshore during the day and offshore at night. There is the occasional "santana," however, a small violent offshore storm that usually hits without warning, to make things more interesting. One of these races is sailed every year, the first Acapulco race having been sailed in January 1953.

More of a spectacle than a race is the annual run from Newport Beach (just south of Los Angeles) to Ensenada, Mexico. This is a short, overnight run that attracts almost everything in Southern California that will float. I made the Ensenada Race in 1968 aboard Bob Grant's Columbia 50 *Robon,* and that year there were 580 entries plus a few tagalongs in 16′ Pacific Cats and the like. More than the number of yachtsmen make the annual pilgrimage to Ensenada overland, and the little Mexican town really rocks with the 10,000 sailors and fleet followers that jam the streets and bars. It is more a carnival than a serious offshore race, but in summing up the experience in the July 1968 issue of *One-Design & Offshore Yachtsman,* I wrote: ". . . Never have I been aboard a boat that beat as many competitors in one race—or in a season!" *Robon* had finished third in Class A.

The Pacific Northwest's Swiftsure

Before leaving the West Coast's offshore races, mention should be made of the Swiftsure Race. This race is little known outside of its local area. It is, perhaps, too short and too far distant for boats based outside the Seattle/Vancouver environs to participate in. Nevertheless, it is a classic in its own right which I would like to sail in someday. Until I do, I will have to be content with the following account by Jay Lewis of the 1971 Swiftsure Race.

> In the lobby of Victoria's stately Empress Hotel, beer-toting sailors lounged about talking loudly of the Transpac and Maui, while the usually dominant little old ladies retreated to a corner with their tea. Out across the manicured gardens and lush lawn, the 191 entries had fastened themselves into the Inner Harbor with a cat's cradle of anchors, mooring lines,

and bumpers. It was the end of May, and the Swiftsure Lightship Classic was about to begin.

Since 1930 the 136-mile Swiftsure Race and the smaller boat 75-mile Juan de Fuca Race have been the premier offshore events in Pacific Northwest yachting. Friday night before the race the halyards began to slap as a Pacific front moved through, packing strong westerly winds. The following morning those who had been celebrating their imminent victories looked without enthusiasm as gale warnings were posted. Somehow, the yachts managed to untangle themselves and make their way to the starting line off Brotchie Ledge Beacon, tying in reefs as they went. The wind, gusting to 35 m.p.h., combined with a tide which flowed at about five knots against it, turned the sea white and lumpy.

As the short-sailed armada hopped along on starboard tack out past Race Rocks, masts began to go over the side. Among the six victims were Bruce Hendrick's Columbia 50, *Six Pack*, and Alvin Narod's Discovery 42 *Sunbird*. In all, some 44 boats failed to finish, due mainly to gear failures and seasickness during the early stages of the race.

Most Swiftsure veterans believe that the quickest route out is along the American shore where the currents are strongest, and the best path back is down the Canadian side. This approach has worked well over the years when wind conditions were normal. Consequently, nearly all the fleet worked out across the strait toward Washington's Olympic Mountains on the far shore.

Before long the weather began to clear, making the ride enjoyable though wet. The big Division I boats such as *Diamond Head, Min-sette, Coho, Adios,* and *Pemaquid* charged up the shore past Pillar Point in a race of their own. The smaller boats refused to let go, however, and dogged their wakes some way back. The wind began to ease as the fleet moved out the strait. All boats were soon back to full sail after a flurry of shaking out reefs and headsail changes.

Figuring that if staying along the shore was a good tactic, getting even closer would be that much better, a number of boats tacked further in, into lighter and lighter air. Many of the early leaders soon found themselves sitting dead in the water, while others moved along toward Swiftsure out in the strait.

The Juan de Fuca Race fleet, which started 15 minutes later than the bigger boats, was having a much faster run of it. The leaders caught many of the Swiftsure boats before they rounded their mark at Callam Bay on the American side and started home. The wind held for them as they surfed with chutes back past Race Rocks toward the finish. David Gibberd in his Spencer 31 *Gypsy G* crossed in a record elapsed time of 13 hours, 23 minutes. The leader in Division II was Gordon Hill's Redwing 30 *Ariki II* and PHRF winner was S. R. Oldham in *Te-pah*. Both races included a PHRF Division (Pacific Handicap) for those not rated IOR.

The bigger boats closed in on the Canadian minesweeper mark boat on Swiftsure Bank near midnight. Missing were several of the early leaders that had gone too far inshore and died. In their place were several of the Division II and III boats that had moved up when the wind softened further and shifted to the southeast. There was a large sea rolling, making progress slow and uncomfortable.

George S. Schuchart's Lapworth 50 *Pemaquid* was first around the carnival-lit, rolling mark boat. Close behind were veteran 73-foot *Diamond Head, Adios, Min-sette, Tyee,* and several smaller boats like Discovery 37s *Winsome IV* and *Sinful,* C&C 35s *Terna* and *Tangent,* and a Discovery 32, *Hyak*. It was a tedious cold beat back toward Carmanah Point on the Canadian shore. There were several clusters of boats with positions shifting back and forth between them. In the lead group, *Pemaquid,* Carl Schiff's 60-foot *Adios,* and Joe Pollack, Jr.'s, 59-foot *Min-sette* maneuvered for the first to finish position. Behind, Ches Rickard on *Winsome IV,* Per Christofferson with *Terna,* and Bonard Davis on *Hyak,* all top Swiftsure contenders over the years, eyed the Swiftsure Trophy for the overall win.

The wind held as the boats shot inside Race Rocks with the current and headed toward the finish line off McLoughlin Point. Further back, out of sight of the leaders, a challenge was being mounted. As *Terna* watched the clock and watched *Hyak* approach the line, Richard Gilbert's Ericson 35 *Firecracker,* Tom O'Brien's Cal 2-30 *Hooligan,* and Dan Brink's Ranger 29 *Tonic* were moving well not far back. As darkness fell, the wind held, and when the sun rose on the weary race committee, *Hooligan* was winner of the Swiftsure trophy.

In spite of the heavy going early in the race, the smaller

boats led by *Hooligan* were able to stay well placed for the light-air run to the finish. Although Skipper Tom O'Brien of Seattle is relatively new to Swiftsure racing, having entered only three, he is a Mackinac veteran. With an experienced crew and a well-prepared boat, it was not surprising to find *Hooligan* on top in the year of the small boat.[3]

The Southern Ocean Racing Circuit

Without doubt, one of the finest offshore racing series in the world is the Southern Ocean Racing Circuit (SORC), held each winter off the coast of Florida and sponsored by a group of yacht clubs banded together as the Southern Ocean Racing Conference. This series, which started as a midwinter series for Florida-based yachts, quickly spread in popularity among winter-weary sailors to the north. Many northern-based yachtsmen were soon sailing or shipping their boats south for the SORC. It has also become popular for new boats to be delivered for shakedown in the Circuit so that one usually can see the latest designs and the best crews assembled there each year. The competition is probably the finest one can find anywhere in offshore racing.

The races themselves are sailed over challenging courses. The first race is a medium-distance run from St. Petersburg to Anclote Key and back. This is followed, starting the next week, by the longest race of the Circuit from St. Petersburg to Fort Lauderdale. This race was originally sailed to Havana, Cuba, but political considerations dictated the course change. The result is a better race, considered by many to be the finest offshore race in the world, but one that is not exotic nor filled with so much shoreside revelry.

I have sailed in many St. Petersburg/Fort Lauderdale races. They are consistently the most interesting, challenging, and roughest races I have sailed. The following account, which I wrote of the 1969 race, typifies the action one usually encounters.

> It started out just great. It very quickly turned into a shambles. There was a big question mark throughout most of it. It ended up just fine. Those four sentences sum up the St.

[3] Jay Lewis, " '71 Swiftsure," *One-Design & Offshore Yachtsman*, vol. 10, no. 8 (August 1971), pp. 38–39.

Petersburg/Fort Lauderdale Race from *outRAGEous*, Charlie Morgan's new Morgan 33.

When Charlie invited me to do the SORC with him, I had visions of *Maredea, Panacea,* and *Rage* with hot showers, deep freezes, heat or air conditioning (depending on the ambient temperature), full-time cook, dry clothes, early finish. That sort of luxurious life swam into view before Charlie said, ". . . on my 33-footer." Visions shattered.

As I said, it started off just great. I hid in the cabin while Charlie and his regulars made a beautiful, clear air start toward the committee boat end of the line. It was blowing light from the southwest but forecast to turn northwest later in the day with the passage of a cold front. We moved out well on our class and soon were in a commanding lead. It got bigger and bigger, and for a while I had visions of our being first under the bridge. That happy thought was dashed to bits after 45 minutes or so. The wind picked up to 10 knots, calling for a headsail change. I was on deck by this time and had figured out where most of the strings were. We made one of the world's worst headsail changes—the genoa had a twist in it and the halyard had a wrap—and by the time we got it all straightened out, 50 boats had gone by. They weren't all in our class, of course, because of the inverted order start (little boats first), but that didn't help our morale any.

All of these shenanigans had a most disastrous effect on *outRAGEous*, and we passed under the Sunshine Bridge not first, not last, but decidedly toward the rear of the fleet.

Then the race ended!

We were comfortably settled down on the starboard tack when, BAM! *outRAGEous* crumpled and her mast took a sickening lurch to leeward. From my vantage point on the weather rail, I watched the mast take another lurch, then I saw the backstay whipping around the leeward spreader (the turnbuckle had broken). The genoa halyard being close to hand, I uncleated it and cast it off the winch, then went forward to gather in the genoa—keeping a wary eye on the backstayless mast. Since we were close hauled, the mainsheet and the vang saved the mast. Bruce Bidwell dived below and undid the turnbuckle, which connects the staysail tack to the forefoot. It was the same size, and in half-an-hour or so we were back in business.

Soon it was time for Bruce, Jimmy, and me to be relieved by Charlie, Sam, and Freddy. During their watch the front

Part of the fleet passes under the Sunshine Skyway as they leave Tampa Bay on the St. Petersburg/Fort Lauderdale Race. (Yacht Racing)

came through, and I was only subconsciously aware that we had driven through several torrential rainstorms, the sails had been up and down as many times, and when I was finally routed cruelly from my warm, dry bunk four hours later, we were booming along with eased sheets.

From then on it was duck soup—only there wasn't any soup or much else to eat. We were all too busy for galley detail, and it was too rough to cook. We did get a hot can of spaghetti and a warm can of beans out of Sam, but for the rest of the race each was on his own. We had a bountiful supply of fried chicken and Charlie's wife had made a shoebox full of brownies, which I devoured singlehanded and washed down with Pepsi. Somewhere in the ice box there was a roast, but it didn't see the inside of our stomachs until after the race. Gourmetwise, this race was a long way from my visions of *Maredea, Panacea, Rage* fare.

We didn't really care about food; *outRAGEous* was moving. With the spinnaker set and the wind off our starboard quarter at 18 knots, we charged down the Gulf of Mexico with the Sum-Log humming 10 knots. Granted, it was reading 10 percent high, but it would hover at "10," burst to the stop, and then sag to "8" or "7" for a second before zooming up to "10" again. *outRAGEous* was phenomenal. We had few sails in sight, but those we did see were quickly left astern. On she flew, and with the steering always well under control, for almost 24 hours to Rebecca Shoal. We began to think we might be in the race after all.

We flashed past Rebecca, jibed, and held the chute to the first of the buoys off the Florida Keys, which are all marks of the course. Then it was down chute and reach out into the Gulf Stream where we gradually hardened up until we were on the wind for Ft. Lauderdale.

It was late afternoon Monday (*Windward Passage* had finished at 10 Monday morning) before we saw any other sails we could identify.

In the fading breeze of Tuesday morning we were beginning to feel hopeful. We hadn't seen anyone in our class, so we must be either first or last—or close to either. With only bigger boats around, we dared hope we were first. As we finished and reported to the Race Committee, we were told we were the third boat to finish in Class D and so far we were second on corrected time.

Our time held, and we ended up second to O. J. Young's Cal

2-30 *Nauti-Cal*. We had apparently made all our mistakes in the first 10 miles. [4]

The other races of the SORC are all on the east coast of Florida and the Bahamas. The Miami–Lucaya (Grand Bahama) race follows the Lauderdale after a week for boat repairs and a chance for crews to put in time at their respective businesses. Following the Lucaya Race is a weeklong series consisting of the Lipton Cup Race—a day race off Miami—the Miami–Nassau Race returning to the Bahamas—and the final Governor's Cup Race—a day race from Nassau around Booby Rocks and return.

Bruce Kirby and I wrote the following account of the 1969 Miami–Nassau Race, which saw many records established:

> The Miami–Nassau Race was over so fast one hardly knew it had started. A fresh SSE wind came in with an advancing frontal system just at the start Monday afternoon, to be replaced by a booming northwester, complete with cold front squalls, early Tuesday morning. The resulting spectacular sailing (there were some equally spectacular accidents including a man overboard) saw Bob Johnson's *Windward Passage* break yet another course record. W. P. had an elapsed time of 15 hours, 54 minutes, 17 seconds (average speed over 11 knots!) to break the record set by Peter Grimm's *Escapade* in 1966 by more than three hours. Even the leading Class D boats, which ended up the first four corrected time winners, had elapsed times barely over 23 hours.
>
> Just as happened to *Escapade* when she set the old course record and wound up 69th on corrected time in '66, *Windward Passage*'s corrected time plunged her to 53rd in the fleet and right out of contention for overall SORC point standings. Ted Turner's converted 12-meter *American Eagle* plunged out of contention for another reason. She was dismasted several miles past Great Isaac light when her running backstay block broke.
>
> Taking Class A, sixth in the fleet and moving into an unassailable lead for the SORC Championship was the Jack Powell/Wally Frank-owned, Bob Derecktor-designed and built, 46-foot yawl *Salty Tiger*.

---

[4] Ted Jones, "Rage? No outRAGEous. Outrageous!" *One Design & Offshore Yachtsman*, vol. 8, no. 4 (April 1969), pp. 51, 71.

Overall winner of the Miami–Nassau Race was the 30-foot, Gary Mull-designed San Francisco sloop *Lively Lady II*, owned and sailed by Mike Shea and sponsored by David Allen. *Lively Lady* averaged not quite eight knots for the entire course. For the run from Great Stirrup Cay to the finish, when the wind blew up to 35 knots, she averaged more than eight knots even though she did not set a spinnaker.

Lively Lady was almost beaten across the line by Charlie Morgan's M-33 *outRAGEous*, which set a storm chute for the last leg and averaged more than nine knots. *OutRAGEous* ended up fourth on corrected time in both fleet and Class D.

It was a race full of records that are likely to stand for a long time, and it will also live in the memories of many as the most spectacular Miami–Nassau contest ever sailed. The first six boats to finish broke the old course record. Only 19 of the 99 finishers took more than 24 hours to sail the 180 miles. That means that even many of the little 30-footers like *Lively Lady* averaged over seven-and-a-half knots for the distance.

Three of the most highly touted boats in the fleet lost their masts. *American Eagle* was leading the series standings and doing well in the race when hers went over the side. The 33-foot, Gurney-designed *Hot Foot*, third in the Circuit last year, lost her mast shortly after rounding Isaac; and *Stubby*, designed, built, and sailed by last year's Nassau Race winner, Lee Creekmore, lost her rig in the Gulf Stream only about an hour after the start.

The weather, too, was spectacular. The wind was never below 15 knots, blew up to about 40 in some of the line squalls, averaged about 25 for the race, and was never on the nose. At the start the fleet was not quite close hauled on starboard tack. The wind veered as the boats altered course around Isaac, so that it was still a close reach. It continued to veer as the fleet blasted across towards Stirrup, hauling further aft with each rainsquall, until it was nearly dead astern. And then, in the middle of one hairy blast, it veered suddenly past "dead aft" and caused some spectacular jibes, some of them quite unexpected, others delayed long enough to be called intentional.

And if it was true that the worst of the rainsqualls obliterated everything more than 10 feet away, it is equally true that some of the prolonged holes in the overcast revealed a moon so brilliant that colors of hulls and spinnakers could be distinguished from half a mile away.

Perhaps more spectacular even than the records, the wind,

and the weather were the surfing and the broaching on the final leg from Stirrup to Nassau. Virtually every boat in the fleet reported hurtling down waves with speed gauges pegged at 10 knots. Bow waves were squirting out aft of the shrouds, and frequently were high enough to hit main booms. Roostertails alternated with wave tops in the cockpit.

Most of the boats that set spinnakers on that rollicking 54-mile dead run to the finish had at least one spectacular "wipe out." In many cases that ended the experiment, and they dropped back to main and "wung out" headsails.

Bill Allen of Los Angeles was steering the beautifully sailed Cal-40 *Melee* with the spinnaker up when a wave threw her stern to windward, threatening to jibe her. He corrected just as another wave picked her up and started her into a broach. Allen, six feet, seven inches tall, stood up to get a better purchase on the tiller, and as the boat knocked down he was catapulted across the cockpit and into the ocean without touching anything.

Bill Samuels of Oxford, Md., threw a horseshoe life preserver and was close to target. Allen swam to the horseshoe with his foul-weather gear on and then got rid of the excess clothing. Meanwhile the spinnaker halyard and guy had been released on *Melee*, she was upright, and the chute was holding her like a sea anchor. One man kept an eye on Allen as the spinnaker was hauled aboard, and the boat was tacked. *Melee* sailed back on the reciprocal course and Allen was brought aboard with little difficulty. Samuels estimated total time for the rescue at between six and eight minutes.

Allen, himself a Cal-40 owner, had been wearing a safety harness, but did not have it clipped on at the time of the broach.

In Class C, one 38-foot centerboarder is reported to have been knocked down and held for so long by a spinnaker that would not get rid of its wind that a crew member on another boat had time to go below and get his camera to photograph the incident.

The 31-foot Corvette centerboard sloop, *Mistral IV*, from Toronto, got badly off course during one of the rainsqualls Sunday morning and was driven in onto the Bahama Bank. She went aground and was stranded when the tide ebbed, then floated at the next high tide. But skipper Ken Johnston and his crew could not pick their way out of the area, which ranges from a few inches to a few feet in depth. The Coast Guard could not get close enough to be of assistance. It was almost a day after she had gone aground that *Mistral* found her way back to deep water and proceeded under power and shortened sail to Nassau.[5]

Great Lakes Racing

Not all the world's great offshore races are sailed in salt water. Three truly offshore events are held in the Great Lakes: the Chicago–Mackinac, Port Huron–Mackinac, and Trans-Superior races, which can vie with the most notorious "ocean" races for both danger and excitement. For one used to salt spray in the face, a soaking in fresh water can be pleasant by comparison, but those who sailed from Chicago to Mackinac Island in 1970 got more than they bargained for, as told in the following account by Bruce Kirby.

Ted Turner hadn't sailed the Chicago–Mackinac Race before. His first experience with offshore racing on the Great Lakes had been in the Port Huron to Mackinac contest the week before, and that had been light and spotty most of the way, with just a bit of a kick from the west toward the end.

So when someone at the Chicago YC told him the night before the start of the longer "Mac" that Lake Michigan could get pretty rough, Ted said, "Yeah, I'm really scared."

An hour or so after the start of the race the pleasant northerly got full of holes and finally stopped altogether. It filled in here and then over there and dropped away again. There were a lot of comments about "lake sailing" aboard Turner's *American Eagle,* which has put thousands and thousands of miles of ocean under her since "the man from Atlanta" bought her less than two years ago.

Then the wind filled in solidly from the northeast, gradually worked into the east, and we had a pleasant night of reaching up the lake on the rhumb line. The wind continued to "clock," and most of Sunday was spent broad reaching and

---

[5] Bruce Kirby and Ted Jones, "*Salty Tiger* Wins SORC," *One-Design & Offshore Yachtsman,* vol. 8, no. 4 (April 1969), pp. 56, 57.

running in 20- to 30-knot winds, low visibility due to haze and fog and building seas, which frequently pushed *Eagle* beyond the 12 knots that marks the top of her speed gauge.

In the afternoon the wind went into the southwest, then into the west. Carrying the spinnaker became difficult, then impossible. We were close reaching on port tack with main and nine-ounce No. 1 Genoa. The wind was from the northwest at about 20 knots and was building. The mugginess of the past two days gave way to a briskness. The Met men would call it "cool Canadian air." As one who had sailed the course before and who has in the past breathed a lot of "cool Canadian air," I warned my watchmates that we were in for a cold, rough night.

That was one time when I really was sorry to be so terribly right. Before long the wind was right on the nose and up into the 25- to 35-knot range. The direction held true for the next 12 hours, but the velocity didn't. It increased past 35, past 40, and then got up into the 50s. Twice I saw the anemometer hit 60 with the boat almost at a standstill, so it was not apparent wind speed, but a real 60 knots.

Before this, with the anemometer needle pegged on 45, I shouted to Turner, "What do you think of lake sailing now?," and he came back with "I hereby publicly retract anything and everything I have ever said about inland sailing."

About then the No. 3 jib came apart. Earlier we had reefed the main about six feet, then we'd changed down from the No. 1 to the No. 3, then we'd reefed the main to below the first batten. *Eagle* was going to windward at eight-and-a-half knots, pointing very high and getting her crew very wet when the clew pulled out of the headsail.

The irony was that we had no storm jib aboard (Ted thinks he has one in his basement) so as the wind rose we changed up to the No. 2 Genoa. *Eagle* continued to make tracks up the lake, and there was no doubt in our minds that we were quickly putting enough time between us and the rest of the fleet to make it impossible for anyone to save his time on us.

Our reasoning went something like this; the one other converted 12-Meter in the race, *Norsaga*, had looked a lot slower than *Eagle* upwind after the start in 10 to 12 knots of air, and we figured that the more wind there was, the more superior *Eagle* would prove to be. Not only that but the crew of *Norsaga* had been boasting before the race that they had never reefed the main, "and didn't know how." We had visions of *Norsaga* with full main in that weather.

Then there was *Dora*, which was the boat we feared most. Knowing *Dora*'s owner-skipper Lynn Williams, his son Lynn, and several of the other hard-rocks aboard, I was able to tell my captain that the new Gary Mull 55-footer definitely would not suffer from crew breakdown. But we convinced ourselves that a boat as new as *Dora* could not possibly hold together under such wind and sea conditions. Something had to break; not that we wanted anything to break, as that would be an unsatisfactory way to beat an opponent. But we were making a considered assessment of the opposition and felt that *Dora*, new as she was, probably would have something give way. We felt that if *Dora* held together, she would be hard to beat for corrected time honors as she was big, fast, well-sailed, and fitted very well into the International Offshore Rule under which the race was being run.

We considered *Bay Bea* a threat, too, but usually with a tough upwind grind *American Eagle* had managed to save her time on Pat Haggerty's red sloop from Texas. And *Inferno* could be trouble, but here too the record showed that *Eagle* usually got far enough ahead in hard going to have her time on Jim McHugh's powerful Chicago machine.

Around the time we were assuring ourselves of overall victory, Lake Michigan began to get the upper hand in its battle with *American Eagle*. Up until then it had been a draw. The lake pounded hell out of the converted 12-Meter, and *Eagle* pounded back, knocking great chunks out of the water and tossing them over her shoulder as she charged north with the wind and sea rising and the temperature dropping.

As the wind climbed off the top of our 45-knot anemometer, we carried more and more luff in the main to make up for having to use the No. 2 jenny instead of the No. 3. Then *Eagle*'s mast (the same one she used as a racing 12) began to shake violently, like a racing dinghy's does when she is overburdened and the main is allowed to flog.

Ted ordered the main down immediately, with a comment to the effect that "that thing [the mast] costs $25,000 and it's not insured." With only the No. 2 jenny up, *Eagle*'s speed remained above seven knots. When the boys got the storm trysail set and sheeted, the gauge went up over eight and the lee-helm disappeared.

Again we had the right combination on for the conditions, and again we knew we must be proceeding towards Mackinac Island faster than anyone else. About this time one of *Eagle*'s "regulars," Gary Wheatley, changed the anemometer from the low scale to the high scale. It had been against the top—pegged at 45 knots—for two hours anyway, so we thought it would be fun to find out what the wind was really blowing. It immediately began to register in the 50- to 55-knot range, which was about where we'd thought it was.

A little while later the clew pulled out of the No. 2 with a whack that brought Turner on deck certain that the mast had gone over the side. And there we were under storm trysail only, making about three knots through the water, and very little to windward. At this point the turning mark in the Straits of Mackinac was only about 18 miles ahead. But it was straight to windward, and we weren't going to get there very fast without a headsail.

Seldom had any of us felt so helpless in a boat. We had no more heavy weather headsails. The next one up was the nine-ounce No. 1 jenny, and we knew that if that blew out, we'd have nothing we could hoist until the wind got down below 15 knots. We thought about using a well-reefed main only, but were sure the leech would blow out of it before it was halfway up; and then we'd really be out of action.

So for a little more than an hour-and-a-half we jogged along under trysail, making a little progress to windward and alternating discouragement with the thought that if *Eagle* was in trouble, everyone else must be too. Throughout this period Turner frequently questioned the watch on deck to see if the wind was abating. He had decided that if it would just fall off to 40 knots or below, we could get the nine-ounce No. 1 up and be on our way. Finally, the wind did seem to be letting up for short periods—sometimes dropping a bit below 45. During one of these "lulls" Turner came on deck, took a quick look at the anemometer, and ordered the No. 1 set.

With the big sail up and half-sheeted home, *Eagle* began once again to do her thing. She bit into the seas, her "steam gauge" quickly worked up over eight knots, and the thunder of the big boat going to windward in a gale returned to the ears of the watch below. Turner kept calling for the sail to be sheeted harder; and at each call the coffee grinders would bring the straining jenny in a few more inches. The men at the winches seemed less anxious than the skipper to take a chance on pulling the clew out of the only sail on board that had a chance of holding together. But Turner insisted that the strain was the same whether the sail was in hard or eased off, and soon *Eagle* was at top form—pointing higher and going faster than any other ocean racer was likely to be able to do.

As the sheet was ground in, Turner took another quick look at the wind gauge, saw the needle at about 30, and called his crew down for being "chicken." "It's only blowing 30 knots," he shouted, ending the sentence with an expletive or two.

"No, Ted," said Chris Chatain from the weather rail, "the anemometer is on the upper scale. It's blowing 55."

Turner said, "Oh, it is?" and there was no more conversation on deck for some time.

But the nine-ounce No. 1 held together, which means we probably could have hoisted it much sooner and not have wasted the hour and 40 minutes almost hove to.

The wind didn't really go down for another couple of hours. The seas were a little smaller up in the straits, but no less wet, and probably no easier on the hull and rig. The temperature kept dropping and the final close reach under the Mackinaw Bridge and across the finish line was bitterly cold.

We were first to finish, and the last part of the race had been so exhilarating that again we were confident of saving our time on the fleet. But an hour and 36 minutes after we'd finished and an hour and 35 minutes after we'd broken into the scotch and rum, *Dora* crossed the line to save her time on us by just under an hour.

She was the only boat that did, so we took a second overall to *Dora*'s first.[6]

Transatlantic Races

There are, of course, many offshore races sailed on the East Coast of the United States in the spring and summer months. The 1960 Bermuda Race has been recounted at the beginning of this chapter. Some of the others are: Annapolis/Newport, biennial on odd-numbered years to alternate with the Bermuda Race;

---

[6] Bruce Kirby, "A Funny Thing Happened on the Way to Mackinac," *One-Design & Offshore Yachtsman*, vol. 9, no. 9 (September 1970), pp. 52–54.

Marblehead/Halifax, also held biennially; Stamford/Vineyard, an annual alongshore race of 240 miles; and many others.

Among the longest and often toughest races sailed anywhere, the occasional, but increasingly popular Transatlantic Races start either on the northeast coast or from Bermuda following the Bermuda Race. All these races are over 3,000 miles in length and have finished in various European ports, such as Plymouth, England; Santander and Bayona, Spain; Copenhagen, Denmark; Marstrand, Sweden; and Travemünde, Germany.

The first ocean race in history was a transatlantic race, rather a bizarre affair, which originated as a bet in the bar of the New York Yacht Club in December 1866. Only one of the three owners of *Henrietta, Fleetwing,* and *Vesta,* each of whom put up $30,000 prize money, sailed aboard his yacht. James Gordon Bennett on *Henrietta* collected the $90,000 for his trouble, and six hands were lost from *Fleetwing.* However historic this race between the 100-foot behemoths, it has almost nothing in common with offshore racing as we know it today—a sporting event for amateurs. All working crew members in 1866 were professional sailors except Mr. Bennett, and he went along mostly for the ride and to protect his investment.[7]

In many ways the Transatlantic Race is the ultimate offshore race. Yacht and crew must be prepared to be completely self-sufficient. They can expect everything from endless calms to hurricanes. They will be at sea for nearly three weeks, which in itself requires a substantial commitment from each crew member and adds immeasurably to problems of logistics and stowage.

The two accounts that follow, the first my own story of what it was like aboard *Kittiwake* in the 1966 race to Copenhagen, and the second, John Rousmaniere's story of the 1972 race to Bayona, illustrate how entirely different two Transatlantic Races can be.

The 1966 race started in a gale. I had the helm of *Kittiwake* at the start, and in my eagerness to be off for Copenhagen, I put us over the line before the gun and we had to return to start properly. It was a good joke on me, but tough on the rest of the crew, which had to handle an extra jibe and tack in high winds and rough seas. Finally, we were off chasing after our classmates who, by the time we had returned, were well ahead. *Kittiwake* liked the rough,

---

[7] Alfred F. Loomis, *Ocean Racing*, rev. ed. (New York: Yachting Publishing, 1946), p. 7.

The Class B start of the 1966 Transatlantic Race in gale conditions. (Bermuda News Bureau)

windward work, however, and before nightfall we were leading our class.

The first leg of the race, from Bermuda to point "A" (an imaginary turning point just south of the Grand Banks), was dominated by light-reaching winds after a blustery start in heavy seas and 30-knot headwinds. The first of many casualties, *Indigo*, dropped out on the second day with a broken centerboard.

Up to point "A" it was strictly a small boat race. From the daily position reports it was apparent that the top boats in Class A like *Ticonderoga, Audacious,* and *Germania VI,* who were vying for the lead, were not making enough distance to make up the four and five days they had to give away to the smaller boats. In class B, *Carina*, though she didn't make position reports, found herself sailing in the same water with some of the 40-foot Class C boats—a very unhealthy position for a 53-footer.

Once point "A" was passed, however, the weather turned cold and windy, blowing 25 knots from the southwest. *Ondine* took off like a shot, carrying a spinnaker almost continuously to the finish. She racked up an uncredible 11 consecutive noon-to-noon runs of more than 200 miles. *Carina* found these conditions more to her liking, and she, too, racked up many day runs of 200 miles plus.

In Class C, *Vamp X*, Ted Turner's SORC-winning Cal-40, surfed her way to victory. She also had many runs of over 200 miles and finished a full two days before the next boat in her class, Humphrey Simson's *Kittiwake*. *Vamp X* had an excellent chance to win the overall prize, but light winds near the finish moved her down to fourth in the fleet.

Light winds were the curse of the remainder of the fleet. The "second contingent," lead by George M. Moffett's new 48-foot yawl, *Guinevere,* and her near-sister *Kittiwake,* fell into a gigantic 1,000-mile diameter calm area off Rockall and the Hebrides. They had days of drifting, recording well under 100 miles. *Guinevere* had a noon-to-noon run of 48 miles, which must be something of a record in ocean racing. When it was finally reached, the North Sea was like a mill pond, and the Skagerak wasn't much better. Class D struggled along, thoroughly mixed in with Classes B and C. *Kirsten,* owned by I. E. Rothe, won in D, placing 13th in the fleet right after the last Class A boat.

Bob Johnson's California-based *Ticonderoga* was first to

finish but tumbled to ninth in Class A on corrected time. "Big *Ti*" had a fabulous run taking just under 16 days for the passage. While there is no direct comparison for this course, "*Ti*'s" run is something of a record. It is the fastest Transatlantic passage in recent years over the longest course, and it compares with the official record set by the 185-foot schooner *Atlantic,* which sailed from New York to the southwest tip of England (3,014 miles) in 12 days and four hours.

The hardest thing about a race across the ocean is the work and planning that precedes it—not only is it a monumental task getting the boat ready, but even though I was in the unique position of having the trip sanctioned by my employer, the preparation both at work and at home caused me to vow "never again" by the time I was aboard Humphrey Simson's *Kittiwake* and ready to go.[8]

That "never again" has been well tempered by the passage of time, and I am eager for another Transatlantic Race. Nevertheless, from the following story by John Rousmaniere of the 1972 Transatlantic, I can't say that I'm sorry to have missed that one!

For many of those who found themselves drifting around in the Azores high for a few days in early and mid-July, the 1972 Transatlantic Race from Bermuda to Bayona, Spain, provided little new in sailing experience.

Dick Nye, of the winning *Carina,* called it the 2,800-mile Block Island Race, and other Long Island Sound and Southern California veterans relied upon the same black humor that they use when discussing the light airs of their own areas.

Steve Colgate, my watch captain on *Dyna* and a veteran of half a dozen or so of these intercontinental races, expressed it best: "This is so awful," he muttered the third or sixth or 10th night out—as he twitched at a quarter-inch sheet attached to a drooping half-ounce spinnaker—"this is so awful that it's indescribable."

It blew 20 knots or more only a couple of times and only once did *Dyna* have a day's run of more than 200 miles. That is, only once did this 55-foot yawl, 40 feet on the water, average as much as 8.3 knots from local apparent noon to local

---

[8] Ted Jones, "From Bermuda to Denmark," *One-Design & Offshore Yachtsman,* vol. 8, no. 10 (October 1969), pp. 30–32, 53.

apparent noon. We averaged only 136 miles a day—5.7 knots—and first-to-finish *Blackfin* averaged only 11 miles more.

The start was promising, with two days of fast running or broad reaching in a gradually dying southwester. The few yawls and ketches held high to the south in order to keep their mizzen staysails full, but some sloops ran off to make northing. *Charisma* was the most extreme of these, and Jesse Phillips' 56-footer was to be first around the turning mark—the island of Flores in the Azores—1,800 miles later. The July pilot chart indicates better odds for winds north of the Great Circle course to Flores, and *Charisma*, the Portuguese *Jessica*, the Bermuda Race winner *Noreyma*, and others played the odds and won. After the southwester caved in on the third day, radioed position reports from the most northern boats showed the pilot chart to be correct.

There were some course changes to the north by boats listening in, probably the most drastic of which was made by *Carina*. When, late on the third day, her crew discovered that *Charisma* was already 100 or so miles ahead, she jibed and sailed at right angles to the course for 23-and-a-half hours before jibing back. This brave decision and the McCurdy and Rhodes 46-footer's extraordinarily good light-air ability got her in sixth to finish, only nine hours after *Blackfin*. This was Nye's third Transatlantic win in a career that spans three *Carinas*, 20 years, and two Bermuda Race triumphs. Some say that ocean racing is little more than an expensive crap game; if so, a few skippers are lucky all the time.

So it paid to listen to the daily position reports. *Dyna*'s experienced owner, Clayton Ewing, chose not to bother with reporting and, with the integrity for which he is renowned, he decided it would be unfair to take advantage of competitors' reports. His decision to neither a borrower nor a lender be was shared by few, and a couple of boats, nameless here, made it clear that they were listening in without contributing anything more than mileage runs.

Dyna is a yawl, so we were well south of the great circle when the wind pooped out on July 1, the third day. It took us another six days to get back to that shortest of all routes, and there, not knowing the good fortune of our competitors 50 or 150 miles to the north, we stayed. A sighting of the 73-foot *Kialoa* on the eighth day cheered us up, but if we had known of her 40-mile day when we made 60, we might not have been so happy. She eventually retired from the endurance contest and dropped off several of her crew at the Azores. *Ondine* also dropped out after several discouraging days.

So we sailed through the high to the Azores, across a weather map that daily showed contour lines stretching all the way from the Pecos to the Steppes. The tropical storms that had battered the western Atlantic in June succeeded in blocking off almost all frontal activity for the next month, and our hard-working navigator, Dick McCurdy, could report no storm warnings for the entire North Atlantic from the race's start until a couple of days before *Blackfin*'s finish. Inexplicably, there was more wind on the top of the high in its plateaus to the west, and we had some lovely nighttime close reaching in light southeasters—aesthetically lovely, that is.

Once around Flores, the hot, slow going became cool, slow going, and longjohns replaced shorts. A depression finally appeared, but those who went to meet it either got on the wrong side or missed it altogether. *Charisma*, leading the fleet at Flores after holding well north, tried it again with poor results; she was ninth to finish and corrected to 7th in Class B and 30th in fleet. *Blackfin* finished late in her 18th day at sea. A day and a half later, we on *Dyna* drifted across the finish line under—guess what—half-ounce spinnaker and quarter-inch sheets. Any more wind would have served an injustice to our memories of this long race.[9]

The first Transatlantic Race in the other direction was the 1971 race from Cape Town, South Africa, to Rio de Janeiro, Brazil, recounted by English yachtsman and author Jack Knights:

Fifteen minutes after the start of the 3,600-mile Cape Town to Rio race, bookies would have given long odds against the ultimate success of one of the smallest runners . . . for there she lay, the Van de Stadt-designed, 42-foot long, *Albatross II*, beam on to the wind, her mast along the water, her giant spinnaker full of the stuff, the white caps of the straits of Cape Town breaking into her wide open cockpit and the remainder of the 59 starters racing out of sight under the heavy hand of a Force 8 sou'easter.

---

[9] John Rousmaniere, "Drifting to Spain," *Yacht Racing*, vol. 11, no. 10 (October 1972), pp. 51, 52.

The start was such an important national occasion that crews overcooked things. Instead of philosophizing that the world's longest yacht race course lay ahead with an infinity of pitfalls and opportunities, they hysterically hoisted more than enough sail for an afternoon's turn around the buoys and then hung on grimly to their tillers and wheels, refusing to be outdone by anyone.

Albatross II has an unusually tall spar for her 42 feet of length and 16,000 pounds of displacement. It is supported by an extremely light rig featuring single spreaders, rod backstay and forestay, and an inner forestay. When *Albatross* broached so soon after the start, she went over with an almighty bang, which threw her crew of six bodily to leeward. When they picked themselves up, clawed the fragments of spinnaker down, and handed the main, they saw that the mast had been bent sickeningly under the savage thrust of the spinnaker pole. It had bent and stayed profoundly bent. They managed to get their yacht to stagger into the lee of nearby Robben Island. At first they tried to anchor, later they came alongside. Each man reckoned the race was over before it had truly begun, but nobody had the courage to say so. So they grimly set to work with the sheet winches to grind the mast back to approximate shape. Then they lashed up extra stays. After four hours they cautiously poked their nose out into the ocean again and under close reefed main and storm jib followed in the path of the others.

Slowly their confidence increased. Slowly it dawned upon them that they might not have to retire after all. Bit by bit sail was increased. After a time, with great ingenuity, a more permanent mast reinforcement was made, part of the sail used to join this spreader to the mast. Tactics were promptly reassessed; the most obvious and important fact in the crew's estimation was that they were now behind. Therefore, they had to do something different. Instead of heading far north of the rhumb line to pick up the theoretically stronger winds and current, they would keep to the south.

Later, when this tactic was obviously paying off, they discovered a big high looming directly ahead. Since south had paid before, they reckoned it would pay again. So they veered to the south of the high and, though this gave them head winds, it kept them moving.

This, together with the yacht's natural ability and the persistence of her experienced crew, won the race for *Albatross II*.

After something like 2,000 miles, *Albatross* had made more westing than even the largest competitors. Like everybody else they now ran into calm, but because they had the wind ahead of the beam for most of the time and because they were small and responsive, they were able to play the fronts and rainsqualls, maneuvering so that the centers always passed to one side or the other. Only once did they get a front wrong, and then they lost a whole day's march.

Albatross (now followed by her sister ship *Mercury*) was hampered by calms for some four-and-a-half days, which probably was less than the calms that afflicted those to the north. Because she was so far south, she now had cross-currents and contrary currents to fight to the finish, whereas the others could expect to be helped onwards by the sea. Here *Albatross* was just plain lucky, much luckier than *Mercury* or another close rival, *Golden City*, a Cal 40. She found a fine breeze to speed her around 200 miles a day, for two days into the finish, and she swept home, with her crew taking one last apprehensive look at their fallible spar, eighth in the fleet for a corrected time of 529 hours, 33 minutes, and 34 seconds and seized the handicap lead from the veteran French 12-Meter *Striana*. No later finisher was able to take the lead from *Albatross II*.[10]

The Royal Ocean Racing Club (RORC) in England has an extensive program of offshore races each season, both in the English Channel between England, France, Holland, Belgium, and in Spain and the Mediterranean. The most famous of all the RORC races, however, and one that many Americans have participated in, is the biennial (odd years) Fastnet Race. The Fastnet course is from Cowes (following Cowes Week) out into the Channel, around the Lizard at the southern tip of England, across the Irish Sea, and around Fastnet Rock just off the southern Irish Coast, around the Scilly Isles and Bishop Rock to finish at the entrance to Plymouth Harbor. This is a tough and varied race, if anything, tougher than the St. Petersburg/Fort Lauderdale Race, and shares honors with the Bermuda Race and the Australian Sydney/Hobart Race as one of the three most prestigious races in the world.

In Fastnet years, the RORC also runs the Admiral's Cup Series, which is a competition among national teams of three yachts rac-

---

[10] Jack Knights, "Capetown–Rio Race," *One-Design & Offshore Yachtsman*, vol. 10, no. 4 (April 1971), pp. 12, 13.

ing in the Channel Race, day races during Cowes Week, and the Fastnet Race. My introduction to this whole scene was in 1969—a disappointing year for the Fastnet Race itself. This was my first trip to England and my first look at Cowes Week and an Admiral's Cup Series. While the climax was disappointing, the "World Series" of offshore racing was anything but that. This is the yachtsman's Mecca.

I had visions of splinters of Dragons flying into the air as the British Rail Hovercraft *Seaspeed* skidded around the corner of the breakwater into the harbor at Cowes, but with what seemed a miraculously close call (I later watched them do the same maneuver 15 times a day for one week), the hovercraft crabbed its way down its orange-balled channel and slithered up the concrete ramp to a stop. The crew of Chris Bouzaid's *Rainbow II* from New Zealand—with whom I had ridden down from London—chimed in with a "Welcome to Cowes, mate."

The prelude to Cowes Week and the first race counting for the Admiral's Cup is the 240-mile Channel Race sponsored by the Royal Ocean Racing Club (RORC). The start was off the Royal Albert Y.C. at Southsea Beach, Portsmouth, on Friday evening. The fleet milled around off the beach stemming the ebbing tide. It was impossible to cross the line on starboard tack so most boats elected a port-tack start, but someone in each class charged up the line on starboard, forcing many boats about. Unfortunately, the beach and the front porch of the R.A.Y.C. constituted the port end of the line; this combined with over two knots of fair current complicated the starting procedure somewhat. (Imagine the awesome sight of big, red *American Eagle* sweeping across the bows of 30 port-tack starters!)

The course consisted of three equal legs first eastward to Bassurelle Light Vessel (after leaving shoreside marks to seaward) in mid-English Channel, then south-southwestward to Le Havre L.V., then back across the Channel passing east of Nab Tower to the finish in The Solent at Horse Sand Fort off Portsmouth.

The first leg started out as a light beat, but roughly halfway to Bassurelle it turned into a run. How one played this wind shift had a lot to do with how one finished. Those who stayed south, into the Channel, made out best; they had less beating, were on the favored tack, and came into Bassurelle on a broad reach instead of a run.

Bassurelle to Le Havre was a close reach which turned into a short beat along the French coast. Some who failed to hold high on this leg (like British Admiral's Cup contender *Casse Tete III*) fell out of contention on their longer beat to Le Havre.

Le Havre to Nab Tower was another reach, without much chance to catch up lost ground. Not surprisingly, Chris Bouzaid's Class IIIa *Rainbow II* was the overall winner. The New Zealanders were fresh from their One-Ton Cup victory and had their three-year-old Sparkman and Stephens sloop cranked up for fair. First in Class I and second overall to *Rainbow II* was Syd Fischer's S&S-designed *Ragamuffin*, largest boat on Australia's Admiral's Cup team. Third overall and first in Class IIa was Dick Carter's radical new retractable swing-keel sloop *Red Rooster* which was to be the hot boat in the U.S. Admiral's Cup team.

Australia jumped into an early lead in Admiral's Cup competition with finishes of 1-4-7 among Admiral's Cup yachts. Italy was second with 6-9-16, while Britain and the U.S. were tied for third with 3-5-28 and 2-8-26, respectively. Germany was fifth, followed by Finland, Holland, Spain, Argentina, and Bermuda in that order. Spain and Bermuda had only two entries each instead of three.

Cowes was a changed place from Friday to Sunday. The famous "trots," where most of the boats lie rafted to large moorings just off the waterfront, were already loaded with all sorts of offshore racers—flying flags from European and South and North American countries as well as Australia and New Zealand—then there were powerboats, boyer yachts, and a Thames barge or two. The narrow streets of Cowes were swarming with people. Any time the bar was open at the Island Sailing Club, you couldn't get near it. The sightseeing-boat captains were packing them in off the Parade with their singsong Cockney call, "See all the ships tu-dey. Are you coming now for 'alf-a-crown?" A five-pound note wouldn't buy a table for dinner at the Gloster before 2230. The brass cannons flanking the signal hoist at the Royal Yacht Squadron boomed a salute you could hear all over The Solent and scared the pants off the passing tourists. It was Cowes Week.

I had always thought of Cowes Week as "big-boat" racing. With 235 offshore boats racing in four classes, it certainly has more than regattas elsewhere. What surprised me, though, was the vast one-design fleets that race also. Most of the

Offshore racers starting a day race in the Solent off the parade in front of the Royal Yacht Squadron during Cowes Week. (Ted Jones)

classes wouldn't be recognized anywhere else in the world—like SCODs, Solent Sunbeams, Seaview Mermaids, Redwings (all with red sails, of course), and Y and X O-D's (the X's number near 100)—but there are healthy numbers of Dragons, Solings, Flying Fifteens, and IOD's, which are, at least, known in other parts of the world. All 13 one-design classes were keel boats.

The two big days for the larger RORC Class I, II, and III boats are Tuesday's and Thursday's races for the Britannia Cup and New York Yacht Club Cup. These races also count for the Admiral's Cup. Tuesday's race saw 90 boats either start or finish in Class I. (The results sheet listed several DNF reasons such as "no time received," "not seen at start," and "disqualified"; therefore it is difficult to tell exactly how many were actually in contention.) With the starting line stretching over a mile to West Bramble buoy nearly all the way across The Solent, it was extremely important if one end happened to be favored.

Shortly afer the start the wind backed, making what had been a close reach a light air—sometimes very light—beat against a foul current. Ted Turner's converted 12 *American Eagle* was around seemingly hours ahead of the next boat, Jim Kilroy's 73-foot *Kialoa II*. Others were struggling against the current on either shore with those to the north having the better of it. The wind filled in while most were on the second leg—a run—and the rest of the twice-around course was a jolly romp in up to 18 knots of wind. Proper playing of the currents and headlands in The Solent is the way to win, and proper timing of strategy is extremely important. The proper tack 20 minutes previously may be all wrong now.

British Admiral's Cup team member *Prospect of Whitby* was the corrected time winner as the RORC Rule and the time-on-time handicap system combined to put *Eagle* down to 40th place in spite of her wide margin. Italy's Admiral's Cup team member *Mabelle* was second, and her teammate *La Meloria* was fourth. Had the third member of the Italian team, *Levantades*, not been disqualified, Italy might have moved into first place instead of slipping to third.

Thursday's race for the New York Yacht Club Cup turned The Solent in the opposite direction (first leg to the east) with less maximum wind but more minimum wind than Tuesday. Dick Carter came through once again for the U.S. team, posting a first. Among Admiral's Cup teams Italy's *Mabelle* was second—which helped maintain their third place—and *Ragamuffin* was third. Once again the Australians led the Admiral's Cup scoring, posting 79 points and giving them a commanding lead.

So it was thought that the Aussies would once again sweep the Admiral's Cup, but the dullest, longest, most frustrating, inglorious Fastnet Race ever did them in. The Fastnet is weighted three-to-one in total score over the day races in The Solent and three-to-two over the Channel Race. Nevertheless, the Australians had such a commanding lead and are always so good in the long races, that it was thought they couldn't lose.

Aside from an invigorating spinnaker reach out of The Solent, past the Needles, and up to Portland Bill—and a protracted beat out to Fastnet Rock—the 1969 Fastnet was a 600-mile dead loss. England had been experiencing unusually warm weather with a series of shallow high-pressure weather systems. This pattern continued, and the Fastnet weather degenerated into fitful, weak thermal breezes. If you happened not to be near land, which is the normal thing in the middle of the Irish Sea, you had nothing.

Through it all, however, Dick Carter's *Red Rooster* came through again to win the Fastnet overall. Among team finishers, *Carina* was third and *Palawan* came through with a fine eighth. Although *Ragamuffin* was second, her teammates *Koomooloo* and *Mercedes III* were caught in the calms and finished well out of contention. The U.S. ended up with high score, winning the Admiral's Cup by 14 points more than the Australians. Britain was third and Italy fourth.[11]

The Sydney/Hobart Race

The Sydney/Hobart Race was inspired by Captain John Illingworth following World War II. While visiting Australia, Illingworth, who was then commodore of the RORC, suggested a race to Hobart over the Christmas holidays. He was the winning skipper of that first race in 1945, which marked the beginning of the third classic offshore racing course to rank with Bermuda and the Fastnet as the three top races.

---

[11] Ted Jones, "Cowes Week—and All That . . ." *One-Design & Offshore Yachtsman*, vol. 8, no. 10 (October 1969), pp. 30–32, 53.

Bob Williams, who sailed aboard *Ondine*, the first American yacht to sail the race and which set the course record in 1963, gives the following account of the race.

The sun glistened in all its magnificence, the River Derwent was alive with the action and color of a flotilla of small craft skipping across the whitecaps, while thousands of shore spectators from South Arm to Princes Wharf cheered and waved as *Ondine*, driven by a fresh 15-knot southeast breeze, surged forward to win line honors in the annual 630-nautical mile Sydney to Hobart Race. A mere 60 seconds astern followed the 73-foot Australian schooner *Astor* (for 36 hours thereafter the other 41 boats crossed the line) ; the finish being one of the most dramatic in ocean racing history, and the closest in the 17 years of what is generally considered one of the toughest deep water races.

Clapping and shouts of congratulations filled the air. The crew was jubilant, and for the first time in several days relaxed, as the yacht slowly sailed to Princes Wharf and then to Constitution Dock, her permanent mooring.

Thirty days earlier, on November 26th, *Ondine* had received a similar welcome as she gracefully danced between the Heads at the entrance to Sydney Harbor at the end of her 11,500 mile voyage, from New York to Sydney, for the Sydney–Hobart Race. Only five of *Ondine*'s crew of 13 sailed her down from New York; the other seven flew down by Qantas early in December to complete the racing crew.

The Sydney–Hobart Race begins on Boxing Day, December 26th, at midmorning. All crew members were aboard by 0830, and anxious to get under way. A few last-minute preparations and decisions were discussed, and crew positions reviewed before departing. A full day had been spent practicing offshore following the arrival of the complete crew. Numerous sail changes, reefing procedures, and spinnaker exercises were practiced.

A rousing cheer went up as *Ondine* slipped her docking lines and bade farewell to Rushcutters Bay. Sydney Harbor was a sight long to be remembered. Every conceivable type of craft, from tugboats to small outboard-powered dinghies towing skiers, turned out to give the fleet a gala sendoff. The shores were lined with spectators from Rushcutters Bay to Hornby Light, a distance of five miles. The effect was that of a national holiday.

Ondine, holder of the Sydney-Hobart course record. (Yacht Racing)

The wind, out of the southeast, blew a steady 30 to 35 knots. Inside the Heads, the sea was moderately smooth, but we observed heavy seas during our initial trial run to the Heads.

"Huey" [*Ondine*'s owner Sumner A. Long] maneuvered skillfully for a windward start, found an opening, and showed *Ondine*'s stern to the fleet by being number one over the line. *Julie*, skippered by Jock Sturrock, was second across the line, and slightly to leeward. *Athena, Caprice,* and *Astor* started further on down the line. *Astor*, shortly after the start, proceeded to foot steadily to leeward.

Solo, off to a poor start, advanced as we approached the spit of land off Hornby Light (just inside South Head). Huey, in order to guard his position, hugged the shore, as *Ondine* approached the open sea. *Solo* made one attempt to go above *Ondine*, and in so doing almost walked away with our mizzen before dropping off to leeward.

Astor was the first yacht through the Heads—*Ondine* second. Once out of the Heads, *Ondine* continued to sea for approximately three miles before tacking, and reaching south. *Solo*, having some difficulty with her headsails, floundered in the open sea before tacking south. As dusk gathered around us, *Astor, Solo,* and *Janzoon* were the only visible yachts—*Solo* being about two miles astern and to leeward.

The race at this time now resembled a typical Marblehead to Halifax event, and nothing like the gear-bursting race across the turbulent Tasman Sea that many of us had expected. During the first 24 hours, noon to noon, 217 miles were logged, an average speed of 8.4 knots.

Shortly after spotting Cape Rowe, our number one spinnaker blew out along the tapes and was quickly replaced with a substitute. By the evening of the second day the wind had increased slightly. The port watch was below enjoying dinner when an exploding "Crack!" was heard on the foredeck. The spinnaker pole had bent to a V shape right at the center. With all hands on deck, the crew successfully hauled down the broken pole and replaced it with its mate in five minutes.

The wind that evening reached velocities of 40 to 45 knots at various times. It was during one of these powerful gusts that a second resounding "Crack!" was heard on the foredeck as the replacement spinnaker pole folded up. Much to our dismay the second pole had suffered the same disaster as the first.

Dereck Baylis, a mechanical engineer who specializes in

marine fittings, assisted Captain Sven Joffs and the port watch in mending the pole. The first broken pole was sawed in half at the breaking point, wood-chocks were inserted, the pole sections were forced together. The broken section was sheathed with the other pole, and then completely bound with all available lines. The jury-rigged spinnaker pole was set after a 3½ hour delay. This time loss seriously affected the handicap results. While the poles were being repaired, *Solo* crept past.

By sun-up, *Solo* was clearly ahead, some three miles off the starboard bow. The sun appeared at intervals through overcast skies most of the early morning, but by noon a brilliant sun gave us ample opportunity for drying out damp clothes.

Huey reported at noon that 219 miles had been logged over the previous 24 hours at an average speed of 9.1 knots—211 miles left to go.

With late afternoon rapidly approaching, it was decided to hold our present course of 180° until approximately 1930, and then jibe over for Tasman Light, which held a bearing of approximately 205°. The one boat that had us worried was *Solo*. We observed that *Solo*, during evening radio position reports, had been constantly ahead and to windward of her actual position, or what we considered to be her position in relation to our own. Taking this into consideration it was decided to hold off jibing until dark so that *Solo* couldn't observe the maneuver. We jibed at 2030. An hour later we had left *Solo* astern. We later learned she held off jibing until 2300.

Surging along on this third evening was a sailor's delight. *Ondine* advanced at a steady 7 knots with a frothy wake kicking up astern, and occasional bow waves tossing sparking diamonds upon the foredeck. At 0140 the loom of Tasman Island light was spotted. The wind, which had been averaging 15 to 20 knots, had begun to drop in velocity.

Don Allen, of the Starboard Watch, roused me about 0630 as we rounded Tasman Light. I was particularly interested in seeing the Light and the surroundings.

Much to our amazement, about two miles ahead, hugging the shore, sat *Astor*, silent and still; the water about her was flatter than a duck's instep. *Astor* had rounded Tasman Light at 0100, and had been becalmed ever since.

Seeing *Astor*'s becalmed condition, we continued along in light winds in the center of the channel.

The breeze freshened somewhat as Iron Pot Light, entrance to the Derwent River, came into view eight miles ahead. *Astor*, only about half a mile inshore at this time, began to advance toward the Light as a gentle breeze came from the shore. We thought perhaps in mid-channel the breeze would be strong enough to drive *Ondine* ahead, but as the distance to Iron Pot narrowed, *Astor* was footing to windward, and obtained a clean lead.

Once past Iron Pot, *Astor* continued on for about half a mile before jibing (starboard tack) for the final miles to the finish. *Ondine*, in turn, once beyond the Iron Pot, headed for the east side of the Derwent, away from center channel, and perhaps away from a slight tide (current) disadvantage. Once clear of land, *Ondine* was jibed over and headed for the finish.

Crowds of spectators lined the beaches for what was later called an "epic struggle down the Derwent."

Ondine now took the lead for the first time, by a mere 100 yards, and headed for the finish. *Astor* while jibing, broke out a new glamorous white and blue Venturi spinnaker. It appeared that *Astor* would overtake us at this point, but with Huey skillfully at the helm and Al Salm and Bobby Symonette directing the spinnaker activities, *Ondine* managed to keep her sails full. *Astor*, attempting several times to cover our breeze, flopped her spinnaker, and it was all over.

Ondine crossed the finish line approximately 200 yards, and 60 seconds, ahead of *Astor*. The gun sounded to wild cheers by thousands of spectators who were on hand as *Ondine* came over. The sole U.S. entry in the Sydney–Hobart Classic had achieved line honors and broken the race record, set in 1957, by 14 hours and 44 minutes.

Once over the line, *Ondine* lowered her sails, and with colors flying, motored to Princes Wharf for one of the warmest welcomes in ocean racing history. It followed what was one of the closest finishes in any major ocean racing event.[12]

There are many more accounts of races, some perhaps more exciting than those related here, and many more races that one could read about. There are never any two races the same, and that's one of the main ingredients that makes offshore racing so enjoy-

---

[12] Robert D. Williams, "*Ondine* Captures Australia," *Popular Boating*, vol. 13, no. 4 (April 1963), pp. 83, 86, 87, 148, 161, 169. (Excerpted from *Popular Boating* magazine by permission. Copyright © 1963 by Ziff-Davis Publishing Company. All rights reserved.)

able. Every race will not be a winner, every race will not be a record setter, every race will not be fun, and every race will not be something you'll want to do again, although in my experience no race has been all bad. If you enjoy racing and sailing in the ocean, every race will be worthwhile—something will be learned, even if you are miserable while learning it—and in the end, you will add to your appreciation of offshore racing. When the call goes out, you will be ready, willing—eager—to go again.

Someone once asked me what was the best offshore race I had ever been on. It took a bit of thought to come up with an appropriate answer. I skimmed quickly through memories of Bermuda, Fastnet, SORC, and Transatlantic, and finally answered as truthfully as I could, "The last one . . . and the next one."

Chapter 18 A Philosophical View

Running Tide. (Roland Rose)

And so we come to the end of what I hope has been a pleasant voyage—a voyage that will mark the start of many real and wonderful experiences racing offshore. This book does not tell it all. No book can, because no author or even group of authors can know it all. The next time I go sailing I will learn something new, and if it is of some significance, I will be frustrated in the knowledge that it should have been included here.

There is more to sailing offshore than pointing the yacht in the proper direction and pulling the proper lines. In fact, the way you go about it is just as important as what you do. The conduct of a race or a passage deserves as much thought as its direction.

Booze

Sailors have a long and close association with drinking, in the pubs ashore and with their ration of grog at sea, and many modern sailors look at their yachts as a refuge from shoreside restraints on liquor.

I learned early that alcohol and seawater don't mix. I was in my late teens and was returning a friend's yacht to her home club from where we had left her the weekend before, twenty miles away. My companions and I had a delightful and relaxed reach up Long Island Sound. It was the sort of day that called for a beer, but there wasn't any aboard—we'd consumed all of it over the weekend. There was an opened bottle of premixed Manhattan cocktails, and we tied into that in celebration of the day. Before long we were flying along with the yacht, whooping and shouting, throwing empty bottles at passing channel markers, and having a wonderfully irresponsible time.

A PHILOSOPHICAL VIEW 253

All was well until it came time to make the mooring. Here was a yacht that I knew as if it were my own. I could, under any conditions—except those in which I then found myself—make her do my bidding. I could put her around a mark with inches to spare, alongside a float or dock no matter what the wind direction, and I could coast her to a stop with her bow just nudging her mooring buoy. But not that day! It took me three passes before we could grab the mooring, and then it was none too sharp a maneuver. I was glad it was a weekday and no one was around to see what a bunch of dummies we were.

Naturally, I knew what was wrong, and I resolved on the spot to stay off the hard booze while sailing. When instant decisions may be needed and when careful yacht handling requires good coordination and a steady hand—cruising or racing—liquor can wait until the hook is down or the mooring is secured.

In my opinion, this prohibition need not apply to beer, which most people can consume in moderation with very little effect upon their coordination or judgment. There is also an appropriate time, when offshore, that hard liquor may be served to the crew: "happy hour."

Nothing binds a crew in good fellowship more than a relaxing half-hour together over a drink of rum or whatever. A good time for this is just before the evening meal. The watch below can come on deck at 1800, socialize with the watch on deck, drink their grog, and retire below for dinner at 1830. One drink normally does not get anyone boiled. The watch on will soon be relieved, and the watch below will have a meal to dilute the effects of the spirits. "Happy hour" is a custom practiced aboard many successful offshore racers. It is great for the crew's morale and thereby brings many benefits.

What is Offshore Racing?

The purchase of a sailboat with living accommodations and the sailing of it across to Catalina or down Long Island Sound overnight do not qualify you for the Blue Water Medal.* Nor does hammering around an Olympic course in a One-Ton Cupper—even though you win a lot—qualify you for the Ocean Racing Champion-

---

* The Blue Water Medal is awarded by the Cruising Club of America whenever deserved to someone who has completed an outstanding sea voyage.

ship. Yet these kinds of activities certainly will help you on the way to successful offshore racing. One would be foolish to step aboard any boat, no matter how well fitted out, and sail or race to Bermuda, Honolulu, or Hobart without any prior experience in offshore boats.

Even though you may have been racing for years in Block Island and Vineyard races, sailed in a Miami/Nassau race two years ago, and have an invitation from a friend to sail to Ensenada Race with him next spring, that still doesn't qualify you as an experienced offshore racer.

Offshore racing is you and your crew taking your boat to sea, where there is little opportunity to run for cover in the event of a storm and where you must be self-sufficient and face whatever comes in the way of wind, wave, sun, and darkness.

Offshore sailing is not a pastime for the casual, the ill-informed, or the unprepared, nor is it a pastime for everyone, even though they be serious, informed, and prepared. There are people who simply won't like sailing offshore.

Let me quickly dispel the notion that I am knocking overnight races, round-the-buoys races, and short cruises in cruising-type sailboats. To me and to countless thousands of others, this can be the finest kind of sailing there is. Some of the best competition, second only to championship one-design races, can be found in racing offshore yachts in sheltered waters. Some of the most delightful evenings in a lifetime afloat may well be spent in a quiet anchorage only a few miles from home or even on your own mooring a horn-blow away from the yacht club dock.

Offshore sailing has its own special delights. The reader should realize by now that these delights are quite different from those enjoyed in sheltered-water sailing.

Racing Or Cruising

The differences between inshore racing and cruising are as vast as two different activities using the same medium can be. In any type of racing, everything is all out. You work as hard as you can and try to make the boat go as fast as it can, day and night. Inshore cruising is relaxed. You work as little as you wish and let the boat go at its own pace. You leave the harbor late in the morning and make port early in the afternoon.

Offshore racing and cruising are much more alike. They are

basically similar because the goals are the same—to get from point A to point B as expeditiously as possible. The longer you are at sea, the longer you are exposed to whatever dangers may be present. You do not anchor at night. With either racing or cruising you must, after all, arrive at your destination, and often, in offshore cruising, that means working almost as hard as the racing crew.

One subtle difference between racing and cruising offshore is the attitude of the crew. The racing crew will carry on longer in the face of a storm. Spinnakers will be flown rather than twin staysails. Helmsmen will be selected for their ability instead of by turns. Navigation will be done daringly instead of conservatively. Of course, the basic problems of endurance and safety are common to both activities, but in cruising the crew is usually smaller and the intensity with which they function considerably lower.

A passage from New York to Florida aboard a 40′ yawl illustrated this difference in intensity to me. We had taken the inside route past the dangerous reefs off Cape Hatteras and planned to sail outside from Moorehead City south to Fort Lauderdale. The forecast was for good weather with easterly winds that would give us a fast reaching passage. A large frontal system was moving across the United States from the west and would most likely reach us in a couple of days, providing strong northwesterly winds to whisk us further and faster southward.

Just as predicted, the easterly winds held true for almost two days, and we made good time. Along with the easterly winds were large, menacing easterly seas and cold, rainy skies. The boat was not comfortable. It was damp below and wet on deck. Whether sitting on deck or trying to sleep below, one had to constantly brace oneself against the incessant and irregular motion. One of our crew of four was actively seasick, and the rest of us were generally uncomfortable. The Atlantic Ocean was making life unpleasant.

Had we been racing, we wouldn't even have considered the course of action we took, but we weren't racing. We were abeam of Charleston; the wind was going soft and coming more from the south (against us); we were running low on bread and eggs (we had plenty else to eat); our seasick crew member claimed to be feeling better but was looking peaked from lack of nourishment; and the engine's ignition switch was acting up. These little things added up to make Charleston harbor look mighty attractive, so we put in.

We motored in the Inland Waterway for the next day and a half until the front came through, then we went outside once more to romp at hull speed before the cold, sparkling northwest wind, our spirits soaring and our bellies full and content.

Had we been racing we would, of course, have stayed offshore and taken whatever came to us. Our seasick crew member would have gotten well, we could have eaten other things to make up for bread and eggs, we could have made do with a finicky ignition switch or done without. We would still have romped at hull speed before the cold front and our spirits would have soared to relatively greater heights. Who knows, we might even have won a trophy.

Regardless of our decision to put into Charleston, we had to be just as prepared for our offshore passage as if we had been racing. We could not count on the availability of shelter in either case, so regardless of our reason for being offshore we had to be ready to stay there.

When cruising offshore, you do the same things, make the same preparations, take the same precautions, and risk the same high stakes as when racing. You just don't worry quite so much about the clock.

Future Shock

So much has happened in the development of offshore racers in the past few years that once-sacred concepts and beliefs have been shattered and sent plummeting to the bottom. All but gone are the days of custom-built yachts designed in an almost leisurely way, with designer and owner in consultation over every detail. In those idyllic days, designer, builder, and owner knew exactly what was wanted, what could be achieved, and where the limits of endurance lay.

It is far different today. Designer and owner rarely meet in the world of production fiberglass yachts. The closest the owner usually gets to the builder is through his dealer, who sells the yacht. Many owners assume that the new boats are built to some of the old standards of handling, probably because no one has told them differently. The intimate communication between designer and owner has been replaced with the salesman's brochure, which will hardly voluntarily admit there are any limits beyond which the shiny new "Bathtub 34" should be pushed. This is a potentially dangerous situation. Every reasonable skipper knows that there is no such thing as an indestructible boat. However, with the lines of communication between designer, builder, and owner broken, it is hard to know at what point to expect things to start coming apart.

While there are many examples of this sort of situation, I can recall one instance in particular that points out how the lack of communication between designer and owner may produce an unnecessary and potentially very dangerous accident.

In the 1970 Bermuda Race, several boats of the same design were dismasted, all for the same reason. All were yawls, and when squalls produced winds between 40 and 60 knots, each owner assumed that the time-honored method of reducing sail in a yawl or ketch—lowering the mainsail and sailing under "jib and jigger"—would see him through the high winds. Each was sadly mistaken and more than a little surprised when the mainmasts collapsed while sailing with no mainsail and a large genoa. I talked with each owner following the race, and all thought that their boats should have been able to sail this way in the winds encountered. One said he expected it—that was why he'd bought a yawl.

These owners had never discussed the situation with the designer. They did not know that this design was never intended to be sailed hard with a large genoa and no mainsail. The mainsail, either full or reefed, was intended to hold up the spar, to keep it from buckling forward under the compression load of a genoa. With no main set, with the yacht pitching in the waves, the spars buckled forward and collapsed. Had the owners known the limitations of this design, they would have shortened sail by reducing both the foretriangle area and the mainsail area. There is also the possibility that more than one of them would not have bought the boat in the first place.

From the designer's standpoint, it is unreasonable for these owners to expect to sail modern offshore racing designs in the same way they would have sailed a heavy cruising ketch. He would have told them, had he the opportunity, that it was impossible to design a winning rig, with its large foretriangle and full masthead height, that would be strong enough to sail under a large genoa and no mainsail. It's tough, but those are the facts. The owner should understand them—and have the opportunity to understand them—before he buys.

Now, as we see more and more responsibility being placed upon the manufacturers of consumer goods to make their products "idiot proof," the owner of an offshore racer finds himself having to buck the trend. No yacht can be made idiot proof; each will have its faults. The owner must be responsible for finding out what the faults are and adjusting his handling techniques accordingly.

In addition, the owner of a new boat must have a basic understanding of the design philosophy on which it was built. The philosophy both of the marketplace and the racing course encourages cutting corners. Certainly there are lots of corners that may be cut without jeopardizing the seaworthiness of a yacht, but you don't want to be leaning on a corner you thought was there and find out that it's been eliminated. That's what happened to the crews of the dismasted yawls.

If in doubt, communicate with the yacht's designer (preferably before you buy, but also as you begin to race). If he won't talk with you, assuming you are reasonable and understand that he has many owners and other things to do, don't buy his design. After all, he should want you to understand what the design can and cannot do. It won't do his reputation any good if you go offshore and have a serious failure.

Do Your Own Thing

The focus of this book has been on the fun aspect of offshore racing. Fun manifests itself in different ways to different people. To me, it is fun to be able to leave the demands of civilization behind. The pressures of everyday life are enough without adding to them the pressures of all-out racing. Oh, I race hard, all right, but I do it in my own way and leave out those things that I find boring routine. For example, in several instances I have recommended keeping notes and writing things down for future reference. This to me is drudgery from the real world. If I can safely avoid it, I will. As a result, I rely upon my memory for local knowledge, downwind tacking angles, and effective sail combinations. Granted, my memory is not as good as written notes, but it is fun for me to try to remember and not so much fun to write it down. I am not as competitive as I could be, but I am as competitive as I want to be.

Navigation is something else. Here, precision is a necessary and challenging part of the art. I am challenged by fog, by unknown currents, and by distant weather systems. I don't face these problems in everyday life, so the detailed analysis of them is not a bore, but an invigorating activity.

There are those who never get enough of competition. They are the dedicated racers who leave nothing to chance, make every effort, write everything down, read it over, ask countless questions, give no quarter, and ask for nothing but the best. This is their idea of ultimate fun, and I do not begrudge their having it, even when they beat me.

There are those at the other end of the scale who want no part of competition. Racing? Couldn't care less whether it's around the buoys or transatlantic. Gentle breezes, sunny days, and a comfortable cruiser are for them. I don't begrudge them their brand of fun either, but the chances are they won't go in for offshore sailing. You must have some competitive urge to go out there and do battle with the sea. It is a demanding master and often keeps those who venture forth casually and in contempt of its wrath.

Figure out what is fun for you. Is it all-out racing? Is it lazy cruising? Is it something in between? Whatever it is, go out and do your own thing!

Why Do People Go Offshore?

It is easy to sit here in comfortable surroundings and think of many moments of pleasant offshore sailing. Even as I look out on the cold rain falling from a leaden December sky it is not hard to recall the excitement of a Fastnet Race start, the exhilaration of wild surfing day after day before the transatlantic rollers, the beauty of a brilliant Caribbean sunset, or the challenge of a thrash to windward in the Gulf Stream. These are the images that are conjured up by the word "offshore" to both the landlocked dreamer and the crusty old salt.

It is another matter for one to find excitement, exhilaration, beauty, and challenge offshore when things aren't so pleasant. When you're double reefed and storm jibbed, and the seas off Portland Bill leap for the sky; when the deck above your bunk and the bilge below combine to soak everything you own with clammy, itchy salt; when the sun beats down on a windless, glassy sea and fries everything you touch; when in both agony and relief you pour your seasick guts into the lee scuppers and wish that you could die—then you would gladly stand naked in that cold December rain for the chance to feel the soggy, matted grass beneath your feet and to stand up straight without having to hang on braced for the inexorable yet unpredictable next lurch from the heaving sea.

Are we offshore *aficionados* completely daft to put up with being alternately frustrated, soaking, blistered, and ill just to get from point A to point B in the world's most snaillike conveyance? Do we just forget the unpleasant times with the incredible relief of the voyage's end? Do the excitement, exhilaration, beauty, and challenge come in sufficient measure to outweigh the awful perils?

One thing about sailing hundreds of miles at a snail's pace is that there is time for everything to change. In a few hours the current will turn off Portland Bill and whisk you off toward the Lizard. Tomorrow or the next day the sun will shine and dry your itchy, salty clothing. Just over the horizon is a rain shower that will cool the steaming decks and wash the sweat from your body. And, God willing, you will sooner or later get your stomach back and feel glad to be alive. It is then that we know *why* we are there. The excitement, exhilaration, beauty, and challenge that took us out there are not for everyone, and maybe that's part of the reason we like it, too. The man (or woman) with saltwater in his boots has done something that relatively few have done or can do. He is apart from the crowd, above it if you prefer. Like the sea bird and the dolphin who accompany him offshore, he is free and full of life.

The fireside is nice, and there are those for whom it will be the ultimate Utopia, but the fireside is nicer still when you can remember the joys of an offshore passage and dream of the time when you can go out and do it *again*.

Appendix I | Bill of Fare, Yacht Astral Bermuda Race, 1960

Saturday, June 18th

Lunch Ham & swiss cheese sandwiches
Tomato soup (3 cans)
Cookies
Pears (2 cans)
Dinner Beef stew, onions (2 cans), potatoes (2 cans)
Green salad, tomatoes
Grapefruit (2 cans)
Coffee

Sunday, June 19th

Breakfast Orange juice (2 large cans)
Soft-boiled eggs
"Brown & serve" sausage
Coffee cake
Coffee
Lunch Scotch broth (3 cans)
Turkey sandwiches
Cherries (2 cans)
Cookies
Dinner Meat loaf
Carrots (1 can), peas (2 cans)
Green salad—shoestring beets (1 can), artichoke hearts
   (1 can), asparagus (1 can)
Pound cake
Figs (2 cans)
Coffee

Monday, June 20th

Breakfast	Orange juice (2 large cans)
	Canadian bacon & eggs
	Coffee cake
	Coffee
Lunch	Clam chowder (3 cans)
	Meat loaf sandwiches
	Raw carrots
	Cookies
Dinner	Pepper pot soup (3 cans)
	Roast beef
	Sliced beets (2 cans)
	Romaine salad
	Peaches (2 cans)
	Coffee

Tuesday, June 21st

Breakfast	Orange juice (2 small cans)
	Corned beef hash (4 cans) with eggs
	Coffee
Lunch	Vegetable beef soup (3 cans)
	Roast beef sandwiches
	Orange & grapefruit sections (4 cans)
	Cocoa
Dinner	Tomato & rice soup (3 cans)
	Creamed turkey or spaghetti & meat balls (2 large cans)
	Brown bread (2 cans)
	Salad
	Cake
	Coffee

Wednesday, June 22nd

Breakfast	Orange juice (2 large cans)
	Oatmeal and honey
	Coffee
Lunch	Cold consommé (3 cans)
	Cold cuts sandwiches
	Pears (2 cans)

APPENDIX I   263

Dinner   Meatball stew (4 cans)
             Onions (2 cans), diced carrots (2 cans)
             Peaches (2 cans)
             Coffee

Thursday, June 23rd

Breakfast Orange juice (2 large cans)
             Bacon & eggs
             Coffee
Lunch   Canned corned beef sandwiches (2 cans)
                          or
             Canned ham sandwiches (1 can)
             Beer
Dinner   ASHORE!!
                and
             PLANTER'S PUNCH!!!

Grub List and Stowage

Meats
2 meat loaf	Icebox
1 turkey (chunked)	Icebox
1 filet	Icebox
cold cuts (assorted)	Icebox
ham (sliced)	Icebox
1 beef stew	Icebox
1 roast beef (sliced)	Icebox
2 packages "brown & serve" sausage	Icebox
Canadian bacon (24 slices)	Icebox
4 cans corned beef hash	Bilge forward
4 cans meatball stew	Bilge forward
1 pound of bacon	Ice box
2 cans corned beef	Bilge forward
1 Danish ham (canned)	Bilge forward
3 cans spaghetti & meat balls	Bilge forward
3 cans tuna	Shelf behind stove

Vegetables
4 cans onions (small)	Bilge forward
2 cans sliced beets	Bilge forward

2 cans potatoes	Bilge forward
3 cans carrots	Bilge forward
1 can shoestring beets	Bilge forward
1 can asparagus	Bilge forward

Fruits

4 cans pears	Bilge forward
2 cans grapefruit sections	Bilge forward
2 cans cherries	Bilge forward
2 cans figs	Bilge forward
4 cans peaches	Bilge forward
4 cans orange & grapefruit sections	Bilge forward

Soups (canned)

3 cans tomato soup	Bilge forward
3 cans Scotch broth	Bilge forward
3 cans clam chowder	Bilge forward
3 cans pepper pot soup	Bilge forward
3 cans vegetable beef soup	Bilge forward
3 cans tomato & rice soup	Bilge forward
3 cans cold consommé	Icebox

Soups (dry)

6 packs varied	Shelf behind stove
M.B.T. (bouillon)	Shelf behind stove
1 jar bouillon cubes	Shelf behind stove

Fruit Juice

6 cans orange juice	Bilge forward
6 cans (small) orange concentrate	
1 can tomato juice	

Cheeses

4 packages Swiss	Icebox
4 packages American	Icebox

Bread & Cake

18 small or 12 king-size loaves white bread
6 loaves rye bread
7 poundcakes (canned)
4 coffee cakes
Assorted cookies
Saltines
Chowder biscuits

APPENDIX I

Eggs
   7 dozen   Icebox

Salad & Fresh Vegetables
5 heads lettuce	Icebox
1 head Romaine	Icebox
6 tomatoes	Icebox
1 bunch celery	Icebox
1 bunch carrots	Icebox
6 red onions	Icebox

Miscellaneous
1 box oatmeal
5 lbs. coffee
2 jars instant coffee
2 cans cocoa
1 jar honey
1 jar honey spread
1 jar raspberry preserves
1 jar marmalade
3 jars sour balls
1 jar peanut butter
2 lbs. fresh butter   Icebox
1 lb. butter (canned)
2 boxes corn flakes (individual packages)
raisins

**Miscellaneous Food Aboard but Not Listed on Menu
(Stored Forward Port Side Locker)**
3 cans beef stew
4 cans potatoes
4 cans baked beans
1 can peaches
3 cans evaporated milk
4 cans codfish cakes
2 cans lobster
1 can green pea soup
1 can string beans
4 cans spinach
2 cans peas
2 cans shrimp
2 cans crab

Appendix II | Marine Weather Information (U.S.)

The following is available from Marine Weather Services Charts obtained from the Superintendent of Documents, U.S. Government Printing Office, Washington, D.C. 20402.
1. Local telephone numbers for recorded weather information, small craft advisories, gale or storm warnings.
2. Local telephone numbers direct to weather station forecasters and hours of operation.
3. Station frequencies and reporting hours of broadcasts of marine weather forecasts and warnings by marine radiotelephone stations.
4. Location and explanation of day and night advisory and warning visual displays. These are flown at Coast Guard stations, on police boats, at marinas, at yacht clubs, and at other display stations.
5. Commercial broadcast station marine forecasts and warnings broadcast direct from National Weather Service Offices showing times of broadcasts, station call letters, locations, AM and FM frequencies, AM antenna locations, and remarks.
6. Commercial broadcast stations which present weather information as part of news broadcasts showing locations, station call letters, AM and FM frequencies, and AM antenna locations.
7. Air Navigation radio stations which broadcast weather showing location, call letters, frequencies, antenna locations, and schedules.
8. VHF-FM continuous weather broadcasts on 162.40 and 162.55 MHz showing locations of transmitters and providing notes on suitable receivers (narrow band FM receivers of ± 5 kilohertz deviation).

Marine Weather Services Charts are available for the following locations at a price of 25 cents each:
Eastport, Maine to Montauk Point, New York
Montauk Point, New York to Manasquan, New Jersey
Manasquan, New Jersey to Cape Hatteras, North Carolina
Cape Hatteras, North Carolina to Savannah, Georgia
Savannah, Georgia to Apalachicola, Florida
Apalachicola, Florida to Morgan City, Louisiana
Morgan City, Louisiana to Brownsville, Texas
Point Conception, California to Mexican border
Eureka, California to Point Conception, California
Eureka, California to Canadian border
Great Lakes: Michigan and Superior
Great Lakes: Huron, Erie, and Ontario
Hawaiian waters
Puerto Rico and Virgin Islands
Alaskan waters

9. *World Wide Weather Broadcasts*, issued in 1973, is a revised publication combining H.O. 118, *Radio Weather Aids*, and *Weather Service for Merchant Shipping*.

The following charts and publications are useful for planning purposes and general weather information:
1. Monthly Pilot Charts for ocean areas show storm tracks, wind roses, and marine climate information averages for the month covered.
2. U.S. Coast Pilot lists telephone numbers of weather bureau offices, radio weather broadcast information, climatological tables, and meteorological tables for offshore and coastal areas.
3. *Mariner's Weather Log* is published by the U.S. Department of Commerce. It is a magazine containing articles relating to weather, a marine weather review, and a marine weather diary. Copies are available to persons or agencies with marine interests from the Environmental Data Service, Page Bldg. 2 (D54), 3300 Whitehaven St., Washington, D.C. 20235.
4. The U.S. Navy *Summary of Synoptic Meteorological Observations*, May 1970, is available to mariners.
5. *Climatological and Oceanographic Atlas for Mariners* is suggested for use as a supplement to Pilot Charts.

All publications except *Mariner's Weather Log* are available from the Superintendent of Documents, U.S. Government Printing Office, Washington, D.C. 20402.

Additional Weather Information Sources

Weather information is available from several privately published marine almanacs such as *Eldridge* in Boston, Massachusetts and *Reed's* in England, and from cruising guides such as *The Inland Waterway Guide, Boating Almanacs*, etc.

Marine weather information is available through the American Telephone and Telegraph Company High Seas Maritime Mobile Radiotelephone Service. Broadcasts are over low frequency bands from 4 to 23 MHz. Station locations, call letters, frequencies, and schedules of weather broadcasts are listed in a booklet on the High Seas Service available from American Telephone and Telegraph Company, 32 Avenue of the Americas, New York, N.Y. 10013.

The information for this section pertains primarily to U.S. coastal and surrounding waters and was provided by Walter J. Stoddard, Port Meteorological Officer (N.Y.), and John A. Mayer, Meteorologist in Charge, New York City Weather Station.

Appendix III | Navigator's Checklist

The following charts and lists were prepared by J. J. Mac Brien. They explain the duties of the offshore racing navigator and provide a checklist to avoid the possibility of missing vital information or leaving important equipment ashore.

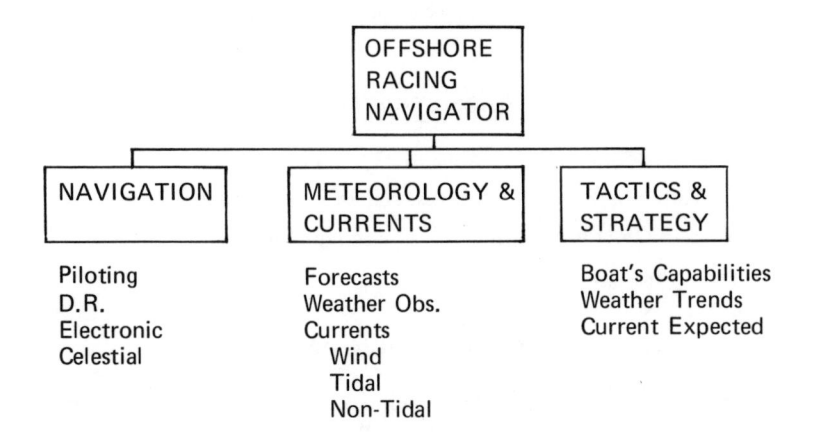

```
                    ┌─────────────┐
                    │  OFFSHORE   │
                    │   RACING    │
                    │  NAVIGATOR  │
                    └─────────────┘
         ┌─────────────────┼─────────────────┐
┌─────────────┐  ┌───────────────────┐  ┌─────────────┐
│ NAVIGATION  │  │  METEOROLOGY &    │  │  TACTICS &  │
│             │  │    CURRENTS       │  │  STRATEGY   │
└─────────────┘  └───────────────────┘  └─────────────┘
```

NAVIGATION	METEOROLOGY & CURRENTS	TACTICS & STRATEGY
Piloting	Forecasts	Boat's Capabilities
D.R.	Weather Obs.	Weather Trends
Electronic	Currents	Current Expected
Celestial	Wind	
	Tidal	
	Non-Tidal	

```
                    ┌────────────┐   ┌─────────┐
                    │ NAVIGATION │---│ HISTORY │
                    └────────────┘   └─────────┘
┌──────┐ ┌─────────┐ ┌────────────┐ ┌──────────┐
│ D.R. │ │ PILOTING│ │ ELECTRONIC │ │ CELESTIAL│
└──────┘ └─────────┘ └────────────┘ └──────────┘
```

D.R.	PILOTING	ELECTRONIC	CELESTIAL
Deduced (Ded)	Fixing	Loran A/C	Sextant
Log (SPD)	Bearings	Decca	
Course	Transits		Time
Errors	Dist. Arcs	Consolan	Chronometer
Compass	Angles		Radio
Log Calib.	Soundings	D/F	
Steering		Accuracy	Astro Triangle
Leeway	Aids	Night Effect	Plotting
Set	Landmarks	Land Effect	Special Cases
	Buoyage	Quad Error	Mer. Alt.
Plotting	Lights		Equal Alt.
	Sound Sig.	New Devices	Polaris
		Omega	Low Alt.
		Transit	Venus

```
        ┌─────────────┐         ┌──────────┐
        │ METEOROLOGY │---------│ CURRENTS │
        └─────────────┘         └──────────┘
```

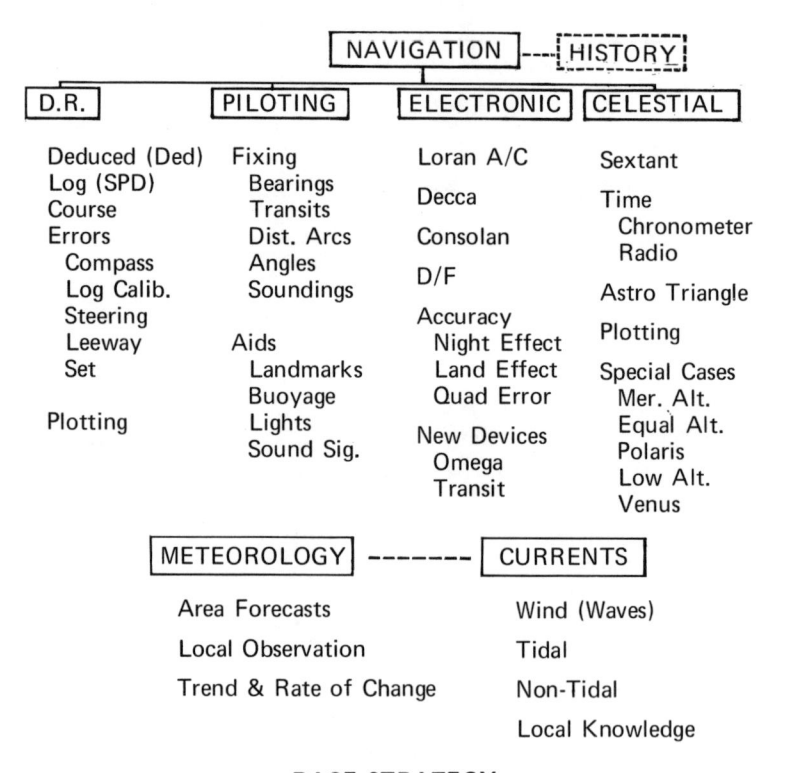

METEOROLOGY	CURRENTS
Area Forecasts	Wind (Waves)
Local Observation	Tidal
Trend & Rate of Change	Non-Tidal
	Local Knowledge

RACE STRATEGY

1. It very seldom pays to gamble everything on the weather.
2. If in any doubt, sail the shortest course in the available wind. (Mitchell)
3. Keep the boat moving—particularly in light air.
4. Watch the competition.

NAVIGATING A RACE

Preparation—charts, publications, calibrate instruments, weather, tides, currents, navigation aids, handicaps, etc.

Execution—position, weather, currents; strategy & tactics; sleep; log.

Post-Race Analysis—What things went right?
    What things went wrong?
    Why?

Appendix IV | Navigator's Equipment Checklist

1. For celestial requirements:
   Sextant
   Almanac
   Sight Reduction Tables (H.O. 214, 229, or 249)
   Sight forms
   Graph paper (for plotting sights)
   Stopwatch
   Starfinder (H.O. 2102)
   Plotting sheets
2. Weather, current, nav. aids:
   Bowditch tables (Part II, H.O. 9)
   Tide and Current Tables
   Radio Aids to Navigation (H.O. 117)
   World Wide Weather Broadcasts (or H.O. 118)
   Light Lists
   Radio aids
   Pilot books (or appropriate H.O. pubs.)
3. Tools:
   Thermometer (suitable for sea temperature)
   Psychrometer (particularly if fog is likely)
   Barometer (check ship's instrument)
   Hand bearing compass
   Radios—
      Time signals
      Direction finding
      Weather broadcasts
      (check antenna arrangements)
   Tape recorder
   Alarm clock
   Dividers

Protractor
Parallel rules
Compasses
Binoculars
Pencils, sharpener, and erasers
Time, speed, distance calculator
Slide rule
Tacking plotter
4. Charts:
Make sure all needed charts are on board
Check chart condition and issue dates
Notices to mariners
5. Radio frequencies:
Communications
Weather
Direction finding
Omni
6. Equipment adjustments:
Compass adjustments (deviation card)
Log calibration
RDF calibration

Appendix V | Sources of Supply

The sources listed are those known personally to the author. Although admittedly limited in scope, they are included as an example of the type of store to look for in one's local area. They can also be considered an ultimate source if items cannot be procured locally.

Personal Equipment:
  Fulton Supply Company, Inc., 23 Fulton St., New York, N.Y.
   Foul weather suits, sou'westers, boots, deck shoes, water resistant oiled sweaters, CPO shirts, iceman's pants, fisherman's gloves, watch caps, thermal underwear, and duffel bags.

Charts, Almanacs, and Books:
  The Hammond Map Store, Inc., One E. 43rd St., New York, N.Y.
   Charts for all parts of the world, nautical publications, almanacs, and cruising guides.

Navigation Equipment:
  New York Nautical Instrument and Service Corporation, 140 West Broadway, New York, N.Y.
   Charts for all parts of the world, light lists, nautical almanacs, celestial navigation tables, starfinders, sextants, chronometers, logs, plotting equipment, pelorus, and compasses.

Bibliography

Blewitt, Mary, *Celestial Navigation for Yachtsmen* (Tuckahoe, N.Y.: John de Graff, 1967).

Bowditch, Nathaniel, *American Practical Navigator* (Washington, D.C.: United States Navy Hydrographic Office, 1958).

Coles, Adlard, *North Atlantic* (Southampton, Eng.: Robert Ross in association with George G. Harrap, 1950).

Dumas, Vito, *Alone Through the Roaring Forties*, English lang. ed. (London: Adlard Coles Ltd., in assoc. with George G. Harrap; New York: John de Graff, 1960).

Dunlap, G. D., and Shufeldt, H. H., *Dutton's Navigation and Piloting*, 12th ed., Annapolis, Md.: United States Naval Institute, 1971).

Ellam, Patrick and Mudie, Colin, *Sopranino* (London: Rupert Hart-Davis, 1958) U.S. ed. (New York: W. W. Norton, 1953).

Hoyt, C. Sherman, *Sherman Hoyt's Memoirs* (New York: D. Van Nostrand, 1950).

Illingworth, John, *Further Offshore* (New York: Quadrangle, 1971).

Johnson, Peter, *Ocean Racing and Offshore Yachts* (New York: Dodd Mead, 1970).

Kals, W. S., *Practical Navigation* (Garden City, N.Y.: Doubleday, 1972).

Mason, C. F., *Ocean Sailing and Racing* (New York: MacMillan, 1954).

Morris, Everett B., and Coulson, Robert, *Racing at Sea* (New York: D. Van Nostrand, 1959).

Phillips-Birt, Douglas, *British Ocean Racing* (London: Adlard Coles, 1960).

Snaith, William T., *Across the Western Ocean* (New York: Harcourt, Brace and World, 1966).

Index

Acapulco Race, 217
Adams, Fred, 30, 170
ADF, see Automatic direction finder
Admiral's Cup, 239, 243, 244
Adriana, 190
Afterguy, 152, 156, 158, 159, 161
Air mass, 83
Air mass thunderstorm, 86, 87
Albatross II, 237
Allen, Bill, 226
Allen, David J., 212, 225
American Eagle, 194, 211, 224, 225, 227, 240, 243
American Practical Navigator, 51
Ames, Henry, 188
Ames, Richard, 188
Ames, Robert, 188
Anchor, 196
Anfossie, Fred, 118
Anemometer, 114
Angle of attack, 104
Annapolis-Newport Race, 231
Apparent wind, 104, 105, 114
Apparent wind indicator, 96, 98, 110
Appendicitis, 199
Astor, 245, 249
Astral, 45, 47, 171, 176, 192, 207, 261
Automatic direction finder (ADF), 58

Backstay adjuster, 132
Backwinding, 139
Baker, Nicholas J., 170
Baker, Toby, 199
Barber haul, 132
Barrett, Peter, 74
Barton, Robert B., 130

Bavier, Robert N., 132
Baxter, Mark, 29
Beam reach, 116
Bennett, James Gordon, 232
Bergström, Lars, 34
Bermuda 40, 71
Bermuda Race, 42, 50, 52, 79, 80, 81, 82, 87, 171, 182, 190, 192, 199, 205, 206, 207, 231, 236, 239, 244, 257
Bidwell, Bruce, 221
Binnacle, 55
Blackfin, 211, 213, 236, 237
Blair, Charles J., 101, 102, 168
Block Island, 69, 72
Block Island 40, 207
Blue Water Medal, 253
Boating Almanacs, 269
Bolton, John, 10
Boom vang, see Vang
Boots, 16, 18, 275
Bosun's chair, 196
Botterell, Edward, 110, 120
Bouzaid, Chris, 240
Bowditch, Nathaniel, 51, 273
Bowker, Peter, 9, 212
Brittania Cup, 243
Broach, 117, 118, 120, 170, 181
Broad reach, 114, 116, 117
Bruynzeel, Cornelius, 2
Buccaneer, 213
Byers, Joe C., 182

C-stay, 130
Cabin heater, 190
Calder, Hugh, 10
Cal 2-30, 219, 223

Cal 40, 226, 234, 239
C&C 35, 118, 120, 195
Cap, 19, 275
Cape Horn, 177
Caprice, 156
Captain, 36, 38
Carina, 11, 25, 32, 33, 48, 90, 122, 234, 235, 244
Carter, Richard E., 241, 243, 244
Caswell, Christopher J., 213
Celestial navigation, 58
Center of buoyancy, 104
Chafe, 185
Chain of command, 37
Changing headsails, 127, 128
Changing spinnakers, 164
Channel Race, 75, 244
Charisma, 236, 237
Chart, 52
Chicago-Mackinac Race, 206, 227
Chimera, 29, 30
Chubasco, 4
Church, Lucia, 195
Church, Peter, 195
Close reach, 116, 162
Coast Guard, U.S., 19, 20, 195, 266
Coffee grinder, 143
Cold front, 85, 86
Coles, K. Adlard, 176, 182, 189
Colgate, Stephen, 235
Columbia 50, 217, 218
Compass, 62, 110, 121, 274, 275
Compass course, 111
Compton, Barnes, Jr., x, 171, 208
Cook, 26, 40
Cooking, 45
Corinthians, The, 11
Coronado Islands, 69
Cotter, Ed, 206
Cotton Blossom, 10
Cowes Week, 239, 241, 242
Cranker, 142, 144
Cunningham, Briggs S., 132
Cunningham control, 103, 110, 125, 126, 132, 135, 138, 139, 140, 141
Current, 62, 71, 74, 76, 77
  charts, 71, 75, 273
  Gulf Stream, 71, 78, 83
  non-tidal, 71
  tables, 273
  tidal, 71
  wind driven, 71

Danforth anchor, 196
Dead reckoning (DR), 52, 53, 54, 57, 60, 61, 62, 78, 79, 82, 176
Deck log, 60
Deck shoes, 18, 275
Demuse, Kenneth, 211
Dental checkup, 199, 200
Derecktor, Robert E., 170, 224
Dip-pole jibe, *see* Jibe
Direction finder, *see* Radio direction finder; Automatic direction finder
Dismasting, 194, 257
Domino, 195, 196
Dora, 229, 231
Double slot, 112, 162, 163
Doubloon, 182, 194
Downhaul, 110, 132
DR, *see* Dead reckoning
Draft control, 102
Drill, 186, 192
Drogue, 181, 196
Drugs, 200, 201, 202
Dry ice, 48
Duffel, 16, 19, 21, 275
Dyna, 235, 237

Eldridge, 269
Ellam, Patrick, 62, 63, 185, 197
Emergency procedures, 186
Emergency tiller, 196
End-for-end jibe, *see* Jibe
English Channel, 74
Ensenada Race, 217
Enzian, 119
Escapade, 224
Ewing, Clayton, 236

Fastnet Race, 42, 206, 239, 244
Fink, Walter L., x, 172, 207
Finnesterre, 209
Fire, 190
Fire extinguisher, 191
First aid, 199, 200
Fischer, Syd, 241
Fisher's Island, 72, 75
Fix, 53, 56
Fleetwing, 232
Flotation jacket, *see* Jacket

INDEX

Foreguy, 143, 149, 151, 157, 158, 159
Foretriangle, 130, 159, 162
Foul-weather gear, 15, 16, 275
Freezer, 48

Galley, 43, 45, 48
Galley fire, 190
"Gearbuster," 26
Geared winch, 143
Genoa, 97, 112, 127, 129, 135, 139, 141, 143, 159, 162, 163, 170, 196, 208
Genoa halyard, 139, 164
Genoa sheet, *see* sheet
Genoa winch, 141, 142
Gloves, 19, 275
Goodwill, 1
Goring, Don, 188
Governor's Cup Race, 224
Grant, Robert S., 217
Graybeard, 213
Gray, William O., *x*
"Great Ocean Race," 1, 6
　　See also Transpac Race
Grimm, Peter, 224
Groove, 100
Guinevere, 234
Gulf Stream, 71, 78, 79, 80, 81, 83, 87, 211, 259
Gurney, Alan P., *x*, 101, 211, 225
Guy, 150, 151, 153, 154, 155, 165
Guzzwell, John, 177, 179, 180

Halyard, 110, 126, 129, 132, 135, 138, 139, 143, 149, 151, 161, 164, 165
Hamrah, 188
Hand-bearing compass, 55, 273
Hat, 20, 22
Havana Race, 220
Health, 199
Heave-to, 181
Heavy displacement, 107
Heavy weather, 169, 202
Heavy Weather Sailing, 176, 182
Heeling, 116
Helmsman, 60, 61, 62, 63, 141, 149, 150, 154, 173, 187, 208
Helmsmanship, 90, 110, 177
Henrietta, 232
Heritage, 198
Herreshoff, L. Francis, 1
Hibberd, Frederick H., 156

Hibberd, Lorna, 156
Hibberd method, 156, 157
High, 85
High-aspect ratio, 100
High pressure, 84
Hiller, Seth, *x*
Hinkle, Gene, 195
Hood, Frederick E. (Ted), 50, 130
Hooligan, 219
Hotfoot, 101, 102, 168, 225

Illingworth, John, 244
Improbable, 212
Indian Harbor Yacht Club, 26
Inland Waterway Guide, 269
Instant Weather Forecasting, 84
Interim jib, 129
Inverness, 145
Isle of Wight, 74

Jacket, 15, 16, 188, 192
　flotation, 20, 192
　life, 19
J.C. strap, 132
Jib, 129, 151, 170
Jibe, 106, 149, 150, 153, 154, 155
　dip-pole, 151, 153, 156
　end-for-end, 151, 154, 155
　two pole, 154, 156
Jibing, 106
Joffs, Sven, 248
Johnson, Howard, 192, 208
Johnson, Mark, 42, 211, 213
Johnson, Robert F., 5, 6, 42, 207, 211, 212, 224, 234
Jolie Brise, 190
Jones, Dorcas D., *xi*
Juan de Fuca Race, 218

Kappel, Albert D., 207
Katama, 30, 31, 170
Kialoa II, 213, 236, 243
Killiam, Lol, 213
Kilroy, Jim, 213, 243
Kirby, Bruce, 34, 115, 118, 224
Kirsten, 234
Kittiwake, 40, 48, 71, 72, 73, 75, 120, 172, 202, 232, 234
Knights, Jack, 237
Knowlton, Elliot B. (Buz), 207
Koomooloo, 244
Kozlay, Clarence, 190

LAN, see Local apparent noon
Land breeze, see Offshore breeze
Lazy sheet, 154, 161
La Paz Race, 182, 217
Learson, T. Vincent, 184
Lee bow, 74, 75
Leech grommet, 126
Lee helm, 100, 229
Le Havre, 74, 77
Lewis, Jay, 217
Life jackets, see Jacket
Life raft, 192
Lift (spinnaker pole), 154, 157
Light displacement, 107
Line of position (LOP), 53, 55, 58
Linked winches, 144
Lipton Cup Race, 224
Liquor, 252
Little Ship Club, 14
Lively Lady II, 225
Local apparent noon, 59
Log, 60, 61, 212, 274, 275
Log entry, 60
Long Island Sound, 67, 72, 170, 253
Long, Sumner A. (Huey), 205, 211, 247
Loomis, Alfred L., 188, 232
LOP, see Line of position
Loran, 58, 62, 78, 79
Lorentzen, Frederick W. P., 75
Low, 84, 85
Low pressure, 85, 87
Luders, A. E., Jr., 145
Luff lacing, 126
Luff grommet, 126
Luff sleeve, 130
Luff strings, 96, 97, 98, 101
Lying ahull, 180, 181

MacBrien, Joseph J., x, 50, 52, 271
MacKenzie, Sandy, 42
Magic, 199
Magnetic bearing, 78
Main halyard, 132, 138, 143
Mainsheet, see Sheet
Mainsheet traveler, see Traveler
Mainsail, 137, 153, 154, 155, 156, 160
Man overboard, 182, 186, 226
Marblehead-Halifax Race, 232
Mariner's Weather Log, 268
Marshall haul, 132, 136, 138

Marshall, John, 136
Masthead fly, 96
Mast jacks, 132
Mazatlán Race, 217
McCullough, Robert W., 145
McCurdy and Rhodes, 236
McKee, Joan, 42
McNamarra, John J. (Don), 145
Medical checkup, 200
Medical officer, 200, 202
Medical supplies, 200
Medication, 21
Melee, 226
Mercedes III, 244
Mexican coastal races, 206, 216
Miami-Montego Bay Race, 9, 209, 210, 211
Miami-Nassau Race, 194, 206, 224
Midget Ocean Racing Association, 216
Midget Ocean Racing Club, 207
Mizzenmast, 164
Mizzen spinnaker, 166, 167
Mizzen staysail, 164, 166
Moffett, George M., Jr., x, 234
Molokai Channel, 2, 216
Morale, 38, 43, 46, 48, 94, 108, 164, 253
MORA, see Midget Ocean Racing Association
MORC, see Midget Ocean Racing Club
Morgan, Charles E., Jr., 198, 221
Morgan 33, 221
Morning Star, 1
Mudie, Colin, 63
Mull, Gary, 212, 225, 229

Nantucket Lightship Race, 71, 73
Nantucket Shoals, 71
Nassau Cup Race, see Governor's Cup
Nauti-Cal, 224
Navigation, 51, 52, 176
Navigator, 26, 37, 38, 49, 50, 78, 113, 114, 187
NAYRU, see North American Yacht Racing Union
Nepenthe, 184
New London, Connecticut, 71
Newport, Rhode Island, 71, 101
New York Yacht Club, 232
New York Yacht Club Cruise, 102
New York Yacht Club Cup, 243
Non-tidal current, 71

INDEX

Noreyma, 236
North American Yacht Racing Union (NAYRU), 19, 58
Norton, Thomas A., x
Nye, Richard B., 32
Nye, Richard S., x, 11, 25, 32, 235

O'Brien, Tom, 219
Ocean Racing, 188
Offshore breeze, 66
Olympic course, 68
OMEGA, 58
OMNI, 58, 274
One-Design & Offshore Yachtsman, 217
Ondine, 10, 205, 211, 213, 237, 245, 246, 247, 249
Onshore breeze, 66, 67, 70
Outhaul, 110, 132, 138, 139
outRAGEous, 164, 221, 225

Pemaquid, 219
Penalty pole, 162
Phillips, Jesse, 236
Physical disability, 199
Physician, 199, 200
Pilot Charts, 268
Piloting, 52
Plotter, 113
Point Loma, 64, 68
Pole lift, *see* Spinnaker pole lift
Popular Boating, 249
Port Huron/Mackinac Race, 227
Pressure gradient, 84
Prospect of Whitby, 243

Races
  Acapulco Race, 217
  Annapolis-Newport Race, 231
  Bermuda Race, 42, 50, 52, 79, 80, 81, 82, 87, 171, 182, 190, 192, 199, 205, 206, 207, 231, 239, 244, 257
  Channel Race, 75, 244
  Chicago-Mackinac Race, 206, 227
  Fastnet Race, 42, 206, 239, 244
  "Gearbuster," 26
  Governor's Cup Race, 224
  Havana Race, 220
  Juan de Fuca Race, 218
  La Paz Race, 182, 217
  Lipton Cup Race, 224
  Marblehead-Halifax Race, 232
  Mazatlán Race, 217
  Miami-Montego Bay Race, 9, 209, 210, 211
  Miami-Nassau Race, 194, 206, 224
  Nantucket Lightship Race, 71, 73
  Nassau Cup Race, *see* Governor's Cup Race
  New York Yacht Club Cruise, 102
  New York Yacht Club Cup, 243
  Port Huron-Mackinac Race, 227
  St. Petersburg-Anclote Key Race, 220
  St. Petersburg-Fort Lauderdale Race, 83, 110, 118, 164, 195, 220, 222, 239
  Southern Ocean Racing Conference (SORC), 118, 200, 205, 220, 224
  Stamford-Vineyard Race, 232
  Stratford Shoal Race, 26
  Swiftsure Race, 217
  Sydney-Hobart Race, 206, 239, 244, 246, 249
  Tahiti Race, 48, 205
  Transatlantic Race, 19, 30, 42, 46, 48, 87, 120, 170, 188, 200, 202, 205, 231, 232, 233, 235, 237
  Transpac Race, 1, 6, 48, 87, 182, 205, 209, 212, 214, 217
  Trans-Superior Race, 227
  Vineyard Race, *see* Stamford-Vineyard Race
Race, The, 72, 75
Race Rock (East Coast), 54, 73, 75
Race Rocks (West Coast), 218
Radio bearings, 52
Radio direction finder (RDF), 57, 58, 274
Raft, *see* Life raft
Ragamuffin, 241, 244
Rainbow II, 240
RDF, *see* Radio direction finder
Reacher, 112, 116, 163
Reaching, 117, 132
Reaching strut, 158, 159
Rebecca Shoal, 83, 196, 223
Redhead, 118, 120, 195, 196
Red Rooster, 241, 244
Reed's, 269
Reef, 102, 106, 125, 126, 170, 196, 208

INDEX

Reef points, 126
Reefing
  roller, 126
  slab, 126
Reel halyard winch, 143
Refrigeration, 48
Rigging knife, 22
Robin, 50, 217
Roller reefing, *see* reefing
RORC, *see* Royal Ocean Racing Club
Rothe, I. E., 234
Rousmaniere, John, 232, 235
Royal Ocean Racing Club (RORC), 14, 42, 239, 244
Royal Yacht Squadron, 241, 242
Running backstay, 139
Running Tide, 252

Safety, 184, 208
Safety harness, 16, 19, 189, 192
St. Petersburg-Anclote Key Race, 220
St. Petersburg-Fort Lauderdale Race, 83, 110, 118, 164, 195, 220, 222, 239
Salm, Alexander, 249
San Diego, 68
Scandinavian watch system, *see* Watch
Sea anchor, 181, 195
Seabreeze, *see* Onshore breeze
Seal, 75
Seamanship, *ix*
Seasickness, 21, 45, 201, 202
Sextant, 59, 273, 275
Shark, 139
Sheehan, Richard F., *x*
Sheet
  genoa, 108, 129, 135, 139, 142, 147, 150, 151, 163
  main, 118, 126, 136, 143, 154
  spinnaker, 112, 118, 147, 149, 150, 151, 154, 155, 159
Sheets, 110
Ship's bells, 27
Simson, Humphrey B., *x*, 71, 172, 234
Sinking, 191
Six-Meter, 100
Skipper, 35, 36, 38, 184, 187, 189, 200
Slab reefing, *see* Reefing
Sliding gooseneck, 132, 138
Slotted stay, 130, 131

Smeaton, Beryl, 177, 179, 180, 189
Smeaton, Miles, 177, 179, 180, 181
Socks, 19
Solo, 247
Sommerset, Robert, 190
Sopranino, 63
SORC, *see* Southern Ocean Racing Conference
Soufflé, 170
Southern Ocean Racing Conference (SORC), 118, 200, 205, 220, 224
"Sou'wester," 15
Sparkman & Stephens, 241
Special Regulations (of ORC), 189, 195
Speedometer, 98, 110, 163
Spinnaker, 111, 112, 114, 116, 118, 146, 148, 150, 162, 170
Spinnaker halyard, 143, 149, 150, 161, 165
Spinnaker, mizzen, *see* Mizzen spinnaker
Spinnaker pole, 149, 150, 152, 153, 154, 155, 156, 159, 170, 238, 247
Spinnaker pole lift, 150, 154, 155, 157, 158, 161
Spinnaker staysail, 120, 161, 163
Squall line, 84
Stall, 118
Stamford-Vineyard Race, 232
Staysail, 111, 112, 129, 152, 161
Staysail, mizzen, *see* Mizzen staysail
Stearn, Timothy, 130
Strategy, 65, 72
Stratford Shoal Race, 26
Stopping, 147, 148
Storm, 145
Storms, 175, 176
Storm trysail, 229
Stormvogel, 1
Stove, 190
Sturrock, Jack, 247
Sunburn, 20
Sunglasses, 22
Surfing, 115, 118, 121, 123, 181
Survival conditions, 169, 175
Swiftsure Race, 217
Sydney-Hobart Race, 206, 239, 244, 246, 249
Symonette, Robert H. (Bobby), 249

INDEX

Tacking, 106
Tacking downwind, 113, 115
Tactics, 65
Tahiti Race, 48, 205
Tailer, 141
Take-down, spinnaker, 149, 158, 160
Tankoos, William G. (Randy), 145
Teazer, 139
Telltales, 94, 98
Thermal wind, 66
Three-speed winch, 143
Thunderstorm, see Air mass thunderstorm
Ticonderoga, 1, 6, 42, 207, 211, 234
Tidal current tables, see Current, tidal
Tidsfordriv, 100
Tiller, emergency, see Emergency tiller
Toilet kit, 19
Topping lift, 143, 158
Touché, 92, 93
Towing a warp, 176, 177, 181
Transatlantic Race, 19, 30, 42, 46, 48, 87, 120, 170, 188, 200, 202, 205, 231, 232, 233, 235, 237
Transpac Race, 1, 6, 48, 87, 182, 205, 209, 212, 214, 217
Trans-Superior Race, 227
Traveler, 98, 110, 125, 126, 132, 136
Trekka Round the World, 179
Trilogy, 56, 57, 136
Tripp, William H., Jr., 92
Trousers, 15
Turner, R. E. (Ted), 224, 227, 243
Turtle, 147
Twin Stay, 130, 131
Two-pole jibe, see Jibe
Tzu Hang, 177, 178, 179, 180, 181, 189

United States Coast Guard, see Coast Guard
United States Power Squadron, 52

Vamp X, 234
Van de Stadt, E. G., 237
Vang, 110, 125, 126, 132, 136, 137, 154
Vector diagram, 74, 75, 83
Vesta, 232
Vineyard Race, see Stamford-Vineyard Race

Warm front, 85
Watch, 24
Watch captain, 24, 25, 35, 37, 38, 60, 187
Watch, Scandinavian system, 27
Watch systems, 27, 28, 29, 31
Waterway Guide, see Inland Waterway Guide
Watts, Alan, 84
Weather, Appendix II, 286
Weather helm, 99, 100, 101, 102, 111, 112, 117
Weather map, 84, 88
Wheel, 91
Williams, Lynn, 229
Williams, Robert D., 245
Winch, 142, 143, 150
Wind and Sailing Boats, 84
Wind driven current, see Current
Windward Passage, xi, 24, 42, 209, 210, 211, 212, 213, 214, 224
Wisner, John N., Jr., xi

Yacht Racing, 115
Young, O. J., 90, 223

Zia, 42